PRAISE FOR TOXIC LOVE

'Indira and Dean have compiled a thought-provoking masterpiece that compels the reader to take a fresh look at the addictive cycle of violence; repetitive behaviour patterns and the build-up of tolerance. Toxic love is an informative discourse and will be useful to a wide audience; victims, perpetrators and therapists as well. The wisdom in this work reflects the authors expertise and profound understanding of the human psyche.'
Pearl Fernandes M. Clin. Psych, Psychologist

'Toxic Love shines a light on understanding the motivations for a perpetrator to abuse their partners, how it develops into such a pattern, why victims can't leave and how people can change. Highly recommend this book! A great read for everyone to gain a deeper insight into toxic love and its underpinnings.'
Julia Green, Naturopath, Health Squad

'Having worked in men's development for many years I've been very concerned about men that commit domestic violence. As a result, I interviewed the co-author of Toxic Love, Dean Quirke, and we explored domestic violence from a man's point of view. Now the book is released, I can see the depth of thinking and experience that has gone into it. I'm sure it will become a valued resource as their new concepts are digested and tested by practitioners in the field.' See the interviews on this URL https://cant2can.com/tag/dean-quirke/
Hilton Barr Director at 'Cant-2-Can'

'Toxic Love is an essential piece of work that affects so many in society today. The book is highly informative and inspiring in a way that will bring so much hope and light to those affected by this challenge. It is a compelling and engaging read that will go a long way to providing hope and inspiring individuals to navigate their way through these challenges.'
Biagio Versace, President & Board Member of MCAS & Founder of 'Mindpositivo'

TOXIC LOVE

BREAKING THE ADDICTIVE PATTERNS OF DOMESTIC ABUSE

INDIRA HARACIC-NOVIC AND DEAN QUIRKE

INGRAM. Lightning Source

The information in this book is not intended to replace professional medical or psychological advice. The content is based upon the authors' personal and professional experiences, opinions and qualifications.

All necessary written permissions have been obtained from patients to pub-lish their individual stories. Names have been changed to protect their identities.

www.toxiclove.com.au

Cover design by Chris Hildenbrand
Typeset in Constantia 9/12pt & Ebrima 14/24pt
Printed and bound in Australia by IngramSpark
Prepared for publication by Dr Juliette Lachemeier @ The Erudite Pen

NATIONAL LIBRARY OF AUSTRALIA

A catalogue record for this book is available from the National Library of Australia

Toxic Love: Breaking the Addictive Patterns of Domestic Abuse – 1st edition
ISBN 9780654028904 Paperback
ISBN 9780645028911 Ebook

Dedication

Dean Quirke

To my best teachers—all the boys and men finding the courage to change their repetitive patterns of behaviours. Their willingness to be vulnerable, transparent and open to learning has inspired my passion for supporting them on their journey towards healing.

Indira Haracic-Novic

To my best teachers—all the trauma survivors who gave me a window into their broken places, helped me understand their inner worlds and find better ways to help them heal.

Foreword

Toxic Love examines intimate partner violence (IPV) as an addiction—not the addiction of the victim to pain and submission as is so frequently the frame—but rather the violent partner's addiction to inflicting this pain and control.

Indira Haracic-Novic and Dean Quirke have produced a timely book that will be widely useful. Timely, because the public discourse about intimate partner violence has entered a new phase. There is now broad acknowledgement of the sheer numbers of women harmed/killed by partners; however, law enforcement practices and legal processes still have a long way to go in protecting women and prosecuting perpetrators.

Written for the reader and hence very engaging, the authors ask us to examine our position instead of just sitting back with platitudes and assumptions. The authors examine patterns in IPV in an effort to understand its repetitive nature, and they present a fair amount of material describing the histories of some men who abuse, with the same aim to understand *why*.

These perpetrator histories have explanatory value, and the reader must resist the urge to disengage from the possibly disturbing content. The authors are not seeking excuses; rather, they are noting the need to seek all plausible explanations to find the turning point in stopping the current cycle of violence. No easy explanations are offered, and the authors present perspectives from a variety of psychological traditions (psychoanalytic, attachment theory) as well as familiar psychosocial discourses. While the book is largely written from a psychological perspective, the political is acknowledged; yes, 'outdated belief systems' are enabling these repetitive patterns of abusive behaviour.

Beyond considering personal history, personality and gender dynamics, this book makes the case for describing patterns of abuse as a cycle of tension and release for the perpetrator; a cycle he becomes addicted to in the process of causing pain to his partner. The authors acknowledge the problems here, particularly around responsibility and choice. They note that some men *do* want to change but will struggle to for many reasons, and that some men will not admit that they need to change.

So what about change? The authors argue that merely changing beliefs and assumptions will not shift men who hurt their partners. There is a discomfort at these men's core that needs to be addressed. It is somatic and often without words. And change will involve him suffering through this discomfort instead of inflicting it on his partner!

The authors suggest a three-step process designed to facilitate tolerance of this discomfort (in other words, to stop him resolving the discomfort by hurting his partner): Awareness, dis-identification and restraint. It is *his* work to do. In describing this work, the authors talk of techniques that are useful and powerful in any therapy, e.g. emotional tracking.

This book is not only about intimate partner violence. It is also about identity and the ways we all absorb and manage the pain of childhood. The chapter on personality (called 'Aspectology') and the sections on trauma are all excellent presentations of some basic principles in psychology.

For the traumatised woman? Her healing is not ignored, nor is the difficulty for her in getting out of the trap created by an abuser's manipulation, further violence and her own processes. At no point does this book become about couple therapy, about healing the couple. The place of change is located in the perpetrator. One complex message is clear: Stopping the violence for one couple does not require them to stay together, yet leaving is the most dangerous process for the victim, as it is a time when most serious violence occurs.

Deborah Gould
Registered Psychologist (M.Soc.Sc. Clinical Psychology)

NSW Service for the Treatment
and Rehabilitation of Torture
and Trauma Survivors

CONTENTS

PART ONE

Is Intimate Partner Abuse a
Pattern of Addiction?

INTRODUCTION

Why another book about intimate partner abuse? Numerous books on this topic have already been written, yet key questions about the nature of abusive behaviours still remain unanswered. For example, why does the repetitive pattern of abuse or violence tend to escalate over the course of an intimate relationship, sometimes to the point where a partner is murdered?

Perhaps you have pondered this question too. Maybe you are in an abusive relationship or you are abusive towards your partner but would like to stop this behaviour? Perhaps someone close to you is trapped in a toxic love relationship and you don't know how to help them? Or maybe you simply want to understand why an abusive partner repeats their pattern of behaviour, even when they are fully aware of the consequences, and why this abuse escalates over time? If so, this book is for you.

It is also for readers interested in masculine and feminine psychology, or for those who'd like to improve their relationships with their partners and children, and prevent transmitting abusive patterns of behaviour from one generation to another.

According to the United Nations' Global Study on Homicide, women are far more likely to be killed by an intimate partner than by anyone else. Breaking the data down by continent, the highest rates of uxoricide (murder of wife or girlfriend) is in Africa, with rates descending in order in the Americas, in Oceania, and in Europe.[1]

Sadly, we are aware of these widespread tragedies behind closed doors, but we are also aware of the limitations in dealing with this epidemic. We blame the legal system, the police or the lack of social support for the victims. We blame the victim for staying with the man who abuses her, asking, 'Why doesn't she leave him?' Of course, we blame the perpetrator and sometimes ask ourselves, 'Why doesn't he leave her? If she hurts his feelings and makes him so angry, so often . . . if he has to "punish her", as he says, or "defend himself" from her attacks and provocations . . . why doesn't he simply leave her?' But we rarely ask, 'Do we really understand the nature of the perpetrator's patterns of abuse?' These patterns lie at the heart of domestic abuse and violence, and it is a well-known fact that they tend to escalate in frequency and severity, yet we still don't understand why.

This book explores these repetitive patterns. Please note that even though women can be abusive and physically violent, this volume will focus on male perpetrators. We, the authors, propose that these perpetrators' abusive behaviours contain a very specific 'ulterior gain'. By ulterior gain, we mean the hidden motivation behind the perpetrator's abusive behaviours. If we shed light on this, we can better explain the repetitive patterns of verbal abuse or physical violence and find more effective ways to break the cycle of abuse. No doubt, the better we under-

stand the sustained patterns of abuse, the mechanics behind them and 'how people can do this to other people',
the more empowered we are. The insights we glean can
help us to deal more effectively with the serious threat
that domestic violence poses.

An equally important goal of this book is to help the
victims to understand what drives an abuser to repeatedly
abuse them. It is easier to relinquish self-blame and protect yourself and your children when you can clearly see
not only *what* is going on in your toxic love relationship
but *why* you are experiencing abuse.

During counselling and consultations with abuse and
trauma survivors, we often witnessed that clarifying the
nature of the patterns and providing the information and
insights into a perpetrator's underlying motivation—the
motivation that is often denied, hidden or totally unconscious—can help them to stop rationalising their
partner's abusive behaviour and acknowledge the true
danger of the situation. Many victims report that counselling interventions, which help them to clearly see the
danger to their children and themselves, are the most
helpful in dealing with intimate partner abuse.

Shedding light on exactly what drives perpetrators to
re-offend can also help the male abuser or the man who is
concerned about becoming an abuser. It is to those men,
and the ones who care about them, that this book is also
written for. Do we really believe that abusive men would
read this book? Yes, we do. There are men who want to
stop abusing their partners. They want to know how they
can overcome the repetitive patterns of emotional abuse
or physical violence. That is why psychoeducation and an
understanding of how the cycle of abuse has been created
in the first place, and why the pattern tends to escalate, is
crucial.

However, the old theories and deep-seated convictions about the 'causes' and 'reasons' for such behaviours can become a hindrance to recovery. A shift in perspective is therefore necessary. Harmful actions are difficult to change if outdated belief systems about what fuels the behaviour are still active. One such belief is that domestic violence is 'all about power and control and nothing else'. Having worked for many years with both perpetrators and traumatised victims of torture, rape and abuse, we have realised that there is more to the repetitive patterns of abusive behaviour than the usual discourse about 'power and control'. We have come to the conclusion that some men use physical violence or verbal abuse addictively. And the urge to inflict pain is what makes them seriously dangerous—more dangerous than we may have initially thought.

Addicted to abusing?

Both behavioural addictions and the repetitive patterns of abusive behaviours in domestic violence share common features. For example, similar to the cycle of addiction, the typical cycle of abuse consists of the tension-building phase, the abuse stage (where the physical violence or verbal assault erupts) and the calm respite. After the calm respite, the cycle will repeat itself. What about the escalation of these patterns?

Despite the recognised fact that the repetitive patterns of intimate partner abuse tend to escalate, with emotional and verbal abuse often deteriorating into more overt threats or even physical violence, there have been very few satisfactory suggestions made as to why abuse intensifies over the course of a relationship. Does the abuse escalate because more severe or additional forms of abuse contribute to an increase in pleasant arousal, or a sense of satisfaction when the perpetrator releases unpleasant inner tension? We claim that it does.

Diminished control and developing tolerance are core defining concepts of substance and behavioural addictions. We know why drug addicts or problem gamblers need more and more of the substance (drug) or behaviour (gambling) over time—it's because of *tolerance*. The reduction in pleasure, termed tolerance, leads to more frequent, more intense or prolonged behaviour in an attempt to recreate the rewarding feelings. The cycle of intimate partner abuse also tends to speed up over time as the intervals between cycles become shorter, and the abuse may escalate in intensity and variety as well.

Of course, there are other factors that may have contributed to the pattern developing and escalating, but an abusive behaviour can in itself be an enjoyable experience for the perpetrator. Violence and anger are often linked to exhilaration. Anger is a high-arousal emotion. When anger is further combined with a sense of righteousness, the resulting action can be pleasant for the abuser.

There are other similarities between the repetitive patterns of intimate partner abuse and the patterns of addiction. For example, a prevalent belief about addictions is that they are, in part, a coping mechanism. They 'help' the person to deal with their unpleasant emotional states by masking them. The repetitive episodes of abuse in domestic violence can also help the abuser to mask his unpleasant emotional states.

Female victims of recurrent domestic violence report that their husbands tend to be more abusive towards them when they feel worried, bored, depressed or anxious, and even when they feel hurt, embarrassed, degraded or threatened by someone else who is not directly related to their partner. When life becomes boring or stressful, or when past traumatic experiences and unpleasant emotional states start to resurface, the perpetrator may need to sedate himself by abusing his partner, thus unleashing his unbearable tension while also drawing satisfaction from it. The abuse can then become habitual. Once this cycle is established, it tends to morph into a chronic downward spiral.

But is it really possible to become addicted to abusing an intimate partner? Physicians Dr Richard Irons and Dr Jennifer P. Schneider, recognised addiction experts and authors of numerous books, studied the parallel between substance addictions and domestic violence and published the article 'When is Domestic Violence a Hidden Face of Addiction?'

These prominent experts view the repetitive pattern of intimate partner abuse within a behavioural addiction paradigm. They published the article in 1997, yet their view has been completely ignored by academic researchers. Why? Perhaps because the notion that domestic violence could be an addiction leaves us bewildered. Some may strongly resist it for various reasons. The first questions and dilemmas usually concern legal and ethical issues, as well as responsibility and accountability for the perpetrator's behaviour. Many people might say, 'If we use the word addiction, we'll stop treating domestic violence as a crime, treating it instead as a problem or a disorder.'

The same behaviour is treated differently depending on the label attached to it—criminals and thieves are imprisoned while kleptomaniacs are prescribed therapy. On top of that, labelling abuse as an addiction may give the violent man permission to excuse himself, based on his 'condition', and he might evade responsibility for his crime.

Addicts are usually portrayed as victims of something that is beyond their control. The term 'addiction' might provide an excellent excuse, not just for his unacceptable behaviour but for the relapses, and make the failure to stop his 'addictive behaviour' (abuse) tolerable. A dilemma then arises: If we use a medical concept by labelling the repetitive patterns of abuse as an addiction, the focus will shift from the crime to the 'disease'. However, implying that the repetitive patterns of abuse could be a pattern of addiction does not mean that we should absolve the perpetrator from being held accountable for his criminal behaviour. Why would we? Unlike psychotic individuals, most domestic violence perpetrators (whether they are 'addicted' or not) are aware of what they are doing. Of course they should be held accountable for their crimes. That is unquestionable. The question is how to stop the repetitive patterns of their abusive behaviour. It's hard to stop doing something when you don't understand why you feel compelled to do it in the first place.

However, some men who have managed to quit domestic violence honestly revealed that they recognised a 'hungry beast' in themselves: the addict who craved fights with his partner. When they decided to quit, they were looking for the 'Uninstall the abuse program' button, but it was difficult to find.

It is our hope that the information presented in this book will motivate the men who are looking for that 'button' to cease their abusive behaviours. The insights into the mechanics behind the repetitive patterns of abusive behaviour can also help to kick-start an awakening in anyone who has a genuine intention to understand what they are doing to their partners and children, and to stop it.

Both victims and abusers have told us their painful stories and shared their experiences, and we are very grateful to them. The stories included in the book are based on our interactions and actual clinical work with these clients. The clients have given us their express permission to publish these stories for the reader's benefit. We have changed all names to protect the identities of the persons involved, but overall, what is written represents the issues brought before us in a counselling setting. The first part of the book covers topics relating to intimate partner abuse, and it explores the similarities between behavioural addictions and the repetitive patterns of abuse that tend to escalate in frequency and severity.

The second part explores strategies to break the repetitive cycle of abuse. It draws on a psychoeducational approach to dismantle the dangerous aspects of the personality that may have become addicted to abusing their partners. The topics also include inter-generational transmission of domestic violence, victim identification with the aggressor and factors that contribute to the 'conversion from terrorised into terrorising'.

Part three focuses on the process of healing from the trauma of abuse and creating healthier relationships. We discuss the domestic violence trap and the manipulative strategies that condition the victim to stay entrapped in an abusive bond, and other related psychological topics, including the differences between female and male psychology.

Chapter 1

WHY CAN'T HE LET HER GO?

The most difficult situation for a researcher is to deal with children who ask, 'Why?', only to meet replies with 'Yes, but why?' While such questions may be annoying, these 'Yes, but why?' questions can actually help us find answers because they invite us to expand our thinking beyond the obvious and dig below the surface. This question also helps us to realise the futility of going around in circles, especially when we feel hesitant to search deeper into the issues we want to understand.

What is it that we, the authors, are trying to understand? We want to know more about intimate partner abuse in general, but particularly the reasons why such abuse escalates in frequency and severity.

Yes, women can be abusive and physically violent, but this book will focus on male perpetrators. Why? There are two types of domestic violence: *situational couple violence* and a *sustained pattern of violence*. When it comes to family conflict and hostility in relationships, women are just as capable of being as abusive as men and can cause serious distress to their male partners. But when it comes to the repetitive and often easily recognisable patterns of abuse, the perpetrators are almost always men. The term 'domestic violence' usually encompasses both *situational* (conflict-initiated violence that results from situations or arguments between partners) and *sustained patterns*, but in this book, we are researching only *sustained patterns* of intimate partner abuse.

Michael P Johnson, emeritus professor at Pennsylvania State University and domestic violence expert, developed extensive typology for describing intimate partner violence. He has made a clear distinction between conflict-initiated episodes of abuse and the repetitive patterns of abuse.[1]

These two forms of abuse have different root causes and consequences for the victims. Situational couple violence, the most common type of domestic violence, usually erupts out of frustration and anger or the need to win or stop an argument. Usually, the violence is mild, and either isolated or sporadic, but sometimes it does warrant a call to police as disagreements can turn into angry quarrelling matches. These can then escalate into violence, even ending with physical injury. Typically, the abusive behaviours stem from a lack of communication skills and poor anger management, and the violence ends when the relationship does. This type of family violence is less likely to become a pattern or escalate over time.

The second type of abuse is the pattern of abuse that most people associate with the term 'domestic violence'. It's the kind of violence that dominates the statistics collected by police, hospitals and shelters for the victims, and it is almost always perpetrated by men against women. The abuse can be either strategic (proactive) or instinctive (reactive); nevertheless, it is the abuse from which women need ongoing protection even long after they have left the relationship. The sustained pattern of abusive behaviour is not necessarily a product of frustration or poor anger management skills, and it is not just about conflicts and disagreements.

Whether proactive or reactive, the abuse is cyclical. Once the cyclical pattern of abusive behaviour has been created, it tends to escalate in frequency and severity, yet we have not known why. Nor have we fully understood why it's hard for women to 'just leave' these abusive men. That's the subject we discuss in this book, but before we embark on a learning journey and explore this query, we must ask another related question: Why doesn't he leave her?

If he is so critical of her or if she hurts his feelings and triggers his anger to the extent that he becomes violent and, in some cases, even kills her in what he believes is self-defence, why doesn't he just get up and leave her? This question might sound ridiculous, naïve and childish, but our search for the answers leads us right to the crux of the domestic violence problem and helps us to understand what motivates the repetitive patterns of abuse.

Post-separation femicide—the most predictable and preventable of all homicides

Many regular folks with nice personalities experience divorce, and divorce does not necessarily mean failure. Some unions simply ought to be dissolved for various reasons. It was a good relationship or successful marriage for some time, but now it has run its course. Other marriages, which perhaps should be dissolved, endure. Couples live together to torment each other, deriving the morbid satisfaction of vengeance. This marriage sounds like warfare, with each seeking to win a victory over the other at any cost. No matter how many times we try, we cannot tell who plays the victim and who takes the role of the perpetrator in these family dramas.

Some marriages endure because the partners fulfil each other's needs and play mother or father to one another. Their needs can be normal or unusual, hidden or overt, infantile or neurotic. Some unconscious needs of the pair can be traced to their early childhood family settings, but they are okay with that, and who are we to say they should stay together or divorce as soon as possible?

Lastly, there are couples who live in the master-and-slave type of relationship. The complementarity of their roles is not voluntary. It is a combination of tyrannical ruthlessness and the victim's fear of opposing the tyrant. Their fear is palpable, and the victim's genuine degradation and pain within that bond is very real. Still, the victim's abuser prefers not to see themselves as an abuser, nor do they see the pattern of their abusive behaviour. Moreover, some intelligent men who know they have a bad temper (and a mean streak) would swiftly write off the idea that domestic violence is a repetitive pattern of abuse that increases in frequency and severity, instead claiming that such a notion is complete nonsense. 'It's not about a pattern! It's just a situation between us,' they believe. They also don't want to acknowledge their urge to repeat the same pattern of abuse over and over again.

These abusers do not like the idea of 'the compulsion to act violently' because it renders them powerless or out of control ('I am in control! Nothing is controlling me!'). They say that they act abusively because they want to punish their partner or defend themselves. However, we suggest that the main reason these abusers use physical violence or verbally abuse their partners is to alleviate their aversive internal emotional states (that may or may not be triggered by their partner) or simply because they crave excitement. But such suggestion does not sound right to them, either. 'It's a conflict between us, nothing else,' they claim.

The debate as to whether the cycle of abuse in their homes is 'conflict-initiated' sounds more titillating, so they would rather stick to that notion (and ignore the phrase 'repetitive patterns that tend to escalate') when discussing the causes and reasons for abusing their wives, and why the abuse gets worse. These abusers may deceive themselves into thinking that they can stop (mal) treating the woman 'in that particular (abusive) way' at any time, if they wished.

But interestingly, as far as many domestic violence perpetrators have been concerned, no inducement has been strong enough and no devastating consequences or circumstances of tragic family life frightening enough to draw them away from abusing their partners. If asked why they repeatedly abused their wives, they would offer a variety of reasons; however, none of their explanations would be that they cannot easily stop because they feel compelled to inflict pain.

What about the wife? Does she see that the man feels compelled to hurt her? It is not easy to accept that he repeatedly says and does things to her because he needs to cause her pain, degrade her and/or induce fear of him. All of the indicators and signs of abuse are there; still, it may not occur to the woman that her partner is a dangerous re-offending abuser.

The thought that a close family member 'needs' to hurt you is hard to digest. Especially when you do not know what to do with that insight or you feel powerless to protect yourself. Also, implicit statements like this one—that

13

the abuser 'craves' his partner's suffering—may sound too simplistic, inappropriate, offensive and frightening. The label 'sadist' is reserved for the mentally ill, criminals and psychopaths. It's not for ordinary, normal, mainstream people, and he is just that—he is one of us, a regular guy. So it cannot be that he repeatedly hurts a woman simply because 'he needs his fix'.

Yet there are esteemed professionals who believe there might be a grain of truth in the notion that the perpetrator 'craves a fix'. This is because they have noticed that some men are hooked on the pursuit of excitement that comes from the conflicts with their partners and the dramas that they tend to create out of nothing. Time after time, even without any provocation or triggers, the abuser will say something to his victim or do something that hurts her, plunging them both into a state of calamity that wreaks havoc in their relationship.

According to the abuser, such a notion that he 'craves a fix' is ludicrous. There are other and better explanations for his behaviour, he claims. For example, he will say that she provoked him. She said or did something, and he reacted the way he did (with violence or abusive behaviour) because he felt threatened or upset; he wanted to punish her for hurting him; he wanted to defend himself; or he felt insecure so he wanted to control and dominate. The victim and bystanders who witness the abuse may share the same opinion about the 'reasons' and 'causes' for his violence. Indeed, she provoked him; it is true that he felt threatened and wanted to defend himself; he has a short fuse; he wants to control and dominate her. But he is not abusive all the time! He can be nice, kind and loving as well.

Even when a woman does see that her partner has a hidden or perhaps totally unconscious need to inflict pain, she also sees the other side of him. He can be a caring and loving man. So, she wants to figure out why he gets angry and attacks her over trivial or totally insignificant things. Or she wants to help him because she loves him. She believes that if she understood his reasons for abusing her, she could correct herself or she could help him break the pattern of his 'up-and-down behaviour': being kind and affectionate in one moment and being mean and violent in another.

The man may also have a sensitive and easily frustrated, though ultimately lovable, Inner Boy aspect in his personality. The woman may be drawn to the child in him as she wants to take care of him. And not just to 'mother' him, but to help him grow into a strong, responsible and competent adult male. She believes there is potential in him, and she feels sorry for her partner when he suffers or when he is frustrated with her. However, if she just 'steps on his toes' or says the wrong thing, she might find herself in trouble. The lovable boy in the man then behaves like the 'King Baby'.

The King Baby persona may have a lot of unfulfilled infantile needs, and his ego is big, inflated and demanding. But there is more to it. If she does not forgive and forget the last episode of his violent explosions, no matter how profusely he apologised and promised that he would change and never hurt her again, he might get depressed, feel miserable or threaten suicide if she leaves him. The victim's problem is that the man's depression and neediness can easily hit her soft spot and make her relent, even though the abuser deeply hurts her or repeatedly batters her. She would feel guilty if something bad happened to him so she comes back home and gives him another chance.

Unfortunately, this man's rage can be intimidating and seriously dangerous. The woman may decide that she cannot stay and tolerate his abuse anymore. She may consider her options, perhaps read self-help books or brochures about domestic violence. She may become determined to either find a solution for her abusive relationship or find the way out of that toxic marriage. Yet, it is not easy. Actually, it can be very complicated, especially if she finds herself entrapped in a relationship with a man who does not want to let her go. It is not safe to stay with him, so she wants out, but is it safe to leave?

Statistics clearly indicate that the prevalence of spousal homicide is highest after separation or when the perpetrator realises that his partner is planning to leave him. That is why post-separation femicide —the intentional killing of females—is considered the most predictable and preventable of all homicides.[2] But why are there so many domestic femicides? And why do so many women get killed trying to escape from their abusers?

Some researchers believe that the triple 'R'— retaliation, restoration and reconciliation—can help to explain motives for post-separation violence.[3] The abuser engages in acts of *retaliation* against his partner as a way of hurting her for leaving him, or if he feels resentful that she is moving on with a new relationship. He may try to *restore* the power and control over her that was taken away from him when she left the relationship. He may also use violence, coercion or threats to their children, to try and force *reconciliation*. But, really, why is he so desperate to reconcile with her?

The stalking phenomenon

The behaviour of some abusive men is indeed quite pre-dictable. The victim knows that if she threatens to leave him or if she 'puts her foot down and stands up to him', his response will become even more violent. When she is determined to divorce him, her violent husband's frustration at losing her can fuel his attacks and cause him to stalk, intimidate, hurt or even murder her. Numerous cases of post-separation intimate partner homicides describe the murderer as a wild animal predator, stalking and chasing his 'prey' (his estranged partner) as though he wanted to squeeze out the last drops of terror and pain from her before he viciously attacked and killed her. Why? We know what the animal predator wants from its prey. The prey is food, and the animal desperately needs it. But what does the man want from the woman?

Much of the literature and statistics on domestic violence highlights separation as a risk factor for homicide. These statistics also found that stalking behaviour escalates when women leave their abusive partners. Alongside emotional and physical abuse, stalking too, may increase in frequency and/or severity. Even more notable is the finding that the length of time a woman is out of the abusive relationship is the strongest predictor of post-separation stalking. The longer she is out of his sight, the more frustrated he becomes.[4]

It seems to be so difficult for some men to not be in contact with their partners.[5] Many women who leave their violent partners continue to experience harassment, maltreatment or threats via phone and e-mail. Their fear is perfectly understandable. The abuse the women have already sustained clearly confirms their worst fear that stalking can easily escalate into more serious, life-threatening violence.

The victims often feel terrorised by this subset of abusive behaviour called *obsessional following*. He monitors her movements or messages, phones her at all hours of the day and night and turns up at her workplace or house uninvited. He often threatens self-harm or to kill her if she doesn't return to him. It is easy to see why intimate partner violence is also termed *intimate terrorism*.

Now it is clear that the answer to our question, 'Why doesn't she just leave him?' is that leaving does not necessarily end the violence, and in some cases, even escalates it. Therefore, we should focus on the question: 'Why doesn't he just let her go?'

Mother/child attachment

Using various psychological theories and schools of thought, researchers have tried to explain the question *'Why doesn't he let her go?'* and understand the (seemingly) illogical persistence of pursuit/stalking behaviours by abusive men when their partners leave, resist or reject them. Attachment theory is one example.

According to attachment theory, we all develop a particular attachment style—either secure, anxious, avoidant, ambivalent or disorganised—based on our relationship with a parent or early caregiver. If the caregivers in a child's life are responsive to the child's needs, they are a source of comfort and safety. However, victims of deficit or lack of care and nurturing generally have had their normal childhood needs unfulfilled at a time when they were most vulnerable. Instead of secure attachment, these children experience disorganised, avoidant or ambivalent attachment adaptations. Such dysfunctional

styles of relating can become cemented in their characters, influence expectations of others and determine the
way they will relate to future partners.

Could a history of early attachment disruptions in
childhood be a risk factor for engaging in stalking behaviour? Is the abuser's intense scrutiny, monitoring and
harassment a form of proximity-seeking behaviour designed to re-establish a secure base in the face of
perceived or actual threats of separation from their intimate partner?

Many forms of obsession have some kind of craving
behind them or a desire to fulfil a developmental need.
The man's obsession with female love can indeed mask
his childhood emotional deprivation and basic needs that
have not been fulfilled. When men with such patterns of
attachment perceive threats to their relationship or possible abandonment by their wives, they may use
desperate means, including violence, to prevent their
wives from leaving. However, there are other reasons why
domestic violence perpetrators stalk their partners.

Typology of stalkers

Some men press for contact with their 'beloved woman'
with oceanic force as if they want to possess the heart and
mind of their mate. They claim they have finally found
their 'true soulmate' and are in a hurry to cement the
bond. Once cemented, the bond may quickly turn into
the domestic violence trap. These men may or may not
use charm and 'love bombing' to allure a woman into the
trap but they almost always use abuse to keep her in it.
They want to feel superior and demand instant gratification, tending to clarify and define their needs as a
priority—and the woman should rally around them. If she

protests, they react with rage and attempt to terrorise her into obedience.

If she threatens to break up the toxic bond, their controlling and violent behaviours become stronger. The abuse can be psychological, physical and/or financial. By blocking or controlling access to money, abusers can coerce their victims into staying with them or coming back if they try to leave. Why do they want her to stay? These types of abuser and stalkers are not afraid of abandonment and may not have early attachment issues or childhood traumas, but they are afraid of losing control over the woman. They like to dominate, so they want to continue with the 'I dominant – You submissive' type of relating. If she escapes her 'I submissive' position, they can't play 'I dominant', and that's what bothers them. They need her so they want her back.

Their stalking tends to be dangerous. These ruthless and cold bullies may begin with phone calls that gradually become more threatening and aggressive, leading to other behaviours that frequently end in physical violence.

Not all stalkers are motivated by the same desires and urges. Stalking is a crime, and stalkers are criminals, but these men do differ. Some of them are psychopaths, others may suffer from borderline or narcissistic personality disorder, and some are paranoid or delusional.

There is also one particular type of a stalker: a man who looks for total, permanent commitment in an intimate relationship and the kind of happiness that can be found only through merging with a soulmate. The soulmate is depicted as the missing piece of a puzzle that joins together perfectly with his piece. He can feel complete only if he has that special person by his side. Enmeshed in his partner's energy field, he can lose his sense of autonomy; nevertheless, he wants a woman he can count on to take care of his material or emotional needs, and in return he will care for her emotional and/or material needs. But there is a flip side to it: If her feelings are not reciprocal, he can become dangerously vindictive. Not only does he tend to merge too closely or too quickly with her, but he expects absolute loyalty and feels betrayed if she wants to leave. So why is her loyalty so important?

He may believe that their shared energy is vital for his psychological survival and that he will not be able to exist without her. Therefore, no reason for his partner's leaving him is acceptable. The desire to have a dependable relationship—to offer everything and have the partner reciprocate with 'everything'—often pushes him too far, and he may become a seriously invasive and aggressive stalker. Not being able to tolerate the frustration, anxiety and the distress triggered by the separation, and especially the fear that without her his needs will not be met, this 'erotomaniac' tends to bully and stalk the woman.

Some other stalkers are not erotomaniacs but narcissists, or they suffer from various personality disorders. They feel entitled to the woman's attention, admiration, time and resources, interpreting every criticism or rejection as an act of aggression, thus reacting with rage. Why rage? For violent men, the quickest way to escape unpleasant emotional states—to discharge unbearable inner tension or mask painful emotions—is through anger.

The impulse to rage in order to release tension is so quickly translated into harsh words or violent actions that the impulse and the action have become one and the same. But there is more to it. Anger and rage can serve not only to get rid of a sense of frustration or tension, but as a substitute for other unpleasant emotions. When these people feel hurt, they get angry. When they feel disappointed, they get angry. When they are sad or afraid, they will switch immediately into anger because grief and fear is disempowering while anger empowers them. Raging can also serve as an excellent anaesthetic. For instance, the abuser who perceives certain situations as humiliating—when others do something that hurts his pride, or others fail to do what his pride requires of them—does not necessarily feel humiliation or hurt directly. He may feel a *substitute emotion*: anger. In many cases, the 'substitution process' is unconscious and not deliberately exploited, especially when it is developed at a very early age.

Either conscious or unconscious, anger helps the abusive man *not* to feel unpleasant emotions. Those who have provoked his rage should feel it! That is why the repetitive pattern of his abusive behaviour—reacting with angry outbursts whenever he feels hurt or upset—has become a conditioned reflex. While some intimate partner abusers use violence instrumentally (in order to achieve a goal), this *reactive abuser* acts out of anger in response to a perceived threat. Unwilling or unable to stay in contact with his internal psychological experiences, he is determined to avoid them. And if his partner threatens him with separation, raging can help him to subdue his pain or fear of living without her.

The inner as well as outer world of some violent men can be both brutal and sentimentally weak at the same time. There is a type of domestic violence perpetrator who is emotionally dependent on his partner and terrified that she will leave him, but also terrified of his own dependency. He often ends up blaming his wife for not satisfying his needs that can never be satisfied, and he tends to keep her everyday movements strictly under his control. He controls her, not necessarily because he wants to dominate her, but out of fear of losing her. He is obsessively jealous and scared she will leave him. At the same time, this may make him resent how dependent he has become on her, and how vulnerable 'she has made him feel'.

When his relationship breaks up, he becomes even more abusive and preoccupied with his partner. He may not react with explosive outbursts immediately upon separation because he may believe that she will return. As it becomes apparent that she will not, he begins to stalk her. His desperation may be such that he'd do anything to get her back—he'd rage, then cry and express remorse, then rage again.

Many abusers behave violently and express rage not only to punish their partner or frighten her so she will come back to them, but to cope with their own weaknesses and dependency needs. It is easy to spot this perpetrator's vulnerable side when he is crying and begging his estranged partner to come back, threatening suicide, making promises of never hurting her again, and that she'll be safe if she returns to him. He is behaving like a desperate little boy totally unprepared for the loss of his mother, and just a few moments later, he is yelling at the woman he feels emotionally dependent on.

The witnesses of these family scenes are often taken aback by how quickly a domestic violence perpetrator's neediness can be replaced with episodes of infantile, primitive fury. His hidden aversion and intolerance for dependency and neediness—in others, as well as in himself—can be very intense, and he wants to avoid such emotional states with the help of rage. Acting like a wounded wild animal, he attacks her not just because she is leaving him, but also for revealing the weak spots that he is supposed to hide at all costs. When he starts stalking his partner, he is like a dangerous pit-bull dog that sinks its teeth into a victim and won't let her go.

Undoubtedly, many intimate partner abusers and stalkers want power and control over their partners. They have childhood issues or an ambivalent relationship with their mothers and/or they may experience deep-seated problems with separation anxiety. This makes them desperate to continue their relationship with their partner. If they feel dependent on the woman (for whatever reason), then separation is a serious matter. But, even if we take into account the perpetrators' early childhood attachment disruptions, their personality disorders, the drive to control and dominate their partner, and the influential traumatic experiences on their current abusive behaviours, we still cannot fully explain the persistence of their abusive behaviours and unwillingness to let go of the woman who wants to escape them.

Stalking as excitement-seeking?

Is stalking always an attempt to get a partner back? Not necessarily. For those who find a thrill in stalking the woman, harassing can be fun, so they abuse her just for the fun of it. When actively engaged in stalking, they are like passionate hunters who find pleasure in chasing their prey. They know that they are annoying her when sending messages or insisting on seeing her. They know that they will scare her when unexpectedly turning up in front of her. They know that she will feel humiliated when they attack her in front of her colleagues, but they don't mind.

On the contrary, her response—her distress, humiliation or fear—may pleasantly excite them. Their pestering serves as a strategy to extract an emotional reaction from their victim, and if the behaviour is provocative enough to trigger the victim's stronger emotional reactions—the 'cocktail' of her fear, pain and degradation— the perpetrators' sense of satisfaction may increase even more.

There is no doubt that the excitement of chasing, abusing, bullying and frightening can contribute to feelings of satisfaction and even pleasure in some abusive men who stalk their estranged partners. Experts believe any behaviour that provides an intense pleasant emotional experience can become addictive. These patterns of addictive behaviours tend to increase in frequency and severity. Could this explain why in some cases, alongside emotional and physical abuse, stalking too, may increase in frequency and severity?

I am not abusing her!

There are men who do not tend to control and dominate their partners, yet they may easily experience an intense feeling of having been wronged by them and a burning sense of injustice. Many domestic violence perpetrators do feel that they have been victims of injustice, so justice has become an important issue. If we ask them about their beliefs on social justice and social values, they will tell us, often with a sarcastic smile, that they have had enough of that so-called 'justice' and other sentimental, sugary stories about social ideals.

Some claim they realised the truth about the nature of human society and its unfairness a long time ago, sometimes even in their early childhood. As children, they would be punished for something they did not do, or were able to get away with something they did do. After having such experiences and witnessing many similar circumstances, they don't trust authorities and the legal social system. As for ideals such as equality, fairness, brotherhood, spiritual values and similar airy-fairy non-sense, they can convince you with absolute certainty that this is simply a shrewd way of exploiting the gullible. Nothing else.

The anger and venom they experience is then an inevi-table emotional reaction to perceiving reality in this way. They blame their mothers who left them, abused them or didn't protect them from abusive men; they are angry at the women they have assaulted 'because they didn't re-spect them'; or they blame the world and are out to make it right.

If they are open enough to show the feelings beneath their reasoning about justice, we may notice something else. If they were severely hurt and humiliated as chil-dren, their innocence and pure goodness derided, or their love rejected, they may have a great fear that they will be tricked by allowing themselves to sense love and good-ness again, only to have it taken away once more. So, they do not believe in the positive qualities in human nature, nor do they believe in love in general. But they do believe in revenge. Those who believe in revenge usually see it as the only way they can balance the imbalances between themselves and others, if they think that others exploited, abused or took advantage of them.

Children sometimes have a similar take on the concept of retribution. Using child-like interpretation, the act of revenge has a magical power to 'delete' the damage done to them as victims. The reasoning goes like this: 'Some-one hurts and humiliates us, so we are in pain. We retaliate by hurting them. That will enable us to rid our-selves of our own pain and sense of shame—the shame linked to our initial powerlessness when we couldn't do anything to avert this person. We couldn't do anything to them then, but we can now! Therefore, revenge restores the previous state of peace and stability in our life. And we get our power back, too.

This is the philosophy of retaliation behind the phrase, 'An eye for an eye, and a tooth for a tooth', and this is why a child may believe that when they retaliate, they will no longer feel offended, hurt, abused or taken advantage of. We may say that it is just childish, magical thinking, but children believe in magic.

The adult believers in the magical power of retaliation are also convinced that revenge can serve to restore their previous state of inner peace and neutralise the damage done. We can find this belief system about the power of revenge to restore the state of balance in many stories and myths in which war lords of all kinds have the leading roles.

How does that magic work? For example, a loss of face has been experienced. We attempt to remedy the situation by taking revenge. What is in revenge that can help? Revenge can be defined as an unconscious attempt to get rid of the shame arising from humiliation. We feel humiliated when someone has power over us, but when we retaliate, we don't feel that type of shame any longer, so we regain our original state prior to the experience of losing face.

Domestic violence perpetrators often share this same belief. The anger and the fits of rage begin in the gut and move rapidly up and outwards, stimulated by perceived injustice and unfair treatment. The perpetrator wants to retaliate: 'If you do it to me, I'll get you back!' The key element in this belief system is that the pain he inflicts as revenge can serve as a painkiller for his own pain. We could call it shifting responsibility and blaming the victim, we could call it personal vendetta, but that's the only thing he believes he could do to bring back his lost sense of peace and calm.

To believe that revenge will help us restore emotional balance means that we will stay unforgiving towards those who inflicted pain. We will continue to hold others accountable and try to set things right; in other words, we will keep fighting, punishing, stalking. As many stalkers know, thoughts of revenge serve to block the feelings of powerlessness, humiliation and betrayal after their partner has left them. When they catch up with the woman and hurt her, her distress, fear, shame and pain calm their own pain. These are the typical domestic violence perpetrators who claim that they do not want to abuse their partners. They only want to punish her. To punish her for what? For something she said or did, (or didn't do) that made them feel hurt, humiliated, frustrated, anxious or tense. Why is punishing their partners so important to these men? Because 'punishing' her (abusing her) for causing the problem is the familiar way to discharge their unpleasant tension or dissolve the distress triggered by their partner's words or deeds. What are the mechanics behind it?

Feeling the pain of disrespect, hurt or humiliation gives rise to the abuser's conviction that he has been wilfully mistreated, betrayed or degraded. He interprets his partner's words or actions as though they not just trigger but *cause* his unpleasant emotional response. He is feeling bad and that is her fault! But he does not want to be her victim. He can protect himself from a painful emotional state if he punishes her for the hurt 'inflicted by her'. From his perspective, the only way he can release tension or 'lift himself up' from the heavy feelings of distress is to say or do something that generates her distress, her sense of humiliation and/or her fear of him.

Putting her through the same or similar suffering that 'she inflicted on him' is dubbed 'punishment'. He can easily justify such behaviour. As he perceives her as the *cause* of his painful feelings, so has he the right to punish: 'If I have been wilfully mistreated, have I not the right to protect or avenge myself?' To him, vindictiveness is the best form of self-protection because it has a very important restorative function. It is a strategy to restore injured pride and suppress pain, grief, hopelessness, helplessness or separation anxiety.

After avenging himself by punishing his partner (abusing her), he can be nice and friendly again, as if nothing had happened. Until then, all his energy and thoughts are dedicated to the one goal of vindictive triumph. He believes that he cannot escape from his unpleasant inner state of tension and discomfort if he does not provoke her emotional response (her distress).

When he feels wronged, the compulsive drive towards revenge can be his governing passion to which everything else is subordinated. As with many other perpetrators, he would likely confirm his worst fear is to find himself in a prolonged state of suffering—when he feels degraded, ignored, inferior, powerless or controlled by others—and not able 'to right the wrong' (retaliate). That's why he feels compelled to hurt his partner, and that's why he perceives the punishment as a protective self-defence mechanism. When he is in anguish, just like a drug addict who desperately needs his fix, the perpetrator needs his partner to suffer. Why? The woman's distress, the 'cocktail' of her humiliation, fear and pain, serves as the painkiller for the perpetrator in pain.

A partner's words or behaviours—interpreted by him as criticism, rejection or disrespect—trigger his tension. The increased unpleasant tension drives the urge to discharge the tension by 'punishing' her, which means 'inflicting pain'. The release of tension creates a feeling of satisfaction. He cannot release tension and draw satisfaction from it unless she suffers.

Now we can answer the question, 'Why can't he let her go?' If his favourite method of protecting himself is revenge, then he wants to take his partner—perceived as a perpetrator who is abusing and humiliating him or a traitor who is abandoning him—through the similar experience of abuse and humiliation.

The abusive man whose intimate partner threatens to separate from him cannot imagine forgiving her for leaving him, unless she has suffered. Revenge is his method of self-defence, and she must pay the price for leaving him. Only this way will she understand the pain that she has inflicted on him! Indeed, the woman is in grave danger when she is about to leave her abusive partner.

So, why can't he let her go? He can, but only after he avenges himself for the distress she has caused by breaking their bond. Only then will he be able to release her from his life. Besides, what he did to her was all her fault. She is the perpetrator! She betrayed him. She abused him. He was only defending himself.

The Women We Failed

Comrie Cullen's ex-husband Christopher Cullen was sentenced last July to 30 years' jail for the callous stabbing of his wife. He had continually threatened and harassed her following their marriage breakdown and accused her in public of sleeping with her clients at a Shire hair salon.

After an appearance in court, he followed her home, assaulted her, forced her into his car boot then stabbed her and left her for dead in a lake. His argument that he had been provoked and was acting in self-defence was rejected.

(From the article 'Voices rise to protect victims of abuse', *The Sydney Morning Herald*, March 12-13. 2016).

Chapter 2

IN THE BEGINNING

What are men looking for in women? Some men feel attracted to women who need them. If a woman presents herself in such a way that she is totally independent, some men will often pick up on this attitude and respond by treating her not as a potential partner but as a friend or like 'one of the boys'. Dating experts warn women that showing you don't need a man is one of the best male repellents in existence.

What about women? What do they want? When dating coaches answer Sigmund Freud's proverbial question, 'What do women want?', and 'psycho-educate' single men about female psychology, they tell them that the two top qualities from the women's wish list are the protector—a good, decent man who cares about her and is capable of supporting and protecting his family; and the empath—the man who can understand her and empathise with her. But how then do we explain the enduring allure of 'bad boys'?

Some women are more attracted to the tough and rough guy than the kind, good and soft guy. And there is a reason for that. The sexual chemistry and close relationship with a carnal, masculine and strong man who openly shows that he is attracted to her can make the woman feel good because she feels wanted and desired. Strong and confident men are significantly more attractive than their soft counterparts who approach women with a permanent 'please like me' smile. This is a big turn-off for many single women. They would rather date a tough guy who shows desire for and interest in them than the kind and sensitive man with the 'I need a girlfriend' mindset—the needy attitude of a man who wants to be taken care of.

Another reason a woman may prefer a tough guy is because she feels secure with him. Relationship counsellors explain that women love the protection these men offer. Okay, tough guys are more attractive than needy boys, but why are the empaths so high on a woman's wish list?

One of the most profound human needs is the need to be recognised and heard. It is amazing how much healing can take place when our problems, feelings or opinions are simply heard. That's why some women appreciate men who are able to listen to and understand their feelings, thus helping them to shed unpleasant emotions or cope with a stressful situation at work and/or in the family.

Women who don't have empathic husbands prefer to talk through their concerns and issues with a girlfriend who listens, shows empathy and reflects back the woman's experiences and views. Feeling 'understood' and having emotions acknowledged and validated will help her to recognise and articulate her distress, sometimes even releasing the painful emotional charge attached to the unpleasant interpersonal or family problem, and eventually move on.

Stroke Seeking and the Need for Recognition

We all need strokes—defined as units of recognition, attention and stimulation through contact with others. Eric Berne, the founder of Transactional Analysis (TA), psychotherapy and a theory of personality, defined a stroke as the 'fundamental unit of social action'.[1] Berne introduced the term recognition-hunger and the idea of strokes into TA based upon the work of Rene Spitz, a researcher who did pioneering work in the area of child development.[2] Spitz observed that infants deprived of touching and cuddling were more likely to experience emotional and physical difficulties.

However, in his formulation of TA, Berne extended the term stroking to mean not only physical touching, but any form of social recognition and human attention. The exchange of strokes is one of the most important activities people engage in. Unfortunately, a large number of human beings are hungry for attention and for recognition of their qualities or unique characteristics. Even negative attention is better than no attention at all. When we are starving for emotional food, just about any kind tastes better than nothing. However, it does not mean this is healthy or nourishing.

Some people manipulate others to get attention. Some people give attention to others to manipulate them as showing interest, kindness and affection can be used as bait that serves to allure.

From the charmer into the perpetrator

When a single woman finds an attractive man who listens to her—he pays attention to her and how she feels; he is kind, caring and gentle—she describes him as charming. Alas, giving loving attention can also be used as bait that serves to allure. Some men who have made a great loving and charming first impression end up as domestic violence perpetrators.

In the beginning, a woman usually does not find anything alarmingly wrong with the man who will later become her perpetrator. On the contrary, she may be delighted with him and feel comfortable with him. She may be in love and feels good and at ease in his presence. She may especially enjoy the man's attention. He looks at her as if she were the most interesting, attractive, beautiful person he has ever met. It is the intensity of his focus on her that can be so seductive and intoxicating.

When Snežana first met her partner, she thought she was a very lucky woman. He was handsome and charming, and he spent all his time with her. He revered her beauty and intelligence, and he claimed that she was the best cook in the former Yugoslavia.

He told her about his life in Australia, and that he wanted to marry her and bring her to this beautiful country. He created the fantasy about what their life in Australia would be like; he made all sorts of promises; he built them a house near the beach.

'He told me all the things I wanted to hear,' she said. 'I was divorced, lonely, unemployed. I really wanted to get married again and start a new life.'

Snežana was in her late thirties at the time, but she disclosed she had still fantasised about being swept off her feet by a handsome man (knight in shining armour) who would make all her dreams come true.

And one summer's day, when this 'knight' visited his country of origin, he met Snežana, offered to rescue her from her dreary life and promised love, intimacy and pleasures.

If a woman was deprived of love and attention in childhood, perhaps she didn't have a family or a caring father figure, and her new boyfriend is offering what she needs the most—she can be particularly vulnerable to a charmer. She is hungry for kindness and recognition of her qualities, talents, goodness and beauty. The charming man comes to her, and he talks about his love for her.

> He was so persuasive! He was pushing for marriage during the first month of their relationship, and Snežana didn't see that their too-quick bonding was a sign that she was heading for some rough waters. On the contrary, she felt flattered and happy because he was ready to commit fully to her. When people fall in love, they want to be together, she thought. But to move in together and start making wedding plans within first two weeks? No, she didn't see it as a red flag.

It is not difficult to get hooked on that type of emotional pleasure, especially if a woman has been starved of it for years. He seduces her by offering what she needs and develops closeness by confiding secrets, sharing intimate details or talking about his painful childhood experiences.

> Ten times a day he would say how much he loved her; he created a nice atmosphere of closeness between them and shared his most intimate details with her. He told her about his unhappy childhood and how his mother used to humiliate him. Snežana became really close to him; she could tell him everything about herself.

The abuse usually starts with words. The victim feels the sting; she feels belittled for the moment and devalued as a person. Nevertheless, she may think there is 'nothing to create a drama about'. His abusiveness is just a temporary difficulty, a rough patch he is going through. Or she may try to correct or change herself to please him. But he keeps inflicting more and more pain.

He was perfect until the day they got married and came to Australia. Not long after the marriage ceremony, Snežana found herself isolated in a western Sydney suburb with a man who suddenly became emotionally cold. He was charming, loving and an attentive listener just a few weeks ago, but now he was moody, brooding and disinterested in her. His controlling behaviour began to show in small ways. For example, he liked her food, but Snežana wasn't allowed to cook what she wanted, only what he'd tell her to cook.

The first warning that he had a dark side occurred during a seemingly insignificant incident when she spent a bit more money in the supermarket than they planned. Out of the blue, his charm turned to rage, and she was under attack. 'You are so stupid! Do you have a brain, you moron?' he said to humiliate her. Snežana froze and became very quiet.

Her initial internal commentary was, 'He has a problem with his anger. Yes, his explosions indicate that he is capable of childish and intimidating outbursts, but he is also a good man.'

Just a few days later, he began what was to become a familiar 'refrain': she'd do something, and he'd verbally attack her. She tried to understand or justify his behaviour. Perhaps the cause of his angry outbursts was in his traumatic childhood? He was abused by his parents...she explained it away to herself.

His intimidation of Snežana became cold and systematic, and yet he would occasionally be sweet and loving, so she hoped that she could bring out the charming and loving side of him that had initially won her attention and love. But his abuse only escalated.

Why does he behave like that?

The Formula is in *Fifty Shades of Grey*

Snežana's relationship was so good in the beginning. But then a nasty aspect in the man's personality started to rear its ugly head. What did he want? Allegorically, *Fifty Shades of Grey* can shed some light for us.

E. L. James, the author of the *Fifty Shades of Grey* trilogy, has fashioned its primary antagonist Christian Grey after the beautiful and rich but corrupt young man Dorian Gray in Oscar Wilde's novella *The Picture of Dorian Gray*.

In *Fifty Shades of Grey*, Christian Grey, a young, handsome and rich guy meets innocent, pretty-girl Anastasia Steele. Anastasia likes him as he is charming. She would like to have a normal relationship with him, a nice romance, perhaps. Then the trouble begins. He starts to introduce an 'I dominant – You submissive' type of relating. She doesn't like it. But on the other hand, he can be a real charmer. This would certainly strengthen her hopes that he is, after all, just a regular guy who is playing a bit of a weird game. It is nothing serious, or so she thinks.

Her first experiences with his sadistic side are disconcerting. She can sense that something is wrong here, but the Charmer in him makes her feel so special. So, she'll stay and try the 'fusion of passion and pain' one more time. She can always leave if she doesn't like it.

Christian gains a great deal of pleasure in Anastasia's submission (pain), and that is obvious. Why didn't she leave him? Yes, she detected the Abuser aspect in Christian's personality. She is not stupid! However, she knows that he was a victim of horrific abuse in his childhood (he has a history of being 'submissive' himself) so she was hoping she might help him to heal his childhood traumas and help him to get rid of his sadist tendencies.

Christian gradually increases the level of pain he wants to inflict on Anastasia. He clearly needs a stronger dose of his 'excitement' and he needs it more frequently. In the beginning, it was from Friday night to Sunday night, but then he desired it in the middle of the week too. Anastasia is not sure she wants to stay, but he is now desperate to keep her. He doesn't want to let her go!

Finally, she understands what the 'game' about inflicting pain and degrading her is all about. She now knows that he is addicted to a special type of pleasure.

Is it possible to become addicted to an 'I dominant – You submissive' type of relating? We believe it is. But why do the women tolerate it? Some people believe that unlike other crimes, domestic violence is complicated by the not-infrequent complicity of victims who love their abusers. Some even believe in feminine masochism. However, the great majority of victims of intimate partner abuse do not want pain and suffering. It is not true that they 'love the abuse'. They want a normal relationship with a normal guy. To say that they want to be humiliated and beaten, or to claim that *Fifty Shades of Grey* tells the story of an affair between a masochistic woman and her sadistic lover, is to completely miss the point.

But if the woman isn't interested in playing 'I submissive', why doesn't she leave an abusive man? What is her problem? Her problem is that the Regular guy aspect in the man's personality shares the same body and psyche with a personality aspect that has become addicted to abusing. She likes only the Regular guy, but the Abuser comes with the package.

An additional problem is having a contaminated mind. She may clearly see both aspects in the man's personality, but she believes that the 'true him' is the one who shows affection, while the 'abusive him' will not last long. She doesn't understand that the Abuser aspect is here to stay. As long as she hopes that the Abuser will disappear from her life, she may be reluctant to leave.

Chapter 3

THE MEN WHO INFLICT PAIN

Evidence for extreme brutality in the sex industry is rich. If a sex worker is beaten and raped, we may consider it an occupational hazard given her field of work. Not many people would ask, 'Why did he do that to her?' A certain percentage of her clientele are the men who find pleasure in inflicting pain through beating and raping. These are the men who do it for pleasure, and they will probably do it again. Why again? One of the most dangerous drugs on the planet is the fusion of sex and violence, and those addicted are not only predatory but persistent offenders.

But how do we explain why ordinary men, who supposedly love their partners and show no signs of such sadism, repeatedly abuse, humiliate and even rape their wives? We often hear the answer, 'Because they want power and control over her'. Or we talk about the 'leading risk factors' for domestic violence such as 'the perpetrator's lack of respect for the woman; his negative communication style and inability to resolve conflict with her; his lack of empathy and inability to care about her feelings; male privileges etcetera'.

However, a lack of respect for women, male privilege or the socialisation of men isn't necessarily a leading risk factor that shapes the repetitive pattern of intimate partner abuse, a pattern that tends to increase in frequency and severity. Consider, for instance, the slogan *'Real men don't rape!'* in campaigns to prevent violence against women. It has been an attempt to send the message that rape is not part of real masculinity. The idea is to create a culture that shames rapists or makes them feel inferior to 'real men'.

While it comes from a place of good intention, the phrase is utterly useless. By saying, 'Hey, you don't need to rape to express or prove your masculinity,' we convey the message that the reason an abuser rapes women is to prove his masculinity. What if he doesn't want to prove anything? He simply craves the thrill when he rapes (his wife or a stranger) and if he is already 'into the habit' of raping or molesting—like paedophiles, for example—he will feel compelled to do it again and again because it is the mechanics behind any addiction.

Theories about the nature of domestic violence

There are many theories that try to explain why people become abusive in relationships, some theories are socially based and some are psychologically based. The oldest and perhaps most widely discussed theory focusses on personality disorders and early life experiences that increase the risk of violent behaviour. In the social science literature, two broad theoretical approaches explaining the phenomenon of intimate partner abuse are the feminist/patriarchal and social learning theories.

According to the feminist/patriarchal theory, the primary origin of male-to-female violence is deeply rooted in the patriarchal ideology. Domestic violence is seen as a reflection of the sexist culture and institutions that perpetuate the oppression of women. Men's intentions are to exercise power and control over women and restrict their autonomy. These men possess a sense of entitlement and hold attitudes that condone the abuse of women. When they experience powerlessness or feel inferior to other more powerful men who control them, the men in patriarchal societies can resort to more aggressive forms of domination or seek to have more control over a woman. Thus, the feminist theory asserts that the goal of male aggression is to dominate his female partner, and domestic violence is defined as a tool used to intimidate and subjugate women.

'Unless we strive for equal power relationships between men and women, women will continue to be victims of these kinds of assaults,'[1] Lenore E. Walker, one of the early feminist psychotherapists and the leading authority in the area of domestic violence, writes in her book *Battered Woman*. Such use of violence in order to control the woman suggests that battering serves as a coercive means of influence. Walker noted that 'A battered woman is a woman who is repeatedly subjected to any forceful physical or psychological behavior by a man in order to coerce her to do something he wants her to do without any concern for her rights.'[2]

No doubt, the feminist/patriarchal theory can help us to understand domestic violence in patriarchal societies, but how do we explain the repetitive patterns of intimate partner abuse in modern societies? The pervasiveness of violence against women even in contemporary societies is still the norm. East or west, rich or poor, educated or illiterate, liberal or conservative, women worldwide suffer the trauma of abuse. Their partners' abusive behaviours include locking women away in their homes, punching, hitting, kicking, slapping or strangling, inflicting permanent injuries, and even killing. At least one Australian woman is murdered by her partner or ex-partner *every week*, and on average more than three women a day are murdered by their husbands or boyfriends in the United States.[3]

How do we explain this? Linda G. Mills, J.D., PhD says in her book *Violent Partners: A Breaking Plan for Ending the Cycle of Abuse*, 'The popular conception of domestic violence, in which the female victim lives in terror of her controlling abuser, only represents a small fraction of the American couples struggling with violence today.'[4]

Even though there is no singular profile of a domestic abuser's psychology, and some seriously violent and re-offending abusers do not tend to dominate their partners, the framework of 'power and control' is still commonly used to explain the patterns of domestic abuse.

Another popular perspective on intimate partner violence is based on Albert Bandura's social learning theory. According to this theory, if an individual learns that a certain abusive or violent behaviour will result in a specific positive or desirable outcome, then this behaviour has a high probability of reoccurring whenever the goal is desired. For example, if a father uses violence against his wife and children with 'successful results' (they do what he wants them to do), children, particularly sons, are more likely to model the father's behaviour, especially when parents encourage or demonstrate approval for such behaviour.

Thanks to social learning theories we know that children not only copy the behaviours of their abusive parents, but internalise their belief systems and attitudes about violence: 'You must punish the woman who is disrespectful!'; 'Threats get you what you want'; 'A person has two choices—to be the aggressor or be the victim—and it is better to be the aggressor than to be a victim' and so on.

Unfortunately, by identifying with our parents and internalising their beliefs, we learn not only how to perpetrate, but how to be victims of domestic violence as well. Many studies show that women who live with abusive men saw their mothers being abused. We often hear them saying, 'My father abused my mother, and I learned that it was okay for men to behave abusively and speak to women in that manner.'

Can perpetrators change their beliefs and attitudes about domestic abuse? The idea behind these two theories (feminist and social learning), and the Duluth model of change, which is based on both theories, is that since perpetrators have learned to use violence as one mechanism to control and dominate women—they have been socialised into rigid gender roles; have attitudes that men are superior; and/or believe that women should be punished (abused) if they do not comply with their gender-role expectations—they can also 'unlearn' it.

The Duluth Model

The Duluth Model is a well-known intervention program derived from the Duluth Domestic Abuse Intervention Program (DAIP) in Duluth, Minnesota. It was designed to address the issue of domestic violence and protect women from the tyranny of abusive men.[5] It is based on the feminist theory and social work perspective, and defines domestic violence as a pattern of abusive behaviour that an individual uses to intentionally control or dominate intimate partners.

The model views assault as a choice, made by men acting in concert with the norms of a sexist society.

The Power and Control Wheel has been developed to diagram the pattern of abusive behaviours perpetrators use to establish and maintain control over their partners. The wheel includes eight items: (1) intimidation, (2) emotional abuse, (3) isolation, (4) economic abuse, (5) male privilege, (6) coercion and threats, (7) using children, and (8) minimising, denying, and blaming.

The aim of the interventions is to reduce patriarchal attitudes and power and control motives, and to re-socialise or convince men to use the nonviolent strategies outlined in the Equality Wheel. The eight items making up this wheel are (1) negotiation and fairness, (2) economic partnership, (3) shared responsibility, (4) responsible parenting, (5) honesty and accountability, (6) trust and support, (7) respect, and (8) non-threatening behaviour.

Critics of the intervention and behaviour change programs based on the Duluth Model argue that the model does not consider the factors beyond patriarchal attitudes of power and control that may contribute to intimate partner abuse. Besides, there is limited evidence that patriarchal attitudes are a primary contributor to the problem. Therefore, targeting patriarchal attitudes may not be the most effective mechanism to reduce abusive behaviour in men.[6] In her award-winning book *See What You Made Me Do*, Jess Hill explains that even the legendary Ellen Pence, co-designer of the Duluth Model, decided that the 'strict feminist model (in which men abuse women because they want power and control) was incomplete and, for some abusive men, not accurate at all.'[7]

So if there are abusive men who are not driven by power and do not tend to dominate women, how then do we explain their repetitive patterns of abusive behaviours? Does the presence of a personality disorder increase the risk of domestic violence, defined as a pattern of violent behaviour that tends to escalate?

Researchers argue that three specific forms of personality disorders are prevalent among intimate partner assaulters: *Anti-Social Personality* (disregards and violates the rights of others with a lack of empathy); *Borderline Personality* (unstable in relationships because of self-image and identity problems, attachment anxiety and abandonment terror, manifesting as outbursts of rage in intimate relationships); and *Narcissistic Personality* (grandiose and needs admiration, but lacks empathy).

The intimate partner abusers who suffer from these personality disorders may or may not be driven by power and control—some indeed want to dominate their partners and abuse strategically (instrumental abusers), and some others abuse on impulse (reactive abusers) when they feel hurt or threatened—yet, they share a few common characteristics.

Many of them have a low sense of empathy for others but a strong sense of entitlement—a self-inflated sense of importance and the belief that they have the right to 'punish the guilty'. No wonder they offend and re-offend their partners; it would be difficult to replay the patterns of abusive behaviour without these two personality characteristics. However, a sense of entitlement and a lack of empathy can't explain the repetitive patterns of these men's abusive behaviours. But there is one more characteristic common to violent men who suffer from these three personality disorders: their tendency to seek excitement.[8] This characteristic could help us to comprehend why some men repeatedly abuse their partners and why the abuse tends to escalate over time.

The abuse 'because of 'and 'in order to'

An abused woman may believe if there was nothing to trigger or irritate her partner, he would not be violent. If she corrected her behaviour and did not give him a reason to blame her, he would stop attacking and abusing her. If she or perhaps counsellors and doctors helped him with controlling his anger or solving his problem with alcohol, he would be okay. He would be able to change his behaviour and finally see how unfair he was and what damage he has done to her and the children!

Even if she has seen that the man actively looks for a provocation to justify his violence, she has been conditioned to believe that his behaviour is only a reaction ('He is angry at me *because* I said that or did that, and that's why he is hurting me') or a result of something ('He is stressed out'), and not as a means to get something ('He is abusing me *in order to* lift himself up by pushing me down').

We are all conditioned to look for the cause of a problem. In attempt to explain intimate partner violence we usually focus on the perpetrator's attitudes, beliefs and issues as *causally* related to his abusive behaviour. We say he is abusive *because* he is jealous or has a short fuse; *because* he suffers from a personality disorder and feels insecure about himself; *because* of the stresses and problems at work or in the family; *because* other people have a negative influence on him; *because* he has financial problems or drinks too much. All of these arguments are plausible, indicative and relevant. However, abusing can become a desirable experience, and the man seeks abusive behaviour not only *because of* but *in order to* boost his mood or alleviate his unpleasant affect.

Two types of intimate partner abusers: instrumental and reactive

Intimate partner abusers share many similar characteristics; however, they differ in the way they use violence. *Pro-active abusers* use violence instrumentally, and *reactive* abusers act out angrily in response to a perceived provocation or threat. In pro-active or instrumental violence, the victim is perceived as a means to achieve a certain goal. In reactive violence, the victim is the target.

The distinction between these two types of aggression—*instrumental* (predatory/premeditated) and *reactive* (impulsive/hostile)—was originally introduced by the American psychologist Seymour Fesbach. Fesbach opined that instrumental aggression occurred when perpetrators felt a sense of lack and coveted what is owned by others, like money or valuable belongings, or they want sex or to feel a sense of power over their victims. Thus instrumental aggressors perceive their victims as a means to acquire specific goals such as money or services, power or sexual gratification by raping their victim, etc. The offenders may not initially intend to inflict pain or cause harm to the victim; however, if it is necessary to achieve a desired outcome, they may use physical force that results in harm, injuries, or even death. This form of aggressive behaviour is more commonly observed in males than females.[9]

On the other end of the instrumental-reactive continuum is reactive aggression, regarded as a reaction to a provocation, where the main goal is injury or harm to the 'provocateur'. The victim has said or done something that triggered the abuser, and the abuser's subsequent intention is to inflict pain or cause harm to the victim. Unlike instrumental violence where the victim is perceived as a means to achieve certain goals, in reactive violence the victim is the target.

Of course, it is a well-known fact that many vicious acts have a mix of cold-blooded, predatory and pro-active instrumental violence (used as a means to obtain power, rewards or goals) and hot-blooded, impulsive and un-planned reactive violence. A domestic violence perpetrator may instrumentally use violence to establish dominance and superiority over his partner, but also re-act with narcissistic rage and inflict injuries when his partner, for example, has made a disparaging remark, dis-agreed with him, criticised him or doubted his grandiosity or fantastic claims. Nevertheless, this instru-mental-reactive dichotomy, and perceiving the victim as a means to achieve a desirable goal versus perceiving the victim as the target, can help us to better understand domestic abuse.

Is it really possible to draw a clear line between in-strumental and reactive intimate partner abusers? The authors of the 2017 study entitled 'Instrumental and Reac-tive Intimate Partner Violence: Offender Characteristics, Reoffense Rates, and Risk Management' argue that it is possible. They claim that 'past research has found that reactive offenders tend to have an almost exclusive pro-clivity for reactive rather than proactive aggression, whereas proactive aggressors may engage in both types of violence. Correspondingly, any single historical example of proactive violence was sufficient for an offender to be classified as an instrumental aggressor.'[10]

Reactive offenders tend to have an almost exclusive proclivi-ty for reactive rather than proactive aggression, whereas proactive aggressors may engage in both types of violence.

The authors of the study describe a reactive aggressor as 'hot-headed' and 'short fused'. This aggressor easily loses control over his behaviour and typically responds to provocation with immediate aggression, but without seriously considering the consequences of his behaviour. In contrast, proactive (instrumental) aggressors are less likely to lose control during the offense, compared with reactive aggressors, and they have a goal or objective associated with the violence, such as services, power, sexual gratification or money. The authors also suggest that instrumental aggressors have more antisocial or psychopathic traits, as well as attitudes of hostility towards women, and they hold attitudes that support intimate partner violence. They may engage 'in more domineering and controlling behavior toward their partners'.[11]

He would watch everything Snežana did. If the kitchen table was dirty, he would attack her with vicious criticism. No matter how reasonable she was in discussing an issue, he would begin a disagreement by immediately becoming belligerent, contemptuous or openly abusive. Snežana started to live her life on eggshells, but she blamed herself and desperately tried to win back his affection. She would even justify her husband's abusive behaviour, saying to herself that he wasn't abusing her because 'it wasn't physical'. But his humiliating and controlling behaviour escalated. He also told her the stories in which he hurt 'those who hurt him'. He was setting the stage for Snežana to view him as seriously dangerous.

What about recidivism rates? Who is more likely to reoffend: instrumental or reactive offenders? It's hard to say, the authors noted. The problem is the victim's fear of reprisal from her male partner and her reluctance to report the abuse or end the relationship. In their study, the victim's fear was more prevalent among the victims of instrumental intimate partner violence (IPV) offenders. 'It is therefore conceivable that underreporting by victims of instrumental IPV offenders may artificially deflate detected violence recidivism rates for that group of offenders'.[12]

Although at present there are no simple screening or assessment tools readily available to distinguish between these two types of intimate partner abusers, the authors share the belief that differentiation could help us create more effective interventions and behaviour change programs for perpetrators, moving away from a 'one-size-fits-all' approach.

Cobras and Pit Bulls

Many other researchers in the field have studied the differences between various types of abusers, and concluded that domestic violence does not always stem from a desire to gain and maintain power over an intimate partner (instrumental violence). Neil Jacobson and John Gottman, psychology professors at the University of Washington, observed 200 married couples and made a significant breakthrough in the understanding of intimate partner abusers. In their a decade-long study, they even examined the changes in heart rate, respiration and blood pressure of male abusers while they were engaged in marital conflict, and concluded that there were two distinct groups of domestic violence perpetrators.

They classified the batterers from their sample as the cold and calculated Cobras (Type I) and the explosive Pit Bulls (Type II). Why the labels 'Cobra' and 'Pit Bull'? 'When Pit Bull perpetrators (about 80 per cent of the violent men who participated in the study) enter into marital conflict, they become physiologically aroused,' the authors noted in their book *When Men Batter Women*.[13] Their heart rate increases, and their anger builds gradually until they are in such a state of rage that they find it difficult to calm themselves. This group of men reminded Jacobson and Gottman of pit bulls, a breed of dogs that grow increasingly aggressive until they strike hard and refuse to let go.

Cobras (the other 20 per cent of violent male participants) are like 'the cobra who becomes quite still and focused just before striking its victim at more than 100 miles an hour.'[14] They tended to be more calm than angry when they entered into the conflict with their partners, and their heart rate dropped. 'We were astonished to discover that anyone's heart rate would lower after a shift from rest to arguing. The heart-rate reduction made no intuitive sense. Cobras looked aroused, they acted aroused, they sounded aroused; yet internally, they were getting calmer and calmer.'[15]

> The man's cold-blooded, reptilian nature frightened her. He controlled her every move, humiliated her at every opportunity, and told her what to do and what not to do. He had to know where Snežana was at all times, and if she wasn't home by a certain time, he'd ring her and accuse her of being with someone else.

Cobras can derive a deep sense of satisfaction from playing their nasty game: when they felt dominant and the woman felt degraded and humiliated, the authors noted. However, in order to play the game, they must first find a woman. And vulnerable women are the easiest prey. 'Cobras, we suspect, have learned to choose their partners very carefully,' Jacobson and Gottman wrote.

'They are adept at finding women who are vulnerable to their macabre charisma, women whose lives are guided by a particular kind of dream, who are new in town or susceptible to an apparently attentive listener.'[16]

One thing that made it difficult for Snežana to leave her abusive husband sooner was not realising she was in an abusive relationship. Her mother had put up with so much from her father, so Snežana thought it was just what you should do: you stay and keep trying. Another thing was her dream. Snežana was single; a family was what she wanted. She was dreaming about a partner who would love her, and he knew it. He came along like Prince Charming to rescue her and start a new life in beautiful Australia, helping her fulfil her dream.

Jacobson and Gottman also studied the reactions of the wives when they were attacked by their abusive husbands. They concluded that the wives of Pit Bulls did not appear as intimidated by them as did the wives of the Cobras. 'In fact, the wives of Pit Bulls often argued as vociferously as their husbands did.' These women tended to fight back and defend themselves verbally, despite their husbands' capacity for brutality, whereas the wives of Cobras were much less likely to fight back.

Why are the wives of Cobras less angry and more frightened than the wives of Pit Bulls? Because they recognise the danger of trying to fight or leave a Cobra, Jacobson and Gottman explained. The aim of the attack— i.e. the effects the Cobras' peculiar way of attacking has on their wives—is 'to suppress the woman's expression of anger, increase their level of fear, and produce significant amount of sadness.'[17] No doubt, the Cobras' tactics of control and intimidation are remarkably effective in terrifying their wives into submission.

She said she knew what he was capable of and lived in a state of terror. He was especially likely to be abusive when he experienced Snežana's behaviour as her trying to control him. 'No woman was going to control him,' he'd say to her. Even when he started physically abusing and raping her, she didn't ask for help. A sense of shame, social isolation and not being able to speak the language were the key barriers. Disclosing what she was going through in her own language would be so difficult, let alone communicate that in English.

The Pit Bulls' motivation for attacking their partners is different. While Cobras can be cool and methodical as they inflict pain and humiliation on the woman, Pit Bulls, whose emotions quickly boil over, are often driven by narcissistic injury, dysphoric moods, deep insecurity or dependence on the mates whom they abuse. Unlike the Cobras who tended to not be emotionally invested in the relationship, the Pit Bulls were emotionally dependent on their wives. This fear is what turns Pit Bulls into controllers, Jacobson and Gottman explained. Their fear of abandonment often produced jealous rages, and they saw potential betrayal in their wives' every move so attempted to deprive their partners of an independent life.

The Pit Bulls dominate their wives in any way they can, and need control as much as the Cobras do, but for different reasons. Pit Bulls are motivated by a fear of being left, while the Cobras are motivated by a desire to get as much immediate gratification as possible. [18] **Neil Jacobson and John Gottman**

Coercive control

Evan Stark is an American sociologist who popularised the term 'coercive control'. In his ground-breaking book *Coercive Control: How Men Entrap Women in Personal Life* he established that coercive control is a very particular kind of violence. Coercive controllers don't just abuse and humiliate their partners; their aim is total domination. He defines coercive control as 'a course of calculated, malevolent conduct deployed almost exclusively by men to dominate individual women by interweaving repeated physical abuse with three equally important tactics: intimidation, isolation, and control.'[19] Here is how Stark describes the tactics of coercive control:

Isolation: 'Controllers isolate their partners to prevent disclosure, instill dependence, express exclusive possession, monopolize their skills and resources, and keep them from getting help or support.' [20]

Control: 'Control tactics also foster dependence by depriving partners of the resources needed for autonomous decision-making and independent living.'[21]

Intimidation: 'Intimidation is used to keep abuse secret and to instill fear, dependence, compliance, loyalty and shame. Offenders induce these effects in three ways, primarily through threats, surveillance, and degradation. Intimidation succeeds because of what a victim has experienced in the past or believes her partner will or may do if she disobeys.'[22]

Degradation: 'Degradation establishes abusers' moral superiority by denying self-respect to their partners.'[23]

Forcing partners to obey rules: 'Since the only purpose of the rules is to exact obedience, they are continually being revised.'[24]

Instilling fear; gaslighting; stalking: Abusers also exploit secret fears to which they alone are privy or play "gaslight" games to make their partners feel "crazy". Stalking is designed to convey the abuser's omnipotence and omnipresence.'[25]

> Snežana was isolated from friends and family so she couldn't borrow any money and return to her country of origin. She was deprived of money because he controlled all bank accounts. He controlled what she should cook and what clothes she should wear. He would give Snežana a small allowance and the set of rules on how to use it. If she 'misused' the carefully monitored allowance, he would intimidate her with fierce outbursts of anger and explicit threats.
>
> When Snežana once refused to obey and questioned the 'rules', he first punched her in the head, and then declared in his cold, metallic voice that the rules were the price that she had to pay in exchange for 'such a good life with him in Australia'. His outburst was an attempt to teach her a lesson, he said. It wasn't easy for Snežana to find the exit from the trap. Not only because she felt ashamed or because she was afraid of her husband – afraid of what he could do to her if she tried to leave but because she lost her self-confidence. She used to see herself as an intelligent and competent woman, but after five years of listening to his 'refrain' ("You are so stupid!"), she started underestimating herself, wondering whether she could survive in the outside world without him. The man was very good at convincing her that she was worthless, Snežana explained.

No doubt, some perpetrators know exactly what they're doing. Their abuse is premeditated and tactical, Australian investigative journalist Jess Hill writes in her book *See What You Made Me Do*: 'Rarely do you see this as blatantly as in this exchange between two Facebook users in the group Aussie Banter:

> Says one: 'Covertly reduce her self-belief and self-esteem to a point where she has to rely on you to survive, then threaten to dump her for being needy.'
>
> Says another: '.... Behave for the first 6–8 months, she'll think he is the perfect one and when she's emotionally invested and reliant then start off as she's an easy picking now and has dropped her guard.... Luring them in is the best sport one can play.'[26]

Luring the woman into a type of a relationship in which she'll end up being trapped and abused is the best sport one can play!

> Despite her intelligence, emotional strength and determination not to be a submissive 'doormat', it took her a while to find a way to escape him. She felt trapped and helpless. There are many migrant women who have been 'groomed' and brought to Australia by abusive men, a case worker who helped her to eventually find the exit from the trap told her. Snežana learned that the wives of these men are less likely to leave the relationship because of the fear of reprisal from their abusive partners in case they attempt to escape.

We know that the major outcome of coercive control is a condition of *entrapment*—a hostage-like condition that arises from the suppression of a victim's autonomy, rights and liberties, as Stark put it. But why is the coercive controller so passionate about keeping the woman entrapped? Is it just because he wants power and control over her? We speculate that 'power and control' is not the coercive controller's ultimate aim; it may be just a chapter, not the whole story. Did Stark have that on his mind when he wrote, 'Advocates have long identified "power and control" as the aim of physical abuse. But a growing body of evidence shows that the presence of control sets the stage for violence and injury, including fatal injury.' [27] The presence of control *sets the stage* for the repetitive pattern of abusive behaviour! Is that why the abuser must have control over the victim and keep her entrapped? If she escaped the trap, he couldn't continue with the abuse. 'To many of these men, assault was a routine, like using the toilet, and not the by-product of overt anger or a "conflict",' Stark noted.[28]

> Snežana recognised the patter. When he'd feel bored or irritable, even in the situations when he felt hurt or disrespected by someone else, he'd look at what she was doing. He'd then find something 'inappropriate' about her or her behaviour, and attack her with derogatory comments and criticism. The pattern was clearly increasing in frequency, as though he craved more and more pleasure from degrading her. The explosions of anger and attacks on her helped him to lift his mood. He needed her pain to alleviate his distress. The abuse also became sexual. If he didn't have intercourse with Snežana every night, he couldn't sleep and he'd become irritable and angry with her.
>
> Snežana realised that there wasn't a day that went by when he didn't look at pornographic films. She also noticed that he was acting out his fantasies, and what he was seeing in porno films, during intercourse with her. Soon, the sex with him became humiliating and even violent. She felt degraded and terribly ashamed.

We know that many people have become addicted to violent video games like *Fortnite* and *World of Warcraft*. Can an intimate partner abuser become addicted to 'the best sport one can play', the nasty 'I dominant – You submissive' relationship game?

It took her time to realise why it was important to him to hurt her and make her feel worthless. She was nothing to him but a 'convenient stepping-stone to gratification'. She was a maid performing domestic chores or serving for the purpose of his sexual gratification and, above all, he wanted a pleasant sense of being superior. He could get a deep sense of satisfaction from hurting her—when he would end up feeling dominant while she'd feel degraded, frightened and in pain.

The coercive controller plays the game . . . not *because of* but *in order to* reaffirm what he believes about himself: that he is superior, dominant, powerful and in control. He can't play dominant (up-graded) unless the woman feels submissive (de-graded). So he uses a set of strategies such as isolation, monitoring her movements, enforcing rigid rules and other manoeuvres to cast her in the role to coerce her to do what she would not otherwise do, and not to do what she would like to do.

As a result, the abused women often feel helpless and trapped. Why don't they pack up their things and leave? The victim of coercive control appears to be willing to stay and tolerate abuse of her own free will. But if we scratch the surface, we'll see something else.

The power players usually present the victim of their power play with an either/or alternative. The coercive controller is a typical power player. He is the controlling, competitive guy who sees the world in terms of mutually exclusive categories: one-up or one-down, either-or, black or white, with nothing in between. The ultimate aim of his control is subjugation, degradation and sometimes even the dehumanisation of women. However, it's not that obvious. He does this in a subtle way. He imposes rules and regulations and sends the subliminal message:

obey or else. His victim has two options: She can accept that she is humiliated, degraded, enslaved, or she'll suffer the consequences (she'll be abused).

No wonder coercive control is referred to as intimate terrorism, and the New South Wales Labor Opposition is preparing to introduce a bill on coercive control. The bill will better define and criminalise coercive control behaviour (penalties could include jail terms of up to ten years). Such an initiative is understandable as the use of force or violence against persons to coerce or intimidate them is a criminal offence. And yet there is even more to it.

'At the intrapsychic level, violence can function to relieve intolerable internal tension, stress or conflict,' Janet Johnston and Linda Campbell write in their article 'A Clinical Typology of Interparental Violence in Disputed-Custody Divorces'.[29] These two notable researchers created a well-known typology of intimate partner abuse based on perpetrators' motivations for the use of violence.

They identified four major profiles of intimate partner violence: *Ongoing or Episodic Male Battering*; *Female-Initiated violence*; *Male-Controlled Interactive Violence*; *and Separation* and *Postdivorce Violence*. Here is how they describe *Ongoing or Episodic Male Battering*: 'The origin of the violence in these cases seemed to be internal to the dynamics of the men, to their low tolerance for frustration, their problems with impulse control, and their angry, possessive, or jealous reactions to any perceived threat to their potency, masculinity, and "proprietary male rights".'[30]

This group of domestic violence perpetrators don't necessarily need a provocation or an external trigger. 'The women who were victims of chronic battering did not generally provoke, initiate, or escalate the physical abuse, at least not intentionally, and indeed they often did not know when the next attack might occur,' the authors concluded.[31] No doubt, some re-offending batterers plan in advance to attack their wives (and later justify it with 'I was drunk') because the abuse is their way of relieving internal tension. 'His aim was to inflict hurt and relieve tension as much as it was to control,' Johnston and Campbell explained.[32] But their aim can be about thrill-seeking as well.

Thrill-seeking is a powerful motivation for violence

Some researchers argue that the traditional distinction—the Cobra type versus the Pit Bull type—fails to do justice to the diverse motivations for violence, including domestic violence. In this instrumental–reactive (Cobra–Pit Bull) classification, violence is either used to control (*instrumental violence*—to obtain tangible goods or goals in a premeditated fashion) or violence is used impulsively (*reactive/affective* type of violence—the motivation is predominantly vengeance).

This classification does not include other violence types, such as, for example, the *appetitive/impulsive* violence type, or excitement-seeking violence. Arousal-seeking as a motive for criminal behaviour has been relatively neglected in criminology and social science, yet Richard C Howard, a researcher at Institute of Mental Health, Nottingham, UK, regards 'the quest for excitement, manifesting as a desire to inflict harm and suffering on others,' as a powerful motive for violent and antisocial behaviour.[33]

According to Howard, the primary motivation behind appetitive violence is inflicting harm on another for thrills. Essentially, these offenders derive pleasure from expressing anger or inflicting pain, and then observing the suffering of the victim. [34] This type of abuse is committed 'just for the hell of it' as high arousal can be experienced as pleasurable and exciting when one feels protected from the consequences of one's potentially hazardous actions.'[35]

> This was the day when Snežana realised that she had been deluding herself, hoping that he would change. It was a nice day, and her husband was in a good mood. Suddenly, out of the blue, he said something that deeply hurt her. 'Even when he is in a good mood, he'd say something derogatory about me. Even when he is happy, he likes to torment me because he draws pleasure in hurting me,' she thought.
>
> Her attitude changed. Instead of shame or a sense of inadequacy, she felt disgusted and contemptuous of him. This shift in her way of perceiving him and his motivation for abusing her—combined with the perception of danger to her if she stayed—helped her to gather up her courage and find the way to escape him.

Do some domestic violence perpetrators also abuse their partners just because they feel a rush of excitement when they express anger and observe a woman's fear, pain or humiliation? But how do they manage to suppress a sense of guilt or avoid feeling empathy for her? Unfortunately, the desire to maximise excitement will overtake any empathy the violent, excitement-seeking perpetrator might have for his victim.[36] Even the man who is not a psychopath and who understands very well what the word *conscience* means, has no feelings of remorse and guilt during an episode of the appetitive/impulsive type of violence. They only desire to inflict pain and observe suffering.

Jacobson and Gottman also noticed the batterer's determination to carry on with the abuse. 'We discovered from our detailed study of the anatomy of violent episodes that once a violent episode starts, there is nothing she (the victim) can do to affect its course,' they wrote in their book *When Men Batter Women*.[37] Many victims of intimate partner abuse would agree. That doesn't mean that the abusive man has always been like that. Perhaps his initial goal was to release internal tension or reduce the unpleasant emotion triggered by his partner's words and behaviour. However, during the episode of abuse he switches to appetitive violence, where the goal becomes achieving a pleasant state of excitement, even if it culminates in his own self destruction.

'One can easily see how . . . the episode might originate in a desire to wreak revenge for some perceived wrong (a state of reactive negativism). But once the violence has started, the perpetrator, viewing the whole episode through a protective frame and feeling excited and empowered by it, might have switched into a motivational state where he seeks ever higher degrees of arousal, culminating even in his own self-destruction, the ultimate act of excitement seeking,' Howard noted.[38]

Indeed, we often hear about the abusers who have killed themselves after killing their partners. How many of those men didn't actually plan it; they only wanted to 'punish' the woman because she had left them? But once the violence started, the abuser felt excited and empowered by the act. In that state, he might have inflicted more injury than he initially intended, and even ended up killing the victim and then killing himself, in the 'ultimate act of excitement seeking', as Howard described it.

Could Howard's insights into the nature of the excitement-seeking type of violence help us to understand why the repetitive patterns of intimate partner abuse tend to escalate in frequency and severity? This type of violence doesn't have a particular aim or 'reason', apart from the lust for excitement and the desire to observe suffering. Such antisocial violent acts, including domestic violence, can reinforce a positive feedback loop, demanding higher and higher levels of excitement.[39] Hence the repetitive pattern of intimate partner abuse escalates in frequency and severity, sometimes to the point when the perpetrator kills the woman and then himself.

We can clearly see the same mechanics behind addictions. One of the major characteristics of addictions is increasingly impaired control over the use of a substance or a behaviour, which then becomes problematic; sometimes problematic to the point when the addict dies of drug overdose.

Chapter Four

ADDICTION

Addiction is one of the most sinister traps that humanity has become ensnared in. We are programmed to seek pleasure and avoid pain, or avoid fear of pain, and that is precisely what can lead us into the addiction trap.

The old biochemical theories viewed addiction as the property of substance—an individual can only become addicted to a substance with addictive properties. Now we know that all characteristics of substance addiction— like *loss of control* (the behaviour has become compulsive and the person has lost the ability to stop); *continuation despite negative consequences* (including loss of job, relationship problems, etc.); *preoccupation or obsession* (the addict spends large, often increasing, amounts of time thinking, planning and doing the detrimental behaviour); *tolerance* (the need for more to produce the same effect); *withdrawal* (distress after a period of abstinence or non-engagement); *craving* (distress associated with a desire to re-engage); *salience* (increasing importance of addiction in lifestyle); *internal conflict* (as a result of increased awareness of negative consequences); and *relapse* (re-engagement after a decision to stop) can be recognised in activities and behaviours such as gambling, or even, perhaps, committing violent offences.

Addiction versus OCD: seeking pleasure versus tension release

People who suffer from Obsessive–compulsive disorder (OCD) seek tension release, not pleasure. They may experience intense anxiety or nervousness that forces them into repetitive behavioural patterns such as frequent hand washing or checking gas appliances. There is nothing pleasant about the monotonous rituals they perform; however, they feel driven to do them.

Those afflicted by OCD say that the tension—often triggered by unpleasant or frightening obsessive thoughts (*obsessions*)—can be almost unbearable, but once they are into the repetitive patterns of cleaning, counting, checking and so on (*compulsions*), their tension starts easing. They clearly understand that their behaviour is unnecessary, silly or ridiculous. It is not something they crave or want to do. They can be very disturbed by their compulsion to carry out a behaviour that defies logic, yet they do it anyway because they feel an intense anxiety or unpleasant inner tension if they try to restrain themselves.

Addicts with a gambling addiction, for example, may also gamble in order to avoid or lessen stress or inner tension. However, while people who suffer from OCD do not seek pleasure, the addict's behaviour is based on the expectations that whatever they're addicted to will be pleasurable. Addicts frequently reveal that their first experiences with the substance, or the behaviour they are addicted to, were pleasant.

A woman who recalled her passion for gambling said, 'I wanted to gamble all the time. I loved it. I loved the high I felt. It took me a long time to realise I was an addict.' Unfortunately, there often comes a point for people with addictions where they don't really enjoy it. They are just seeking relief from the urge to use the substance or engage in the behaviour. Although this can look like obsessive–compulsive behaviour because the pleasure is gone, the original motivation was to feel good.

There is one more significant difference between addicts and those who suffer from OCD. Obsessions (thoughts) and compulsions (behaviours) are often characterised as ego-alien or ego-dystonic, which means foreign to one's sense of self. The people who suffer from OCD may not see the reason they carry out the compulsions. They may relate to the obsessive thoughts not as 'my' thoughts but 'the thoughts', as if they were a foreign idea, voice or even a foreign entity in their mind. In contrast, drugs or gambling are uplifting, so the addicts find purpose in what they do, although they tend to rationalise their actions. The person's thoughts, impulses, attitudes and behaviours are felt to be not foreign (ego-dystonic), but consistent with the rest of the personality (ego-syntonic), 'Of course it's me. Of course I know why I am doing that!'

I can't live without it!

Many drug addicts clearly remember their initial feelings of pleasure or even ecstasy. They talk about powerful transcendental experiences and very pleasant states of consciousness. Alas, the flip side of this is that once they've 'come down', they can become even more conscious of the dullness of ordinary everyday life. The euphoria is often followed by sadness, depression or even dismay, and the addicts find themselves in a thick grey mental fog again. 'The gates of the prison—the banal, everyday reality I was living in—would close in once again,' a heroin addict described how drugs made him feel. 'It is difficult to imagine that the same magical experience is possible without heroin, and you begin to long for it to be repeated.'

But no matter how special the early drug experiences are, they cannot be sustained. Over time, it takes higher and higher doses of a drug to achieve a lesser result. In other words, the repetitive patterns in behavioural addictions become more frequent but bring less satisfaction, and soon the addiction loses their close links with pleasure. In the meantime, a dreadful fear has been instilled in the addict: 'If I stop, I'll suffer!'

Seeking pleasure is one key characteristic of addiction. Another is the belief that it would be extremely difficult to live without what the addict is addicted to. The fear of pain, discomfort, cravings, withdrawal symptoms or emotional suffering, which would occur if one was to stop, is the powerful force that perpetuates addiction problems. This fear enslaves us to the 'master with an ugly face' (the demon of addiction) and keeps addiction in place. We find ourselves entrapped.

What, exactly, is the 'addiction trap'? There has been some confusion about the terms *physical dependence* and *addiction*. Addiction is a pattern of harmful behaviour. It is not the same as dependence. Physical dependence on a substance does not imply addiction unless it is accompanied by behaviours that are harmful, disruptive, or cause problems for an individual. There's a huge difference between addiction and dependence.

Physical dependence is a property of many different classes of drugs (for example, people with diabetes must use insulin), not just drugs that can be abused. 'Opioids also can, and usually do, cause physical dependence. The body makes changes to adapt to the opioids and if you stop suddenly, you get this unpleasant withdrawal syndrome. That's what physical dependence is; it has nothing to do with addiction. Addiction is not necessarily a physical thing. 'Addiction is a psychological phenomenon consisting of three elements,' noted Dr Jennifer Schneider, a leading expert in both the management of chronic pain with opioids and in addictive sexual disorders.[1]

The three well-known fundamental elements of every addiction are: (1) compulsive use of a substance or behaviour, which is the same as loss of control; (2) continuing use in spite of significant adverse consequences; and (3) pre-occupation or obsession with obtaining, using and recovering from the effects of the substance or behaviour. It is also a recognised fact that this repetitious pattern of harmful behaviour (addiction) tends to increase in frequency and/or severity because of tolerance. How does tolerance develop? The substance or behaviour may initially provide a pleasurable feeling. This feeling can be a result of activating the dopaminergic reward pathways and endorphin release in the brain. Experts are still studying exactly how the neurotransmitters dopamine, serotonin, endorphins and oxytocin work in the context of addiction, but many believe they train the brain to seek pleasurable experiences.

Happy Chemicals
'When you feel good, your brain is releasing dopamine, serotonin, oxytocin, or endorphin,' Loretta Graziano (L.G.)

Breuning writes in her book *Habits of a Happy Brain*.[2] 'Each happy chemical triggers a different good feeling: Dopamine produces the joy of finding what you seek—the "Eureka! I got it!" feeling. Endorphins produce oblivion that mask pain—often called euphoria. Oxytocin produces the feeling of being safe with others—now called bonding. Serotonin produces the feeling of being respected by others—pride.'[3]

Each chemical motivates a particular type of behaviour. 'Seeking and finding social rewards stimulate the excitement of dopamine. People invest years of effort trying to become a heart surgeon or a rock star because each step along the way triggers dopamine,' L.G. Breuning noted.[4] Serotonin motivates you to get respect. 'Getting respect feels good because it triggers serotonin. This good feeling motivates you to seek more respect.'[5]

Is there a connection between social dominance ('I dominant –You submissive' relating) and serotonin? We argue that many domestic violence perpetrators exhibit what L.G. Breuning calls the dominance-seeking urges: 'Mammals seek the one-up position because serotonin makes it feel good.'[6] One study clearly showed this. The alpha monkey made the dominance gestures typical of his species, but his subordinates did not respond with the expected submission gestures. The alpha got agitated and his serotonin level fell. 'He needed their submission to keep up his serotonin,' Breuning concluded.[7]

It's this role in reinforcing the brain's quest for pleasure that has led researchers to associate these neurotransmitters with addiction. But it's not that simple. Dopamine, for example, plays an important role in addiction; however, it's just one piece of a puzzle. Although often described as a 'feel-good' chemical, dopamine doesn't work by triggering feelings of pleasure and happiness. And, contrary to popular belief, you can't be addicted to dopamine. Nevertheless, dopamine is a powerful motivator! It does play an important role in motivating you to seek out pleasurable experiences.

How does it work? Dopamine is a neurotransmitter. Neurotransmitters are the messengers of the nervous system. They are molecules that carry information across synapses from a nerve cell to its neighbouring cells, like school kids pass hand-written notes. By exchanging neurotransmitters, brain cells work together to process information and direct behaviour. Experiences that make you feel good activate your brain's reward centre, which responds by releasing dopamine. As a result, you're left with a strong memory of the pleasure you felt. This strong memory can prompt you to make an effort to experience it again. When you're, for example, exposed to environmental cues that remind you of the past pleasant experience, you'll begin to feel the drive to seek out that same pleasure. This drive can be incredibly strong, creating an urge that's hard to resist.

But dopamine also contributes to tolerance. Consistent (mis)use of drugs or behaviours eventually leads to overstimulation in the reward centre in the brain. Its pathways become overwhelmed, making it harder to handle the high levels of dopamine release. The brain tries to solve this problem in two ways: decreasing dopamine production and reducing dopamine receptors. Either change generally results in the substance or the behaviour having less of an effect due to a weaker response by the brain's reward centre. Still, the craving remains. Now, it takes more of the drug or behaviour to satisfy you—you need more to get the same effect. This reduction in pleasure is termed tolerance. As a result of tolerance, the pattern of harmful behaviour tends to escalate.

What is the addict really addicted to?

In his book *Power vs Force: The Hidden Determinants of Human Behaviour*, David R. Hawkins, a renowned psychiatrist, consciousness researcher, spiritual lecturer and mystic, points out that a person is not addicted directly to a substance or a behaviour, but to re-experiencing certain higher levels of consciousness. 'The common belief is that it is the addictive substance itself to which the victim has become addicted, because of that substance's power to create a high state of euphoria,' Hawkins pointed out.[8] 'The high state which people seek, by whatever means, is in fact the experience field of their own consciousness (Self).'[9]

Here is how he explains the effect of drugs: 'The actual effect of drugs is merely to suppress the lower energy field, thereby allowing the user to experience exclusively the higher ones. It is as though a filter screened out all the lower tones coming from an orchestra, so that all that could be heard were the high notes. The suppression of the low notes does not create the high ones, it merely reveals them.'[10]

Hawkins defined a *high* as 'any state of consciousness above one's customary level of awareness. Therefore, to a person who lives in Fear, moving up to Courage is a high. To people who live in hopeless Apathy, Anger is a high.'[11]

To people who live in hopeless Apathy, Anger is a high.
David R. Hawkins

The keyword for understanding how we experience a *high* is the word 'masking'. The actual effect of a particular behaviour or drug is to conceal or mask the lower unpleasant states such as anxiety, fear, shame or hopelessness and helplessness, thus allowing us to experience exclusively the higher and more pleasant ones.

'Higher states are so powerful that once experienced, they are never forgotten and are sought ever after. It is to this experience of higher states that people become addicted,' Hawkins writes.[12] This means that the desire and the object of the addiction may be one thing, what lies beneath it and what is being covered over or denied by addictions—depressed mood, a sense of helplessness, anxiety or fear—may be another.

Shopping, for example, can lift our depressed mood. The uplifting effect does not last long, but when we buy something nice, we feel better. But there is a flip side to it: We can become hooked on shopping. The afflicted consumer may have an uncontrollable, chronic and repetitive urge to buy stuff as a means of alleviating unpleasant feelings of stress, depressed mood or anxiety.

Alcohol too can mask our lower, unpleasant emotional states such as depressed mood, a painful sense of loneliness or being neglected by family members or partners. It can help us not to think about our problems, make us feel that everything is fine or help us to feel good about ourselves.

Drugs can take us into a different world, or a less unpleasant world. Food smooths over the cracks in life, helping us to fill an inner emptiness, sweeten a sense of bitterness or temporarily replace what is missing or what has been lost. Rage can also mask our fears and empower us. No wonder some people have developed 'rageaholism' or the compulsive pursuit of a mood change by repeatedly engaging in episodes of rage, despite the adverse consequences of such behaviour.

Behavioural addictions

The fifth edition of the *Diagnostic and Statistical Manual of Mental Disorders (DSM-5)*—a widely established system for psychiatrists and psychologists for classifying mental disorders—officially recognises only gambling disorder (previously termed pathological gambling) as a behavioural addiction. However, growing evidence indicates that extensive, repetitive and problematic engagement in activities such as playing video games, using the Internet, shopping, engaging in sexual activities, exercising, eating and even tanning, can share some similarities with addictive disorders. Therefore, researchers in the field are considering classifying them as behavioural addictions as well.

By the way, is it really possible to become addicted to tanning? The researchers, Doctors Stapleton, Hillhouse and Coups have found the strong biological evidence that tanning releases endorphins and stimulates dopamine receptors. These two biological effects have clear similarities to those associated with substance abuse.[13]

What exactly are behavioural (non-substance) addictions, and how do we become addicted to gambling, for example, or watching pornography or shopping? Behavioural addictions are patterns of harmful behaviours that follow a cycle. Sadly, we can become addicted not only to alcohol, heroin, opioid painkillers or sedatives, but to behaviours that help us feel good, elated or less tense. When we experience pleasant emotional states or the sense of satisfaction when an unpleasant emotional charge is discharged, we want to repeat such experiences. That's how the pattern is created, and once created it may increase in frequency and duration because of tolerance.

Over time, the behaviour itself may become less pleasurable and more of a habit or compulsion. It may become motivated less by positive reinforcement ('I want to feel good') and more by negative reinforcement (e.g., relief of dissatisfaction or unpleasant symptoms of withdrawal). For example, similar to some domestic violence re-offenders, the people addicted to gambling may gamble because they like the thrill and seek excitement, or because they want to escape unpleasant emotional states.

Problem Gambler Subtypes

Researchers suggest that there are three relatively distinct subtypes of problem gamblers. These subtypes are differentiated based on their motivations for gambling and their psychopathological and personality presentations.[14]

1. **Gamblers are motivated to gamble to relieve or escape dysphoric moods:** The first subtype of pathological gambler demonstrates high level of depression and/or anxiety. They have been referred to as emotionally vulnerable, depression prone, psychologically distressed and demoralised gamblers. They desire to escape or regulate unpleasant emotional states.

2. **Impulsive and sensation-seeking gamblers:** The second subtype of pathological gambler shows marked impulsivity and gambles to increase levels of arousal and/or decrease boredom. They are usually described as antisocial 'impulsivists' who display sensation-seeking tendencies. Psychopathic factors also represent aspects of this type of gambler.

3. **Simple gambler:** The third subtype of pathological gambler does not exhibit serious premorbid signs of psychopathology or maladaptive personality traits. They have been referred to as a normal, social, low-emotion regulation, and simple gambler. These gamblers are characterised by little psychopathology and low impulsivity or sensation seeking. Their erroneous beliefs and experiences of 'wins' capture this type of gambler as well.

As is the case with intimate partner abuser subtypes, the three problem gambler subtypes are not necessarily mutually exclusive. For example, those with depression who predominantly gamble to cope with distressing feelings may, at times, gamble to enhance excitement. Or, the problem gamblers with high level of impulsivity or antisocial personality disorder may, at times, develop depression and gamble to cope with feelings of sadness.[15]

Sexual addiction is also a good example how addiction can mask the lower, painful emotional states. 'Sex addicts typically struggle with underlying emotional or psychological problems often stemming from early life abuse such as physical or sexual trauma and emotional neglect. Male sex addicts more frequently report profound histories of covert childhood emotional abuse (being used emotionally by a parent or caretaker to buoy their parent's ego strength, sense of self and emotional stability), whereas female sex (and relationship) addicts are more likely to report histories of overt childhood sexual and/or physical abuse,' Robert Weiss, a clinical sexologist and psychotherapist, noted.[16]

What about pornography addiction and its strong impact on partnership abuse? Experts claim that intentional exposure to violent pornography increases the risk of domestic violence and sexually aggressive behaviour, but in what way, exactly, does domestic violence intersect with pornography?

Pornography fosters abuse by normalising and depicting verbal and physical violence as enjoyable. For example, mainstream Internet pornography often features slapping, gagging, and spanking as something normal. Perpetrators of such aggression are usually male, whereas the targets of aggression are overwhelmingly female, and most targets show pleasure or respond neutrally when spanked, gagged, or slapped. That's how watching porn can normalise sex acts viewed in porn and cause people to want to imitate it in real life. Many survivors of marital rape report that their abusive partner watched pornography and forces or threatens them to participate in sexual behaviours that the perpetrator saw in porn.

> Rape is a significant or major form of abuse in 54 percent of violent marriages. Of women over the age of 30 who have been raped, 58 percent were raped within the context of an abusive relationship. Among battered women who are first identified in a medical setting, 75 percent will go on to suffer repeated abuse.[17] **Richard Irons and Jennifer P. Schneider**

The domestic violence perpetrators addicted to pornography tend to watch hard-core porn filled with increasingly more violence and sadistic acts as previous images, less violent, are no longer stimulating. Some want to enact with their partners what they had seen in porn, and their sexually aggressive behaviour tends to increase in severity and/or frequency. That's why there's a chance that the raped, degraded and humiliated victim will be assaulted by her abusive husband again.

Sexual Sadism

The essential feature of sadism is a feeling of excitement resulting from inflicting pain, humiliation or suffering on another person. The word sadism is derived from the name of the Marquis de Sade (1740-1814), a French aristocrat who became notorious for writing novels around the theme of inflicting pain as a source of sexual pleasure. The *Diagnostic and Statistical Manual of Mental Disorders* outlines the essential features of sexual sadism. Among them are:

• The focus of sexual sadism involves acts in which the individual derives sexual excitement from the psychological or physical suffering (including humiliation) of the victim.

• The sadistic fantasies usually involve having complete control over the victim, who is terrified by the anticipation of the impending sadistic act.

• In all of these cases, it is the suffering of the victim that is sexually arousing.

• Sadistic fantasies or acts may involve activities that indicate dominance over the victim.

• Sexual sadism is usually chronic.

• When sexual sadism is practised with a non-consenting partner, the activity is likely to be repeated until the sadist is apprehended.

• Some individuals may engage in sadistic acts for many years without a need to increase the potential for inflicting serious physical damage. Usually, however, the severity of the sadistic acts increases over time.

• When sexual sadism is severe, sexual sadists may seriously injure or kill their victims.

What about withdrawal symptoms in non-substance abuse addictions? Gamblers continue with gambling despite the diminishing sense of satisfaction. Why do they keep gambling even when they don't draw much satisfaction from it? To avoid gambling withdrawal? Is the fear of being without a mobile phone one of the symptoms of withdrawal as well?

Some say that many of us have become smartphone junkies who developed nomophobia (fear of being without a mobile phone). We can't go an hour without checking messages, scrolling through Facebook, Instagram, Twitter. If it is just a waste of time or even stressful, why do we do it then? Because it feels good.

Primitive biological responses can explain the allure of social media. When others acknowledge and validate us through positive comments or likes, this can help us to feel good so we succumb to the endless pursuit of the micro-dopamine release that affirmation (likes) provides. That's why we feel compelled to check our phones. If social media can help us fulfil our basic needs for recognition and validation, no wonder we need our digital validation and can't control how much time we spend online. Some even say that we can develop a dependence on the affirmations of others or, like pathological narcissists, become addicted to what Sam Vaknin calls narcissistic supply—attention, both positive and negative.[18] Those addicted to narcissistic supply often use every form of behaviour—or every form of abuse—to make sure that their needs are met.

Indeed, many victims of domestic violence live in a 'war zone' with their abusers who suffer from narcissistic personality disorder and who tend to react with so-called narcissistic rage whenever they feel neglected or disrespected. It is a serious mental disorder in which people have an inflated sense of their own importance, and a deep need for attention, recognition, respect and admiration. When starved of narcissistic supply (arguably a form of addiction), they may experience intense irritability, depressed mood or other symptoms that resemble the symptoms of withdrawal.

Clinicians argue that withdrawal symptoms associated with behavioural addictions are similar to those experienced by long-term drug users. The unpleasant sensations usually involve irritability, restlessness, anxiety and cravings—the same symptoms seen in addicts quitting drugs and alcohol.

Interestingly, many abused women claim that their violent partners also experience some kind of craving for violence. 'I could feel that it was building up; I could feel it coming,' Snežana disclosed in our counselling session. Her abusive husband would seek conflicts and pick fights for no apparent reason other than to hurt her. Even in the situations when nobody or nothing external triggered him, he would seek violence and direct it towards her to release his tension and derive satisfaction from it. His outbursts worked like a drug. After his 'explosions', as

Snežana put it, he would feel calmer. He softened. If he craved it but didn't have an opportunity to act abusively or violently, he'd experience 'symptoms of withdrawal' when he felt irritable, restless, anxious or tense.

Humans Crave Violence Just Like Sex

The study, detailed in the journal *Psychopharmacology*, reveals that the same clusters of brain cells involved in other rewards are also behind the craving for violence. That can be the reason why some individuals will intentionally seek out an aggressive encounter solely because they experience a rewarding sensation from it. 'This shows for the first time that aggression, on its own, is motivating, and that the well-known positive reinforcer dopamine plays a critical role,' said study team member Craig Kennedy, professor of special education and pediatrics at Vanderbilt University in Tennessee.[19]

Addicted to the 'war games'?

Is it possible to become addicted to pleasurable arousal associated with crowd violence? Researchers have found that one of the major motivating factors for soccer hooliganism is the excitement of battle in the 'war games' with other hooligans and the police. Some superthugs intensely crave the fight (they may even have withdrawal symptoms) and strategically plan it in advance, weeks before the soccer game. No doubt, soccer hooligans often use behaviour such as bullying and hooliganism to deliberately stir up conflicts simply because they enjoy the feeling of an adrenaline rush. 'I had not expected the violence to be so pleasurable. This is, if you like, the answer to the hundred-dollar question: Why do young males riot every Saturday?

They do it for the same reason that another generation drank too much, or smoked dope, or took hallucinogenic drugs, or behaved badly or rebelliously. Violence is their antisocial kick, their mind-altering experience, an adrenaline-induced euphoria that might be all the more powerful as it is generated by the body itself, with, I was convinced, many of the same addictive qualities that characterize synthetically-produced drugs,' Bill Buford writes in his book *Among the Thugs: The Experience, and the Seduction, of Crowd Violence*.[20]

We say that an adrenaline junkie is a person addicted to the thrill of the adrenaline rush—the exciting effect produced when the adrenal glands dump a large dose of adrenaline into the bloodstream. The heart rate increases, and the breathing rate ramps up, providing more energy in the body. One of the results of these hormones and extra energy is the adrenaline *high*, a euphoric feeling that can last for hours. 'It is in this way that soccer hooligans become addicted to the experience of the high-felt arousal associated with violent confrontation and assault,' John H. Kerr stated in his book *Understanding Soccer Hooliganism*.[21]

It's not only soccer hooligans and thugs who are addicted to the pleasurable arousal associated with violence. Intimate partner abusers may also enjoy the 'war game' with their partners. Some men who managed to quit domestic violence honestly reveal that they recognised a 'hungry beast' in themselves: the fighter who craved verbal conflicts and sometimes even physical fights. In some cases, the 'beast', or the aspect in the personality addicted to abusing, was not present at the beginning of their relationships but gradually formed and developed over the years. 'Even when you feel disconcerted and ambivalent towards such impulses to abuse your wife, you became attached to the sense of satisfaction you experience in conflicts and fights that intensified over time,' our client Senad admitted.

The drama in Senad's family life operated as a simple program that repeated the same steps over and over again. His sense of satisfaction was reinforced when the couple experienced harsh emotions such as anger and violence, fused with his wife's distress and humiliation. It was important for him to generate these emotions, but it was also the rise in intensity of the emotions that seemed to satisfy this abuser's ever-increasing appetite.

But, really, is it possible to become addicted to abusing your partner? There are striking similarities between repetitive patterns of intimate partner abuse and behavioural addictions. Yet when we ask the question, 'Why does a perpetrator repetitively abuse his partner?' the literature on domestic violence provides three usual answers: 'He likes being in control'; 'He feels entitled—he feels he has a special status that no one else in the family has'; and 'He gets what he wants by his abusive behaviour'. Of course, he might want to control and dominate. But is there something deeper and more sinister behind the repetitive patterns of abusive behaviour towards his partner?

The gruesome stories of the victims of domestic violence, widely spread all over the planet, clearly confirm that an act of violence can provide emotional relief and help the abuser to improve his mood. If such behaviour lifts him up, he is more likely to repeat it when he feels down; hence the repetitive pattern of his abusive behaviour. Indeed, many victims claim that an experienced domestic violence perpetrator has learnt how to use even everyday stresses (mostly clustered around the sense of irritation, moodiness and boredom), or the narrative about being disrespected, humiliated or jealous, to justify a wife-beating or any other form of abuse that lifts him up. When he craved that elevated effect of physical violence or verbal abuse, he would pick a fight with his partner whenever the circumstances permitted.

The narrative about his jealousy is one of the most popular narratives. We often label the intimate partner abuser as controlling or jealous when he monitors the kilometres on his partner's car to see if she is meeting someone outside the house or accuses her of having an affair. Yet many women tell us that his attacks are not actually fuelled by his 'pure jealousy' as he knows very well that she is not having an affair with other men. However, when he feels tense and craves a particular form of 'excitement' (abuse) that can help him to discharge his unpleasant inner tension and draw satisfaction from it, he will initiate a story that features him in the role of a male character who is having fits of anger fuelled by jealousy. The drama will end with the female victim being beaten and in pain. Once he has generated her pain and degradation, he feels better.

What about when there are no external triggers for the man's abusive behaviour? Victims report that their abusive partners sometimes actively seek situations in which they can be triggered. Even when the woman does not provoke them in any way, they would 'provoke her to provoke them'. Especially when they felt low (depressed, distressed or bored).

We usually think about lows as negative emotional states, and such states are always undesirable, we claim. But are they? Without the low there is no high. Without tension there is no pleasure in discharging tension, and in order to get a high, the perpetrator may also need a low. What is a low? Problems, conflicts, dramas. And if there is no one around to create drama, he triggers others to trigger him. Why? In some cases, the abuser's state of tension, similar to pre-orgasmic tension, is not necessarily something he wants to avoid; on the contrary, it can make his blow-up more pleasant.

Once engaged in the excitement-seeking type of violence, he will suspend whatever feelings of empathy he may have for his partner. His empathy will be temporarily overridden by the compulsive desire to maximise a state of high excitement. He may blame the victim or develop a tendency to create arguments for his irrational or violent behaviours. When his abuse escalates, he may tell stories to explain why he believes that more severe 'punishment' is necessary.

We may try to explain the escalating pattern of abusive behaviour using the familiar discourses of 'power-and-control', 'a sense of entitlement' or 'a lack of empathy for his partner'. However, the deepest reason his abusive behaviour tends to get worse could be that he has become addicted to abusing the woman, and he's developed tolerance. Just as drug addicts increase their substance abuse, or gamblers spend more and more time gambling, some domestic violence perpetrators become more and more violent.

As we've already established, the word addiction describes a compulsion to repeat a behaviour regardless of its negative consequences, and many abusers do just that. Some may feel guilty or they may promise that they will not do it again; nevertheless, they feel compelled to repeat an abusive behaviour regardless of its catastrophic consequences. So could the repetitive cycle of intimate partner abuse be a hidden face of addiction? Many of us would disagree. The idea that the pattern of intimate partner abuse could be about behavioural addiction may sound too simplistic to be taken seriously, or too frightening and confusing if we don't know how to deal with the problem.

Moreover, we may claim that there is no evidence that the re-offending perpetrator derives pleasure from his abusive behaviour. We can decide then to ignore the fact that addicts commonly continue their behaviour even when the substance or behaviour is no longer pleasurable.

Parallels between domestic violence and addictive disorders

In their article, 'When is Domestic Violence a Hidden Face of Addiction?' renowned addiction experts Richard Irons, M.D. and Jennifer P. Schneider, M.D. point out that domestic violence and addictive disorders such as alcoholism or drug addiction do not just frequently coexist. They also share many similarities.

> 'The addictive cycle (Carnes, 1983), which is applicable to all addictive disorders, consists of preoccupation with the addictive behavior, rituals associated with the behavior, acting out, and remorse or guilt and shame. The remorse is relieved by preoccupation, and the cycle continues. The battering cycle (Walker, 1979) consists of the tension-building phase, the explosion or acute battering incident, and the calm, loving respite which is based on the batterer's remorse'.[22]

Indeed, if we compare the cycle of addiction and the cycle of intimate partner abuse, we'll see the three similar phases. Here is what the typical cycle of addiction looks like:

Phase 1 Preoccupation: The addicts' thoughts get focused on the object of addiction.

Phase 2 Rituals/Acting out: Rituals of addiction ease internal tension. Acting out provides temporary relief of inner tension or pain.

Phase 3 Consequences: Guilt or shame, but the abuse of substance or behaviour continues.

The *assault* cycle follows the same pattern:

Phase 1 Tension building: A real or imaginary trigger or a provocation is necessary for the anger outburst. For example, the abuser feels ignored, threatened, annoyed or wronged. He uses strategies such as nit-picking, accusations, engaging his partner to argue, destroying property, yelling, crazy-making behaviour, etc. The abuser's behaviour intensifies and reaches a point where a release of tension is inevitable.

Phase 2 Acute Explosion: This is the point where the perpetrator commits an act of abuse on the victim. The victim experiences terror, pain and degradation. The tension eventually subsides.

Phase 3 Consequences: This phase usually goes through sub-stages: remorse; pursuit and honeymoon; and calm. However, something will trigger him again.

Both cycles—the cycle of addiction and the assault cycle—can occur hundreds of times. Irons and Schneider also emphasise that repetitive patterns of abuse and addictive behaviours have a number of common characteristics, including loss of control (domestic violence also involves a *loss of control*, but in this case it is a loss over the control of anger and abusive behaviour rather than substance use); *continuation of behaviour despite adverse consequences* (as with substance addiction, in domestic violence there are characteristically periods of contrition, when the abuser promises to reform and refrain from ever using violence again); *preoccupation or obsession* (over time both the abuser and battered partner become preoccupied with the behaviour, even when violence is not presently occurring); *withdrawal* (withdrawal is often experienced in these relationships as

a period of nervousness, tension and tendencies to manu-
facture conflicts or dramas that would lead to abusive
behaviour); and *development of tolerance* (the violence
escalates in frequency and/or intensity and/or diversity).
The victim can become desensitized and tolerate ever increasing levels of physical, emotional, and sexual trauma
and pain.[23]

> The victim as well gets desensitized and tolerates ever-
> increasing levels of physical, emotional, and sexual trauma
> and pain. **Richard Irons and Jennifer P. Schneider**

The evidence regarding similarities between the repetitive pattern of substance abuse and the repetitive pattern
of intimate partner is compelling. The overlap exists in
terms of phenomenology (craving, tolerance and withdrawal), natural history (onset, chronicity, and relapsing
course), and even in the way the drug addicts, alcoholics
and intimate partner abusers use defences such as denial,
blaming others, minimisation or rationalisation to justify
their behaviour.

In their article, 'When is Domestic Violence a Hidden
Face of Addiction?' Richard Irons and Jennifer P. Schneider also describe the similarity between the partners of
addicts and the partners of abusive men. 'Both victims of
domestic violence and partners of addicts often have difficulty leaving. In addition to realistic fears of escalation
of violence and consideration of financial and parenting
constraints, both types of domestic partners often get
caught up in a cycle of codependency, where they blame
themselves for the current situation and feel that if they
are only able to do particular things better, the situation
will improve'.[24]

The authors state that attending Alcoholics Anonymous (AA) Groups and similar 12-step programs can help both types of partners to develop their self-esteem and place themselves in a situation where they are able to make appropriate choices for themselves. They also emphasise that addressing the similarities between these two social and family behavioural disorders, and being aware about the addictive potential of abusing intimate partners, is crucial to the success of the treatment and prevention of domestic violence.[25]

Taking into consideration the fact that the repetitive pattern of domestic abuse exhibits features of a behavioural addiction could help us better understand this problem and perhaps create more successful behaviour change programs. Of course, it is likely that many domestic violence perpetrators may be resistant to change. If they are addicted to abusing their partners, the fear of having to sacrifice the pleasure they derive from abusive behaviour, or the pleasure derived from discharging unpleasant inner tension by acting abusively, is a big hindrance. However, there are many others who would like to stop abusing their partners. How to help the men motivated to change their abusive behaviour is the topic we focus on in part two.

PART TWO

Breaking the Pattern of
Abuse: Dismantling the
Abuser Aspect

Chapter 5

WILL HE EVER STOP ABUSING HER?

'It's not a problem to say, "I'll never do it again", and really, honestly mean it!' Senad admitted. The problem is when in a moment of rage, you just find yourself doing that (abusing). Your rational mind says, "Stop. Don't do it! You'll feel guilty again." I know I should stop, but that doesn't help much.'

There is a big difference between the words reason and excuse. Reasons explain why you did what you did, and you use excuses when you know that you should have done one thing, but instead, you did something else. You cannot believe in excuses; therefore, you need solid reasons to fuel your behaviour. Without reasons, there would be no need to do something. Why would you punish your partner without a reason?

A man who abuses his wife does not necessarily enjoy it. He may feel guilt and shame when he hurts her, yet he finds it difficult to stop. Why is this? Is it because he believes he has a good reason to punish her?

I will suffer if I stop!

When he is irritable or angry, an abuser believes he is simply responding to something external or to someone who is attacking or hurting him. If he is triggered, it is as though a button has been pushed that activates a compulsive knee-jerk reflex. He has been insulted! He has been disrespected! 'My offence is nothing else but perfectly justified self-defence! Wouldn't anybody normal react in the same way? Do you expect me not to protect myself, or not to get angry when she hurts my feelings? If I feel satisfaction when I defend myself, so be it!'

The man believes he has a real reason for reacting in this particular way, and if he has a genuine reason to do something, then he is making a genuine sacrifice if he doesn't do it. And if he sacrifices something significant, such as self-defence or an urge to 'punish the culprit', he suffers. He does not like to control his angry outbursts because self-control increases a sense of sacrifice, hence frustration. That's why re-offenders find it difficult to stop abusive behaviour. They will suffer if they stop!

Nonetheless, the man may decide to control himself and sacrifice his sense of satisfaction when he punishes the culprit. But that's not easy. His partner's words and behaviour, interpreted by him as disrespect, rejection or criticism, keep triggering his tension. The increased irritation and tension intensify his urge to release this tension through angry outbursts. He may still try to restrain himself; however, the problem with self-control creates a sense of discomfort. Besides, when he experiences a high level of tension in his body but prevents the 'explosion' or doesn't allow the discharge of inner tension—the resulting feeling is agitation. It's difficult to tolerate this unpleasant sensation. This is why re-offenders have difficulty stopping their abusive behaviour. They experience unpleasant agitation when prevented doing what they would like to do. And what would they like to do? Punish their partner because they believe they have a genuine *reason* for that.

Nasty games people play

Silly aspects in our personalities think silly thoughts, but the rational mind will filter them through and decide what is nonsense and what is reasonable. However, our rational thinking can be *contaminated*. This term is borrowed from Transactional Analysis (TA). The rational ego state, named as the Adult in TA, is contaminated when he/she accepts as true some unfounded beliefs, distortions, prejudices or delusions. '*Contamination* is best illustrated by certain types of prejudices on the one hand, and by delusions on the other,' Eric Berne wrote in the book *Transactional Analysis in Psychotherapy*.[1]

In the TA school of psychotherapy, decontamination of the Adult's rational thinking is an early therapeutic requirement in the treatment of any kind of psychological problem. It's an important first step in healing our relationships, too. If the abusive man is resolute to quit playing the same old 'hot potato game'—trying to rid himself of whatever guilt, fear, pain or humiliation he feels by passing on them to his partner—and genuinely wishes to understand what drives his abusive behaviour, he will see that these so-called 'reasons' for abuse are not reasons at all, but triggers and excuses.

The domestic violence perpetrator who repeatedly abuses and then blames his wife with, 'It's your fault!' often does it as though he wants to get rid of his guilt—a potato too hot to handle—and pass it on to her. Using the familiar methods of shaming and blaming, he shoves the uncomfortable emotion onto her, so he can feel justified in 'righteously' attacking her, because 'she deserves it'. Yet there is more to it. Because he feels justified, he can continue to abuse her and draw a guilt-free sense of satisfaction from that. Senad's experience clearly confirms this.

Thirty-seven-year-old Senad, a mechanic who came to Australia as a refugee from Bosnia, was diagnosed with PTSD and agitated depression. He experienced numerous highly traumatic events during the Bosnian war and spent two months in the concentration camp Manjača, in northern Bosnia and Herzegovina. He described camp life as hellish, impulsive and chaotic. His abusers, especially those called 'weekend soldiers' who worked somewhere else but came to camp on the weekend, were relentless in committing atrocities. Some of them would dream up sadistic fantasies and make the detainees enact them. The favourite was to force the younger men to kiss one another and after that brutally beat them, asking, 'What are you doing? Are you crazy? You are homosexuals!'

When Senad started the counselling treatment for his symptoms of intrusion (mostly traumatic nightmares and flashbacks), he didn't want to talk about his experiences in Manjača. Nor did he remember the fear, anger and humiliation he felt as a child raised by two abusive parents. His father was an alcoholic who would beat his wife and children, and his mother was a disempowered victim of domestic violence who 'empowered' herself by abusing Senad. Senad described her as a strict disciplinarian who believed in corporal punishment for the slightest transgression, imagined or real.

A few months in the intensive treatment program for the victims of torture and trauma at STARTTS (NSW Service for the Treatment and Rehabilitation of Torture and Trauma Survivors) helped him to recover from some symptoms. His flashbacks and nightmares stopped, so he was able to sleep without medication. But the problem was his rage. He would react with rage every time his small business took a downturn or when his wife would 'provoke' him. Even without her provocations he'd find something wrong with her, flow into rages and go after her. Obviously, he needed to continue the treatment and go further into the unhealed childhood trauma and the reservoir of pain, anger, fear and humiliation he carried inside. He had to confront his trauma of being victimised not only by the 'weekend soldiers', but by his parents. He didn't deny it; however, it took him some time to acknowledge that he was indeed a victim.

Therapists working with combat veterans know that when a man is subjected to trauma, the trauma itself is often compounded by the soldier's sense of having been disempowered and 'emasculated'. Being overwhelmed by emotional pain, the symptoms of intrusion and uncontrollable sensations of hyperarousal that accompany intrusions are synonymous with being 'unmanly'. Senad didn't want to feel weak and vulnerable. Shortly after he was released from the concentration camp, he joined the Bosnian army and received a medal for bravery. He saw himself as a soldier and defender, not a victim! When he felt hurt, he'd react with anger, not grief or anguish. When his wife would say something that he interpreted as disrespect, criticism, humiliation or attack, he would lash out at her.

Like most domestic violence abusers, Senad medicated himself with the narcotics of rage and dominance. He'd ward off the threatening emergence of unpleasant feelings and inner tension by playing 'I'll make you feel bad so I don't have to' with his wife.

He unconsciously wanted to get rid of his disturbing or unpleasant feelings by inducing similar feelings in his partner. When he'd manage to do that—when he'd generate her fear, humiliation or pain—he'd swell with a sense of power and satisfaction. Playing this vicious game with his wife became a habit. Not that he was fully aware of it, but he instinctively knew the easiest way to elevate his mood was through the use of rage and violence—when he played out his position of superiority and dominance by putting her down. That's how verbal abuse and violence became his addictive defence. It also served to pump up his plummeting self-esteem. Like alcohol or drugs, rage became an elixir, transforming what he perceived as his weaknesses into grandiosity, shifting him from a sense of powerlessness to a sense of being in control. Raging—needed for fuelling his violent outbursts—made him feel invincible; it helped him feel like he had power and control over someone or something in his life.

How does rage work? Rage simultaneously releases adrenaline and endorphins. Adrenaline lifted Senad up. It worked like magic and gave his body extra strength so he didn't feel fearful and vulnerable anymore. Unpleasant body sensations and disempowering emotional states such as feeling disrespected, mistreated, devalued or humiliated disappeared. He would feel strong and in control. Endorphins acted as his body's own opioids; they diminished his perception of pain and also acted as sedatives. The combination of adrenaline and endorphins was a powerful internal cocktail which, like any other form of intoxication, offered Senad short-lived relief from distress, fear, grief or a sense of inferiority, especially with the sense of inferiority or being 'put down' by his wife. It served to move him from the helpless, 'one down' position to a grandiose 'one-up' position. The experience was very pleasant. No wonder it was difficult for him to stop abusing his wife. Rage helped him with depression, too.

Senad was diagnosed with agitated depression. Agitated depression is a type of depression that, along with depressed mood and emptiness, involves symptoms like restlessness, insomnia, extreme irritability, anger, snapping at friends and family, or being annoyed by small things. This diagnosis worried him; mostly because he interpreted the doctor's words, 'You suffer from depression' as a warning.

In Senad's mind, 'You suffer from depression' meant 'You may sink into deep grief or despair and kill yourself.' He didn't know that there is a difference between depression and sadness or grief. Depression is not really a feeling. It is a condition of numbness or non-feeling. Depression freezes and can be long-lasting, but grief flows so it has an end. No matter how painful they are, feelings are not endless. But our attempts to avoid them can last a lifetime. Senad wanted to avoid them.

To avoid his painful emotional states and mask his depressed mood he needed his rage; therefore, his abusive behaviour towards his wife continued. If he stopped, he would suffer. So whenever he felt hurt or humiliated, he'd abuse her. Whenever he needed to lift his mood and pump up his sense of deflation, he'd abuse her. If he felt tense and nervous for reasons that had nothing to do with her, he'd find a 'reason' and abuse her. His parents did

the same to each other and to Senad. He learned the
'How-to-regulate-your-mood' technique from them. He
copied their reasons for repetitive patterns of abusive behaviour, too.

Chapter 6

FROM TERRORISED TO TERRORISING

The majority of abused children do not become abusive. Nobody knows for sure, but statistics indicate that only a small percentage of people who are victims of abuse will become abusers.

If we take children from the same background and same age and expose them to the same abuse, one child may develop depression and self-destructive tendencies, another turns into a perpetrator, and others may become successful professionals who help victims of abuse.

On the other hand, it is a well-known fact that many perpetrators of violence or abuse were also victims of abuse in childhood. How do we explain that? For example, we know that being sexually abused does not cause someone to sexually offend because the majority of boys who are sexually abused do not go on to commit abuse. And yet, the majority of those who commit sexual offences, like paedophiles, have been sexually abused themselves. So if being sexually abused is not the only factor, what are the other factors that contribute to sexual offending?

In a domestic violence context, the discourse of 'victims becoming perpetrators' has been recognised and studied. However, we still struggle to understand what distinguishes those abused in childhood who grow up to be non-violent partners and parents from those who go on to become abusers themselves...and some of their children will become abusers, too.

There is longevity to domestic abuse. The trail of evidence confirms that abuse colonises itself in families, becoming a trans-generational pattern. The grotesque relational cycle repeats itself through the simple pattern: A family member is abused, and it comes out that the perpetrator was also abused. The same tragic script may go back generations. To outsiders, this cycle appears counter-intuitive. If one was wounded by their abuser, why do victims abuse others, including their own children?

In addition to the trans-generational pattern, what is also 'transmitted' from one generation to another is a particular belief system, for example, internalised messages that doing certain things such as 'punishing' is okay, or that being a certain way is wrong and deserves 'punishment'. The major function of such beliefs is to propagate abuse. Indeed, in some family histories, domestic violence is a never-ending story.

Is it possible to be a never-abusive parent? It isn't; however, there is a difference between an abusive parent and the one who is not. Even the best parents have moments when they lose control and say hurtful words or do something harmful, but abusive parents do that regularly. Abuse in families is usually not just one incident but a pattern of inflicting harm and attacking a child's sense of self-worth and wellbeing. It occurs on a continuous basis, over time, and it may imply intent or even desire to hurt the child. The abused child may grow up and go on abusing his children. Why?

When abuse is accepted as 'normal', 'enjoyable' and 'inconsequential'

Are there any factors that contribute to the creation of the next generation of abusers? The researchers Freda Briggs, Russell M. F. Hawkins and Mary Williams argue that the context in which the abuse occurred is particularly important. 'Where the context included an acceptance of the abuse as "normal", "enjoyable" or "inconsequential" the chances of replication were enhanced. Where the context resulted in negative reactions, including feelings of shame, guilt and anger, the victim was less likely to replicate the abuse.'[1]

These researchers from the University of South Australia compared a group of incarcerated child molesters (paedophiles)—who had been victims of sexual abuse themselves—with a group of non-offending males who admitted to being sexually abused as children. They concluded that prisoners convicted of sexual abuse differed in a number of ways from men who did not reproduce this abuse. For example, most prisoners 'denied that they had been sexually abused; the information relating to their victimisation came from detailed questions relating to their sexual experiences in childhood.'[2] Most prisoners 'accepted the abuse as "normal", "enjoyable" or "inconsequential".[3] 'Prisoners were more likely than non-offenders to have become promiscuous and sexually obsessed. They said, "I became hooked on sex...I never stopped thinking about it"; "I couldn't get enough of it"; "I never said 'No' to anyone"; "I went looking for it"; "I was into sex with any-one, anywhere, at any time."'[4]

Could the same three key factors: 1. Perpetrators tend to deny and/or normalise their own childhood experience of abuse; 2. They do not see how they have been damaged by their experiences of abuse, so they discount the damage they do to their victims; and 3.They link abuse with pleasure—which contributes to the creation of the next generation of child molesters—help us to understand trans-generational transmission of intimate partner abuse and domestic violence, including child abuse?

We know that the majority of individuals who experienced maltreatment as a child are not violent towards their own children.[5] So what differentiates a non-abusive parent with a history of childhood abuse from an abusive parent who was a victim of a similar child abuse? Can we predict whether or not the victim of abuse will turn into the perpetrator if we explore these three factors that play a part in the transmission of maltreatment across generations?

The abuse is normal: 'I wasn't abused!'

Sins of My Father

Jelena Dokić is one of the brightest tennis stars Australia has ever produced, but her fans always knew there was something dark about the relationship between her and her powerful, overbearing father Damir Dokić.

'Every morning I wake at home and worries assail my mind before I have even lifted my head off the pillow. How can I make sure he doesn't hurt me today? How can I make sure he doesn't explode? These days that's hard – he is getting more aggressive.

And he has become more violent. The belt is brown, its leather thick and hard, it feels as sharp as a knife when it's whipped against my skin. A mediocre training session, a loss, a bad mood – any of these trigger him to bring out the belt. I stand in my bra, my back to him, and he orders me not to move as he hits me. Often he almost slices my skin with the belt.'

In an interview with a Serbian newspaper in 2009, Damir Dokić admitted to hitting his daughter. 'If I was ever a little more aggressive towards Jelena it was for her sake,' the newspaper has quoted him as saying. 'When I was young, I was beaten by my parents,' Mr Dokić said, 'and I am now thankful to them for that, because that helped me to become the right person.'

'**Always Beaten, Never Broken**', *The Sunday Telegraph*, **Sunday, November 12, 2017**

No doubt, people who normalise their own childhood experience of abuse, like Damir Dokić, father of famous tennis player Jelena Dokić, may be more likely to become perpetrators. The intimate partner abusers who experienced or witnessed family abuse in their childhood homes; the paedophiles who were themselves sexually abused as children; and the physically abusive parents who were physically abused by their own parents—all of them tend to normalise not only the abuse they inflict on others but the abuse they experienced themselves.

How do physically abusive parents normalise their abuse? Through rationalisations and justifications. The eyes-shut attitude towards the maltreatment of children stems from the 'fear of spoiling the child by permissiveness', and the necessity of using force (harsh punishment) to condition the child's 'unreasoning mind'.

The old Calvinist doctrine—the idea of the antisocial nature of human basic needs and instinctual impulses—also supports the rationalisations that make a virtue of parental cruelty. And while some violent parents tend to normalise or rationalise their abusive behaviour, others don't even bother to justify the repetitive pattern of brutally and sadistically beating their children. Some of them indeed could be described as 'getting hooked on beating

children' because of the compelling intensity and frequency of the repetitive child abuse patterns; the
elaborate measures pursued to achieve satisfaction when
'punishing' the child; and the 'withdrawal crisis' that occurs when the parent is deprived of such an outlet for
their unpleasant pent-up tension.

And what is the impact of their violent crime? When
faced with uncertainty regarding the motives of parental
cruelty (a parent is capable of calculated torment using
sudden, unprovoked savagery) and sensing the sadistic
character of 'disciplining', what children find painful is
not only the violence itself but the denigration, helplessness and trauma of being used as a scapegoat. The parent
takes advantage of the child's position of defencelessness
to vent rage often rationalised as 'good for the child'. The
child's sense of security and trust is shattered. However,
the young victims may create a defence against this reali-
sation. They may use dissociation as a defence
mechanism or deny the negative consequences of the
abuse they have been exposed to.

The denial of negative consequences of abuse

Not only do domestic violence perpetrators and paedophiles ignore the damage they do, but so do the abusive
parents. We usually explain such tendencies to deny or
ignore the negative consequences of the abuse as the offender's attempts to avoid a sense of guilt and shame for
what they have been doing, and/or to escape punishment
and legal responsibilities for the crime they have committed. However, in some instances, portraying the abuse as
inconsequential may also be based upon repression and
dissociation. Many studies confirm that a dissociative

process—which allows children to protect themselves from the full impact of the trauma, especially ongoing physical and sexual abuse—plays a part in the trans-generational transmission of maltreatment.

Indeed, the defence mechanism *dissociation* might have an important role in the transmission of maltreat-ment across generations. How does this work? The overwhelming trauma of being abused causes the person to use dissociation as a coping strategy. As in the film *Precious*, when her father rapes her, Precious dissociates and shows no emotions. She lies there and slips into her fantasy world.

Dissociation is a hallmark characteristic of traumatic experience and serves the purpose of protecting the psy-che from an unacceptable reality and buffering the central nervous system under conditions of hyperarousal. As a result, the abused child may have a variety of prob-lems in the area of memory and perception of what has happened during the traumatic event. Instead of 're-membering', 'metabolising' and eventually healing the painful experience, the traumatised person unconsciously re-enacts or acts-out the traumatic event. For example, a man abuses his child in a particular way—he is copying the abusive behaviour of his parents, but seems unaware he is repeating similar abuse that he himself experienced in his childhood. Dissociation also allows him to emo-tionally distance from the offense and maintain minimal empathy for his victim. As he doesn't have a clear picture of what happened to him, he can't see the negative im-pact of the experiences of abuse so he discounts the consequences of abuse.

Now we have a better understanding why perpetrators normalise abuse, minimise negative consequences of their abusive behaviour and deny that their childhood experiences constituted abuse, despite the high levels of violence and emotional damage they experienced. But many other highly traumatised children dissociate, minimise or discount the consequences of the abuse they experienced and deny that they were the victims of abuse. Yet only small percentage of them will turn into abusers. Why do the majority of those abused do not become abusers? Because they don't identify with their aggressors?

Identification with the aggressor

A little girl is rebuked and punished by her mother. Sometime later, she does to her doll what her mother has done to her. Another example: a boy pretends that he is a dangerous monster. Through this play he can transform his own intense anxiety about being attacked by frightening creatures. If he becomes that powerful creature, he is not a frightened little boy anymore. Now he has the power of the dangerous monster!

By identifying with the punitive parental figure or taking on the characteristic of someone or something that causes distress (a dangerous monster), children manage to reduce their painful emotions by switching from the passive role of a helpless victim into the active role of a powerful perpetrator. We create our identity depending on what we identify with, and in the situation where there is only a victim and an abuser (and no middle ground) the majority of victims who will not become perpetrators clearly identify themselves as victims of abuse. That is not necessarily the case with victims-turned-perpetrators.

The boy, for example, may be abused by his sadistic father. The child lives in a world of threat and responds to it with fear. But he does not like his position of 'poor, vulnerable me'. To accept that he is a victim—to give in to the power of others—may feel like degradation or loss of self-respect. He refuses to feel like a victim even when he is and splits off his wounded or traumatised Inner Child aspect perceived as 'weak' thus unacceptable.

Instead of identifying with the object of abuse— instead of seeing himself as a victim—an abused boy may race for the high ground and identify with his abuser. If he succeeds, he is not a powerless, helpless or a broken little boy. Just the opposite! He'll become tough and powerful! The abused child's simplified interpretation of the 'switch' goes like this: 'The perpetrator has abused me. I am hurting. I can keep complaining and crying. I can sit here and be a poor, helpless victim, or I can stand up for myself and decide to build a strong fighter in me so I'm not going to get beaten up anymore.'

Identifying with the aggressor (as a defence against fear or painful emotional states) was described by Anna Freud, daughter of Sigmund Freud. This coping strategy explains how the abused boy can introject his punishment from parents and then project this same punishment on another. The payoff is some element of control and satisfaction: 'Now I can make others feel as bad I am made to feel!' That's how a new aspect in the personality starts crystallising. The new aspect may call himself the Protector, the Tough Guy or the Warrior; alas, he can easily become as abusive as his role model: the perpetrator who has abused him.

When the victims of abuse identify with their aggressors, they also internalise the aggressors' beliefs and attitudes, blame victims, normalise abusive behaviour— their own or in general—and minimise the consequences of the abuse in the same way their aggressors did.

The pleasure factor

Normalising the abuse and discounting the damage that abusers do to their victims are undoubtedly important factors that contribute to transforming the victim into the abuser. But even if we take into consideration these two factors, it is still difficult to understand why someone who was victimised would become the victimiser (the victimiser who offends and re-offends) and develops a repetitive pattern of abusive behaviour. A pattern that tends to escalate in frequency and severity. There must be something more to it. Indeed, there is. A third factor, called the 'pleasure factor', can help us to explain this strange phenomenon.

The sex offenders who use a 'grooming' strategy carefully minimise violence, coercion and psychological pressure on the child. They add the elements such as loving attention ('You are special to me') and affection and pleasure, so the child will find the experience not only 'normal' but pleasurable too. Another example: An abusive parent may derive a sense of satisfaction and superiority from the position of a powerful, controlling authoritative figure that can inflict pain and punish others. In his childhood, he was the abused boy who identified with his abuser and idealised these 'qualities': superiority, strength and having authority or control over others. Now he wants to share the pleasure of being in control and having the power to punish others—the pleasure once reserved for his abusive parent only.

This is how victims-turned-perpetrators link abuse with pleasure. If abusive or violent behaviour brings a sense of satisfaction when the inner tension is released or a sense of pleasure when he 'punishes', the Abuser aspect who craves the pleasure of abusing may start crystallising in the boy's personality. Once formed, it can be activated or easily triggered in the person's relationship with a partner and/or children, and in extreme cases, some become rapists and sadistic serial killers who delight in the suffering of their victims. But will the Abuser always keep offending?

The refusal of domestic violence perpetrators to acknowledge the disastrous consequences of their behaviour; the denial of child molesters to accept responsibility for the effects of traumatising children; and the failure of abusive parents to acknowledge the impact of abuse on their child have frequently been noted as problems when being treated. The offenders from all three groups—intimate partner abusers; physically abusive parents; and child sexual abuse offenders—are usually expected to re-offend soon after release if they have no access to successful treatments and offender re-education programs. Why? They feel compelled to feed the habit. They simply must continue to feed their appetite through the same tedious cycles of molesting children, abusing partners or beating children. And unfortunately, a certain number of their victims will become the perpetrators who will also abuse partners and molest children.

Chapter 7

WHY DO WE NEED A FATHER?

There is a great deal of evidence that shows the presence of a good, healthy father-child bond prevents children, especially boys, from engaging in maladaptive, delinquent or violent behaviour. It does not have to be a biological father. It can be an uncle, a teacher, a mentor or anyone who likes the boy, has the boy's best interests in mind and is willing to support his growth and psychological development.

The boys who are exposed to abuse and do not have an involved, protective and supportive father figure are the most vulnerable and susceptible to convert and join the team from the 'dark side of the Force'—criminal groups, gangs or terrorist organisations—when under the pressure of various manipulative people. Indeed, we need a father or father figure. We need a father for protection and love, guidance and identity. These are the key components in the healthy psychological development of a father's children.

Protection

The childhood memories of being protected and safe are often associated with the presence of a good father. The themes related to the father archetype are those of support for his children's wellbeing, but also about the protection of life in general, not just for the individual.

The qualities of immense strength and solidity are associated with the masculine capacity to protect. This capacity gives children a sense of safety and security because they are looked after. 'He is my rock!' people say when they want to describe the specific rock-solid father quality symbolised by the image of a huge immovable mountain. There is a sense of largeness and majesty about it. But children also experience the pleasant, relaxing sensations of tranquillity and softness, as though they were enveloped in a velvety blanket, when carried in their father's strong arms.

There is another form of a father's protection, especially in situations when we are emotionally hurt, which can be as equally important as protection from physical danger. When exposed to abuse, we are in a desperate need for the protector who would help us to heal the trauma of abuse. Abuse is a specific subset of traumatic experiences, and if we are to heal the emotional wound, we must go through the process of healing. A compassionate father figure can help us to heal quicker.

How can a father help to speed up the healing process? When harmed, we tend to repress the pain and avoid thinking about painful events, or we may want to distract ourselves with alcohol and drugs, or divert the pain through endless fights, dramas and conflicts. But a father knows the process that will facilitate healing is not about avoiding emotions ('Big boys don't cry!') and dissociating from or suppressing the hurt. Nor is it about expressing it—ventilating anger and rage or acting it out ('Be a tough guy and fight back!'). We need to go through it—to experience grief, for example—in order to metabolise it and eventually heal the wound. That's why the positive father (our biological father or a teacher, doctor or a counsellor) will 'hold the protective therapeutic space' so we can safely experience and release the pain of being harmed. With him on our side, we will heal quicker.

Without a supportive father figure, we may feel not just vulnerable and endangered, but betrayed. We may not know who deceived us or why we have been betrayed, or we may not be able to articulate that vague and bitter sense buried somewhere deep within us, but that is what we feel. Sigmund Freud, the father of psychoanalysis, explored the link between the way we relate to our fathers and the way we relate to the masculine deity. Being betrayed by a father figure often transpires into being betrayed by God. Unsupported by their fathers, children may think to themselves, 'God is supposed to be all-loving, all-merciful, but if that's true, why are we suffering so much? Why are innocent people tortured and killed? Why is this world such a mess?' Or, 'If God isn't with me now when I desperately need Him, God is no good. I believed in Him, I trusted Him, I was a good person, I was doing everything I should do, yet He betrayed me. He doesn't care about me, so I don't care about Him. I don't need Him—I hate Him!'

Young children cannot understand abstract concepts, so they can't soothe the pain with adult rationalised thinking such as 'God is testing me', or 'There is a higher reason for suffering'. Children think God is some kind of a superhuman person who will help them. But they don't see anyone or anything like that showing up to take away their suffering so they feel disappointed and abandoned by God the Father. They feel angry. 'He has done nothing to help me! Staying on His side means that I would stay helpless, vulnerable and unprotected. I don't want to stay on His 'good' side. Does His 'good side' exist at all? I'll join the other side—the side that offers me help and gives me hope. That side is the good side!' That's why the children whose basic needs for safety and protection are not met are the most vulnerable when criminals, manipulators or demagogues offer violence as a solution for their problems, and the sense of power that comes with it.

Identity

Identity is not some kind of a static psychological state or attribute. Creating identity is a continuous developmental process. It is an ongoing journey of creating various new aspects of ourselves. It also includes self-discovery about the existing ones and the healing journey of integrating dissociated and suppressed wounded parts of the old personality.

Our identity—who we take ourselves to be and what we identify with—is related to family, nation, culture, religion, gender, roles, values and beliefs. Some of these factors are inherited vertically from our parents and ancestors, so we talk about vertical identity.

Horizontal identities are related to parts of who we are that have nothing to do with our parents. Engineers, blind people or people with a particular artistic talent and skill have their own separate identities; they may develop their own world that they share with others through the horizontal network of communication. Being a refugee could be an example of horizontal identity, too. Ethnicity, on the other hand, is a vertical identity. And while homeland is, in some traditions, seen as related to the mother ('Mother Russia' is closely connected to the word that Russians use to mean 'homeland', usually translated as 'motherland'), national identity is often associated with the father archetype. The words and expressions such as the 'Land of our fathers', can be found as the title of national anthems in some countries.

To create our identity, we need others. As small children, we do not see clearly who we are and what we are capable of. We create our identity based on how we perceive ourselves through the eyes of others. We need others, especially parents, to hold up the mirror and support us through the development of our unique potentials and skills, our personal characteristics, qualities and talents. These are often seen as the gifts we offer to the world. We also need a parent who can be a role model so we can copy him or internalise his values and identify ourselves through them. That is why the boy who has a good or relatively 'conflict-free' relationship with his father usually supports the same soccer team as his father or might share similar world view and political ideology with him. That often means that the son will support the ideology—whether healthy or harmful—his father supports, and believe in what his father believes.

On the other hand, a son's conflicted relationship with his father may lead to the son doubting his father's guidance. The son's resentment and his lack of trust in father's directions and 'definitions of good and bad' can turn him away or against his father's beliefs or world views. Hence, taking different perspectives—choosing different sides in social and national upheavals and wars, the clash of ideologies or religious frictions—can become a central theme in the conflict between son and father.

What about abusive men who have learnt about abuse from their violent fathers? Their fathers also served as role models. A boy can be in terrible pain inflicted by his father, sickened by what he has seen or experienced, and yet he grows up and abuses his wife and children just like his father did.

The issue of identity is generally different for daughters. While abused sons may refuse to see themselves as helpless victims and identify with the aggressors (their abusive fathers), daughters of the same fathers may see themselves as victims. Besides, daughters usually do not identify with fathers but with a self-image that the father holds of them. For example, if her father sees her as intelligent and enjoys intellectual discussions with her, the girl may create the self-image as being smart or an intellectual. But if her father does not recognise her beauty, she might have difficulties seeing herself as physically attractive. Her father's impressions about her can be deeply ingrained in her self-identity and also generalised or projected onto other men. It means that she may believe that other men see her as intelligent but not pretty—the same way her father saw her.

A father's support is precious for his daughter's personal development and growth. He can block or help his daughter to achieve her professional or career goals, especially if he does not believe that her gender is an obstacle to success. A daughter also needs her father's encouragement, his 'empowering support', to be able to stand up for herself. If she had such a father's support, it would be much easier for her to protect herself from male manipulators or domestic violence perpetrators. There are, of course, many empowered girls being raised by single mothers, but the support from a positive father figure can significantly contribute to her good life and healthy relationships with men.

Guidance

The third quality associated with positive father figures is guidance. Its function is to assist with objective perception and understanding ourselves, others and the world in general. We need guidance to comprehend the external world and distinguish the ethical aspects of good and bad, right and wrong. When a young warrior-son decides to fight for a noble cause, his father's definition of noble is often crucial in deciding which side to choose.

A good father figure provides guidance and leads by example. He is a model of adult confidence, responsibility, honesty and competence in the areas of work, creativity, family and society. He indirectly offers himself as a role model—the role model who guides and teaches, not preaches, lectures or demands. He clearly owns his values but does not rigidly impose them on his children as 'the only right way'

The father wound

How many sons remember their violent fathers beating them and yelling, 'Look me in the eyes when I'm talking to you!' The boy would be petrified. There was no point defending himself. Anything the victim did to fend off the blows only outraged the abuser more. He would try to look at his father's face, but there was something in the man's eyes that was terrifying—something that could literally turn him into stone. Some boys formed an image or created the belief that their father was not human at the time of abuse but was an agent of pure evil that somehow emerged from the ether and occupied their father's body and soul. During the episodes of savage beatings, the boy would find himself caught in the 'eye of the hurricane of the evil force'. He could not escape nor could he defend himself. The core of his being was frozen. He was just waiting there for the storm to pass.

David Nugent, a counsellor and facilitator of the behaviour change program for abusive men Heavy METAL (Men's Education Towards Anger and Life), said in the ABC documentary Call Me Dad that 'most of the men he deals with grew up in fear of their own fathers.'[1] As much as they didn't want to be like their fathers, these men—victims of domestic violence themselves—became domestic violence perpetrators, just like their fathers.

Nugent understands this very well as he was one of them. Once he lost it and 'smashed up the family car, bashing in the windscreen. Seeing the look of terror on his children's faces reminded him of his own childhood. It was a turning point. He knew he had to change.'[2] Today he counsels men with a history of violence and teenage boys in schools in Victoria, Australia.

So what motivates domestic violence perpetrators to stop abusing their partners? Some say their children. When they decided to quit abusing their partners, the motivation that often drove the decision was because they wanted to protect their children. They didn't want their sons to become violent or they didn't want their daughters to become victims of abusive men. Men who want to change their abusive behaviour and dismantle their Abuser aspect want to be positive role models for their children. They don't want to 'educate' their daughters to accept abuse or 'teach' their sons to be abusive.

George Lucas, an American film director, best known for creating the *Star Wars*, once said that the relationship between father and son, and the tragedy of Anakin Sky-walker turning into Darth Vader, are the central defining plots in the *Star Wars* films. However, it is the theme of redeeming hope for a father who has fallen to the 'dark side of the Force' (given in to his darker urges of violence and abuse) that makes the films so exciting and appealing to many sons who were raised by abusive fathers—the sons who carry the 'father wound'.

Chapter 8

INTRODUCTION TO ASPECTOLOGY

There are times when I look over the various parts of my character with perplexity. I recognize that I am made up of several persons and that the person that at the moment has the upper hand will inevitably give place to another. But which is the real one? All of them or none?[1] **Somerset Maugham, the English playwright and novelist**

The word 'aspectology' is not used in this book as a new clinical term.[2] There is nothing new about aspectology. Many writers and psychotherapists—Carl G. Jung, Roberto Assagioli, Virginia Satir, Eric Berne, Hal and Sidra Stone, Richard C. Schwartz to name just a few—have pointed out that our personality is not a single entity but a composite or a mosaic of units called 'parts', 'self-representations', 'complexes', 'sub-personalities' or simply 'aspects. Yet, 'most therapists have been trained in a "uni-consciousness" model of personality and are less familiar with working in a "multi-consciousness" paradigm,' Dr

Janina Fisher, known as an expert on the treatment of trauma, noted in her book *Healing the Fragmented Selves of Trauma Survivors*.[3]

Various terms in psychology describe distinct psychological formations in the normal personality, and 'aspects' are just one of them. However, we are much more than a sum of aspects. Both in Western and Eastern philosophy and spiritual traditions there is the widely held belief that every human being has a true self or spiritual centre, known as the Self. '*Self* refers to innate qualities possessed by all human beings in undamaged form, no matter how much abuse and trauma they have experienced,' Dr Fisher writes.[4]

Nonetheless, we all have a host of different characters inside of our psyche whom Richard C. Schwartz, the founder of the Internal Family Systems (IFS) model of psychotherapy, calls the 'internal family'. These 'parts', as they are called in IFS, are described as seemingly autonomous personality aspects with their unique way of thinking, e-moting (they have their own set of emotions) and patterns of behaving. 'What Schwartz learned was that the existence of parts is not pathological; it is a normal structure of the mind.'[5]

Different parts have different functions; they operate in different areas of our life and represent various aspects of us such as the parent, the businessperson, the musician, the driver, the friend and more. They also express our talents, abilities and disabilities: the good singer, the bad cook aspect and so forth. Some aspects are charged with strong emotions, so we call them my 'angry self' or my 'compassionate self'. Some others are our unconscious creations. Cut off from our everyday awareness, they may take on a life of their own as if they were little personas with separate identities. And they keep perpetuating their identity. Why? Because that's in the mechanics of the aspects.

Once created, they perpetuate their identity by attracting the types of experiences that confirm their beliefs about themselves. For example, you have formed an 'I am not so smart' aspect in your early childhood. There is a judgement attached to it, and you have accepted it as a truth. You tend to live out your beliefs, so the 'dumb' aspect, who doesn't feel as worthy as other 'smart' people, will find life circumstances and experiences to perpetuate its 'I am stupid' identity. It will follow you through life, causing you to spend a tremendous amount of life energy trying to prove yourself to you and to others.

But no matter how many good marks or degrees you get, something deep within is still nagging you that perhaps you're not as smart. That's because the aspect will keep proving that it is dumb as that's its identity; it cannot behave differently. The good news is that although you have unconsciously created your dumb aspect through a particular judgement and belief about yourself, you can consciously un-create it.

Each aspect has his/her own 'face' or a unique way of communicating and behaving. When active, these aspects do not just think, feel or react through their usual patterns of thinking, feeling and behaving, but they also occupy the physical body in a specific way. The stronger the aspect is charged with emotional energy, the more control it has over the physical body and the person's behaviour.

Aspects communicate between each other. They can influence, sabotage and contaminate each other or fight for control and dominance. Aspects with different belief systems can be in conflict and create unpleasant intrapsychic tension—a nagging feeling of being stuck in an endless fight between 'pros and cons'. Some aspects are very loud and opinionated. The Inner Critic is one of them. Some others are not that visible—they hide in the shadow of our personality.

Shadow aspects

We all have a shadow part of our personality. The shadow, a term coined by famous Swiss psychiatrist Carl Gustav Jung who founded analytic psychology, is typically conceived of as the part of ourselves we are not proud of and want to hide from others and ourselves. When the undesirable aspect, hidden in the shadow, is pointed out by a friend or partner, our first reaction is to deny it. Then we defend against it using various distractions to keep it at bay or project it onto others.

A good example of shadow projection is a domestic violence abuser who denies responsibility for his violent behaviour and blames his victim. Unwilling or unable to consciously experience his sense of guilt and remorse for his repetitive patterns of abuse, he accuses and blames his partner. Projecting his guilt onto her not only protects him from this unpleasant emotion, but allows him to 'self-righteously' keep using violence for the gratification of his sadistic drives—the drives he hides from others and/or himself.

Unfortunately, many victims of domestic violence buy into this and start believing that they are indeed guilty or somehow responsible for the abuse they endure, thus unconsciously helping their perpetrator to feel justified in abusing them. Why? There is a saying that when someone is projecting their shadow onto us, there is often a grain of truth in the projection. 'The grain of truth' (the woman indeed has certain negative qualities; or she did say something that triggered him) may serve as a hook on which the abusive man, unconscious of his dark aspects, 'hangs' his shadow parts of the personality. But when the abused woman realises that she has been hooked by the abuser's shadow projection, she'll stop buying into it— she'll stop believing his rationalisations and accusations, even if there is a grain of truth in them. The insights into the dark and dangerous aspects of her abusive partner's personality, and understanding the mechanics behind the insidious and entangling trap of shadow projection, can help her to find the exit from her toxic bond with him.

Not only inferior and undesirable, but the parts of the psyche that have split off due to trauma also live in the shadow realm of the psyche. Although pushed into the shadow, these fragments of memory from past traumatic experiences, charged with intense, frightening or painful emotions and bodily sensations, may encroach on our everyday life and influence us in an unconscious and often detrimental way. They intrude in the form of symptoms of intrusion—intrusive images and memory; traumatic nightmares; flashbacks; and so-called behavioural (traumatic) re-enactments—and they can be the basis for various mental and even physical illnesses.

These parts of the psyche—fragmented and dissociated as a result of traumatic experiences such as abuse, serious illness, accident and overwhelming or catastrophic events—can create little aspects that tend to form their own seemingly independent identity. Why are they dissociated? So the memories, images, overwhelming emotions and physical sensations related to the trauma do not impede daily functioning.

One of the reactions in situations when we are exposed to extreme violence is to seemingly 'withdraw from the scene of injury'—the painful experience continues but it is not happening to 'me'. The victims of torture, rape and domestic violence sometimes report a feeling of 'not being there' during their ordeal, as though they were observing the event from a distance, detached from emotions and physical sensations. They learn how to move out of the body so that they do not feel the harrowing enormity of what's happening to them. They become 'disembodied observers', cut off from the terrifying experience. The name for this defence mechanism is dissociation. Dissociation is the essence of trauma.

Trauma is not the same as stress. Trauma is any experience that causes overwhelming and unbearable emotional pain or terror. Stress is inevitable in everyday life, but trauma can take us to a much darker place. When we are traumatised by an overwhelming experience that couldn't be metabolised and assimilated in the usual way, a fragment of our psyche becomes frozen in time and 'stuck' in the shock of the traumatising event. The feeling is as though a chunk of crystallised psychic structure—thoughts, impressions or beliefs about what happened, loaded with intense unpleasant emotions and bodily sensations—splits off. The inner world is no longer coherent.

Dissociated 'chunks' of memory and images from the traumatic event, charged with intense affect, float like little satellites in the psyche in a disconnected way. However, the painful experiences that could not be metabolised do not disappear. They are just 'removed' from conscious awareness to protect the psychological and sometimes even physical survival and everyday functioning.

Jung called these parts of the psyche *autonomous complexes*. They have split off due to shock, trauma, abuse or breach of our personal boundaries and have developed a seemingly autonomous life and independent will of their own. 'In most cases where a split-off complex manifests itself it does so in the form of a personality, as if the complex had a consciousness of itself. Thus the voices heard by the insane are personified. I dealt long ago with this phenomenon of personified complexes in my doctoral dissertation,' Jung noted in the book *Memories, Dreams, Reflections*. [6]

The dissociated parts can morph into seemingly separate aspects, and the wounded Inner Child aspect is one of them. These aspects can have a particular emotional charge, belief system and even life of their own as though they were a separate entity. If we are not aware that these distinct parts of ourselves exist or how they operate from the inner psychic plane, we say that the aspect is not fully integrated. They will stay dissociated until the time when they can be re-connected.

For example, the wounded Inner Child aspect holds the terror and shock from painful childhood events, as though patiently waiting for the person to grow up and become strong enough to get back to the traumatic experience and release the emotional charge attached to the painful memory. When the traumatised person feels safe and ready to heal, the emotional charge can start gradually discharging. The exiled parts—the repressed or dissociated aspects—are finally re-collected (re-membered), and the healing process can begin.

Unfortunately, our attempts to heal traumatised aspects can be dysfunctional, even re-traumatising. For instance, if unrecognised, the wounded Inner Child aspect of a woman who was abused by her father may seek love, acceptance or protection from the very types of men who cannot give it to her. Being in relationships with abusive men—perhaps because she is unconsciously trying to undo the past, gain mastery over the situation and get love, or because she is repeating the painful experiences in attempts to release the emotional charge generated in the original trauma with abusive father—she recreates the very trauma she is trying to heal from. Or the man, abused as a child by his parents, may unconsciously act out the unhealed wound, traumatising and terrorising his partner. Instead of opening to the pain in his wounded Inner Child aspect and releasing it, he inflicts pain onto others. If he has identified with his violent parents, he may feel compelled to unconsciously act out the role of the perpetrator and abuse his partner in a similar way he was abused. It is recognised fact that re-enacting victimisation is one of the major causes of violence. Abusers have often been physically or sexually abused as children. Acting out his unhealed trauma of abuse, the man induces in his victim the experiences of pain, fear and humiliation—the emotions he himself is unwilling or unable to feel and release.

Our inner demons

We all have dark aspects. Some people refer to them as 'monsters' or talk about battling with their inner demons. Various destructive and self-destructive tendencies such as addictions are drives and behavioural patterns of the dark aspects within us. We are afraid that they might take over, 'possess' us, wreak havoc in our relationships with other people or 'run the horror show', so we tend to deny or dissociate from them. We push them into the cellar of our subconscious and shut the door, never to open it again. If they come up to the surface, we may claim that we have no control over them or that these aspects are not me. But they are still ours, and just as they have been created, they can be un-created, even if we don't know how they have been created in the first place.

However, some dark aspects can be challenging to deal with. Addict aspects are particularly nasty. They tend to dominate not only other aspects but the person's everyday life. Addict aspects often develop various strategies to influence or manipulate—even posing as protectors in the inner drama of the person's psyche—in order to get what they are addicted to. They may be addicted to heroin, a behaviour such as gambling or watching pornography, or they may be addicted to hurting others. They all have one common characteristic: The more you supply them with what they crave (the more you feed them) the stronger they are and the more they come to the forefront of your personality and life. Everyday life may then start revolving around them and your life energy is invested in feeding your addictions. You've become addicted to alcohol, for example, which creates the problem-drinking aspect. The aspect has found a way to consume your life force.

This is a sad story because from now on, your life energy will be invested in maintaining the habit—keeping the Addict alive. The stronger the problem-drinking aspect is, the more energy is tied up into feeding that addiction. On top of that, the Addict can mess with the mind, contaminating your common sense, so you use various stories to rationalise why you do what you do to make sense of the Addict's agenda. There are many examples and descriptions how the Addict operates. Consider this story:

A woman decides to lose weight. She wants to look better and be healthier, so she makes a plan to quit sugar. But that's not in her sugar addict aspect's interest. That aspect says, 'I want ice-cream.' Sometime later, as though hypnotised, the woman finds herself searching the fridge.

However, she is determined not to eat it, so she moves away from the fridge.

Not long after, she starts feeling bad; a vague sense of bitterness, depression and anxiety creeps in. She sinks into a heavy, gloomy mood while the scary thoughts about her empty life and suicidal ideation trigger her anxiety. The anxiety is getting worse and it'll soon become almost intolerable. She knows that awful emotional state well. She's been diagnosed with depression and that diagnosis worries her. Besides, she has a history of childhood abuse, and when the suppressed painful memories start to resurface (sometimes in the attempt to be addressed, released and eventually healed), she eats. The sense of pleasure she gets from eating temporarily sedates her painful emotions. Nevertheless, she tries not to think about the ice-cream in the fridge. But after a couple of attempts to resist the temptation, she gives up.

We can observe the opening scene in the woman's inner drama with the Rational Woman in the foreground, the Addict in the background and the molested wounded Inner Child aspect hidden in the subconscious. The dynamic that unfolds on the home stage—with the ice-cream in the fridge, on the stage—reveals an interesting interplay between the aspects. The Addict wants sugar. However, the Rational aspect is in control and will not yield to the Addict's pressure. The Addict doesn't care about the woman's weight, looks, health. The only thing that matters is ice-cream! Powerful Addict aspects, bolstered through many years of behaviour or substance (in this case sugar) abuse, can mess with the mind. They develop various strategies to influence or manipulate other aspects.

For instance, they can create a 'problem' and then offer a 'solution to the problem'. The solution is always to use

130

the substance or the behaviour the Addict is addicted to. In our story, the problem was the unpleasant emotional state when the woman's traumatised Inner Child aspect was triggered.

The woman wanted to lose weight and decided not to eat sugar, but 'suddenly' started getting depressed and anxious. Her mind might also get involved and become busy rationalising why it is good to eat ('I'll feel better if I eat a little bit of ice-cream') and that it is better to be overweight than to sink into depression and kill herself! The Child doesn't mind her overeating because this vulnerable, timid aspect somehow feels protected by the walls of fat around the woman's waist.

The Child is hiding behind this, metaphorically speaking. Besides, if the woman is physically bigger and less sexually attractive, she could repel potential new molesters, or so the Child believes. The Addict, misusing the rationale that says, 'Eating is how you can lift yourself from your gloomy mood!', thus poses as a protector in the inner drama, convincing the other aspects that eating ice-cream helps avoid pain and elevates her depressed mood.

No doubt, the human psyche consists of many aspects and multiple belief systems, and some of them can be in serious conflict. Especially when it comes to dealing with addictions. The rational aspects may try to control the addicts, but the resulting intrapsychic conflicts between them drain a lot of energy. Yes, the addicts can be suppressed, with an effort of will, but not argued out of existence (you can't tell them, 'Please leave me alone!'). At the first suitable opportunity they reappear in all their original strength. That's why many behaviour change programs focused on suppressing or controlling addiction don't work.

Reasoning and negotiation skills do not help much in dealing with these aspects, either. You cannot negotiate with them or convince them that what they are doing is wrong. They are not open to being influenced, educated or corrected by 'reality'. They cannot be re-educated or re-programmed to stop their harmful behaviour. Nor can they be healed with love, kindness, compassion or self-acceptance. But they can be eliminated.

The question is not how to heal and integrate them—as in the case of traumatised aspects—but how to get rid of them. Even if we have created such aspects unintentionally and unconsciously, we can still un-create them. To un-create the Addict aspects in the personality means to stop feeding them with what they are addicted to and leave them to starve to death. Computer experts would say that this type of personality aspect resembles the corrupted computer programs and files that need to be deleted or uninstalled. Many people have succeeded at dismantling their Addict aspects. Many of us remember the moments or situations when we hardly recognise our former-self, the aspect of our personality that once existed, but is no more.

How to create and un-create the Smoker aspect

Habits can also form aspects in our personality. The more we repeat a certain behaviour that is charged with emotions, the stronger the habit is—personified as an aspect. How can we create an aspect? For example, imagine that you have associated the sensation of pleasure with fishing. You used to go fishing with your father who was a passionate fisherman. You were a kid and it wasn't easy in the beginning, but you trained yourself to tolerate the initially unpleasant sensation of being tired and bored, and eventually you found pleasure in that hobby.

As you invested time and energy into the activity charged with pleasant sensations and emotions (especially when you catch a fish) you created an aspect in your personality. Today, you are a passionate fisherman, and you really enjoy your hobby. On the other side of the coin, you may feel frustrated, depressed, irritated or have an empty feeling when you'd love to go fishing yet for some reason are prevented from doing so. But the moment you grab your fishing rod and do the activities associated with this familiar, exciting and pleasant hobby, your Fisherman aspect is 'satisfied' and will stop pestering you, at least for some time (till the next weekend, perhaps).

Smokers know all about this. It took them some time to get used to smoking and tolerate the awful sensation in the throat and lungs. Every smoker remembers the difficulties with inhaling nicotine and toxic chemicals. It wasn't easy; it takes time to become a smoker. But once the Smoker aspect has been created, it will not give up without a fight! The created aspect wants to keep living. Its only agenda is to exist. You starve it, and it will generate a familiar empty, annoying and irritating sensation of frustration in your gut and depressing feelings in your chests. And not just that. The Smoker aspect is cunning. It may contaminate your clear thinking with various stories and rationales why you should keep smoking ('Smoking helps me with the stresses at work') even when you know you shouldn't.

You still believe that smoking in itself is pleasurable, so not smoking (not inhaling toxic chemicals) feels like suffering because you think that you sacrifice the pleasure. But what really prevents you from breaking the habit is fear. Fear of what? Fear of being in an unpleasant state when you crave something you want to do but can't. If you don't give the Smoker aspect what it wants, it 'punishes' you with a sense of frustration, leaving you feeling sensations of emptiness or irritation. Stop feeding the Smoker aspect and you'll suffer! Once you have dismantled your Smoker aspect (you have starved it to death) you do not have the feeling that you will suffer if you quit, and you are free.

Allen Carr's Easy Way to Stop Smoking

Quitting smoking feels like suffering because smokers believe they are sacrificing pleasure. However, the pleasure they experience doesn't come from the nicotine itself, but from relieving the withdrawal pangs. 'It is fear that keeps people smoking, the fear of that empty, insecure feeling that you get when you stop supplying the nicotine. Because you are not aware of it doesn't mean it isn't there,' Allen Carr, writes in his popular self-help book *Allen Carr's Easy Way To Stop Smoking*.[7]

The best way to quit smoking is to remove your desire to smoke. With no desire to smoke, it takes no willpower not to, he explained. But how to remove the desire to smoke? The nicotine monster lives in the smoker's gut, figuratively speaking, and the person addicted to smoking will have to feed it for the rest of their lives, unless they get rid of it by starving it to death. 'Think of the nicotine monster as a sort of tape worm inside your stomach. You have got to starve him for three weeks, and he is going to try to trick you into lightening a cigarette to keep him alive,' Carr writes.[8]

The Abuser aspect

We (the authors) believe that humans can create not only personality aspects such as the Fisherman or the Smoker, but the Addict aspects that feed on abusing other people. We call them the Abuser aspects.

As with the Smoker aspect, re-educating, negotiating or reasoning do not help much in dealing with the Abuser aspect either. You cannot convince a perpetrator that abusing his partner is wrong. When you try, they react with, 'Yes, but...'

Some people attempt to suppress or control the inner Abuser in a similar way some smokers, for example, try to suppress the urge to smoke—with sheer willpower. But this is difficult.

Behaviour change programs for addicts or domestic violence perpetrators that are focused exclusively on re-educating and/or controlling by suppressing or resisting the impulses of the Addict or Abuser aspect have limited results. The real solution for the problem is to un-create the Addict or the Abuser aspect. How? Starve it to death.

Please note, there are violent men who wouldn't even think about 'un-creating the inner Abuser'. To them, the notion that they have an aspect in their personality addicted to abusing is sheer nonsense. Unless prevented by an outside force, these men will keep offending and re-offending. Some can be deterred from re-offending through interventions that limit opportunities for re-offense and/or those that increase the probability that new offences will be detected and punished. Some will not stop abusing their partners even when they know that they will be detected and punished.

The killer monster

In the advanced stages of serious drug addictions, the addict's life revolves around drugs and nothing else matters. The process can take over the person so completely that we could say the person, whom we used to know, or perhaps love, is no longer there. We can observe the same tragic destructive process in one particular type of domestic violence perpetrator.

Like a hungry and dangerous animal predator preoccupied only with its prey, this man is obsessed with a partner who has escaped him or is hiding from him. He is almost constantly angry, and the only thing that matters to him is to restore contact with the 'object' of his obsession—the woman who lives in mortal fear of him.

In the most severe cases of such violent perpetrators—usually after years of serious domestic violence dramas—you can no longer recognise the man who once was. His body looks like an empty shell that carries a hungry, furious monster in it. Some would say that, in a sense, there is just the monster operating through what appears to be a human being. The man has long gone...

Chapter 9

KNOWING THE ABUSER ASPECT

Is it possible for a re-offending domestic violence perpetrator to leave his position of the disgraced Perpetrator and become a noble Protector? Some would say that there is always a possibility for human beings whose development has been arrested and distorted to be 'redeemed'. This is especially true when perpetrators have their children's best interests at heart.

Domestic violence perpetrators who love their sons, for example, and do not want them to become abusers themselves, have a better chance to overcome their own dark Abuser aspects and stop their abusive behaviour. There are also re-offending intimate partner abusers who perhaps don't have children but genuinely wish to heal their relationship with their partners. They say they would like to understand what drives them and why they act and react violently. The insights and deeper understanding of their behaviour would help them to stop abusing their partners. But, really, what does drive an abusive man to abuse his partner? Is it a psychological trait called aggression? Is it his attitude towards women mixed with the impulsivity and inability to properly control his violent impulses? Is an abuser's impulsivity inherited or acquired? Is the man's abusive behaviour something he learned in his family and social environment? Or is it genetic? Is it nurture or nature, or a combination of the two?

Nurture versus nature is a popular dilemma not only in the world of science but also in politics. Even in politics today—with the endless debate about how to deal with violence, including domestic violence—we can see two camps. Some claim the cause for all evil deeds and suffering can be found internally in psychological weaknesses and genetics. The simplified explanation used by some conservatives, Republicans and those who believe that 'nature' is stronger than 'nurture' is: 'If you are criminal you are born criminal'. Others tend to look for external, environmental and social factors. Of course, the majority of people would agree that both aspects must be taken into account when we discuss human psychology. However, the nature versus nurture debate is still active when researchers are concerned with the extent to which human behaviour is a product of inherited (genetic) and acquired (learned) characteristics.

The Warrior Gene Maoa: Genetic Culprit for Violence?

In the ongoing search for inborn characteristics and genes underlying aggressive behaviour, none has sparked more curiosity, and controversy, than the infamous monoamine oxidase A gene (MAOA), nicknamed the 'warrior gene'. 'Its presence has been used successfully in some courtrooms to lessen sentences for impulsive murders,' Robert M. Sapolsky noted in his popular book *Behave: The Biology of Humans at Our Best and Worst*.[1]

But bad genes don't cause bad behaviour. Genetic factors interact with environmental factors to influence violence, so environmental factors too must be taken into account. Researchers warn that 'MAOA genotype alone typically does not play a role in forming aggression in individuals. MAOA genotype will predispose a person to aggression only in the particular environmental context, such as early traumatic experiences, maltreatment, strict parenting style, etc.'[2]

When we talk about *nature* in the nature versus nurture debate, we usually think about biological and genetic factors such as the 'warrior gene' MAOA that has been linked to aggression and violent behaviour. But can certain personality types, not only genes, make a person more violence-prone than other personality types? And if it can, are we born with predispositions to develop a particular type of personality? 'We are born predisposed to develop one personality type. According to enneagram theory, then, we are not entirely the products of our conditioning, but rather arrive predisposed to interpret that conditioning in particular ways,' Sandra Maitri, a renowned enneagram teacher and author, writes in her book *The Spiritual Dimension of the Eneagram*.[3]

Enneagram Theory of Personality

The Enneagram theory of personality combines spiritual wisdom from different ancient traditions with modern psychology. It maps out the nine distinct personality types (*enneagram types*)—the ways in which people think, feel, behave and relate to each other. Each of us contains the characteristics of all nine ennea-types, and most people can understand and relate to every single one of them. But according to this theory, one type is predominant in our personality. That particular personality type is with us from birth. However, this doesn't mean that the environment and conditioning is less important. This theory of personality claims that the environment *activates* the ennea-type, and then that particular type of personality *mediates* the experience and the behaviour.

From the perspective of enneagram theory, nature (the sensitivity we arrived with) and nurture (the effects of our conditioning) go hand in hand, Sandra Maitri noted.[4] This is where the mother and father play their important roles. If the boy's family environment is nurturing and supportive, if parents respect the needs and integrity of their children, the boy with a particular personality structure—let's say ennea-type Eight—has a good chance to develop into a strong, honest, dependable protector and noble warrior for the social cause: to shield the weak and defend the innocent. If his environment is violent, intrusive, abusive, unjust, or the child feels helpless, exploited, humiliated or misused, the same potential and qualities can diverge into overpowering and violating others.

Instead of becoming a noble Protector, the person would grow into the vicious Perpetrator. He can be an abusive partner, a persecutor, a delinquent or a school bully. As a father, he is the embodiment of a negative father figure: a tyrannical, oppressive, jealous authoritarian.

We can recognise this ennea-type's negative characteristics in some ruthless and despotic CEOs, vicious Mafia bosses and corrupt political leaders. They can be workplace disasters who gravitate to positions of power and control with the focus always on 'Me first!'

As they evolve, Eights move higher on the Perpetrator-Protector continuum, from lower egocentric positions (preoccupied only with their own personal interests) to higher positions of protectors who know how to take care of others, too. Instead of controlling and diminishing subordinates for selfish purposes, they are generous and giving, working for the good of everybody.

Of course, perpetrators of domestic violence can be any of the nine ennea-types, but it would be interesting to learn if people with certain personality types are more prone to develop the Abuser aspect in their personality than others. That would certainly help us to understand the nature of the domestic violence epidemic better. It may even help us to answer the question why certain people develop the Abuser aspect and turn into a perpetrator, while others, from the same background and experiences, don't.

Addicts and abusers

Personality aspects are real; they are not just theoretical constructs. They are like little living personas within us, each with his or her unique pattern of thoughts and beliefs, emotions and behaviours. Relationships, especially marital relationships, are not just between two persons, but rather two interacting groups of aspects. Once we understand how they have been created and how they operate, it is much easier to dismantle them and deal with the intimate partner abuse problem.

There are a lot of similarities between the Addict aspect and the personality aspect that thrives on abuse and violence. How do they come into being? If you are to create the Gambler aspect, for example, you start by playing on poker machines. If you are to create the Abuser, you start by hurting someone. You inflict either a physical or an emotional hurt. It may have been intentional or not, justified or not, but you inflicted pain. Perhaps you were partially conscious or even fully aware of what you were doing, yet you believed you couldn't help yourself. Your rage overcame you and you did something that you shouldn't have. The moment you did that, you loathed yourself. Or you didn't. You wanted to punish those who humiliated or hurt you, or you wanted to avenge yourself for the pain others inflicted upon you. You felt a sense of satisfaction and pride, because you managed to protect or avenge yourself. Perhaps you even felt pleasure because you were dominant and 'in control' in that situation, and your brain's pleasure centre was activated. You felt good about yourself when you did it so you, consciously or unconsciously, wanted to re-experience it. In other words, you wanted to keep inflicting pain to recreate that pleasant feeling again.

The sense of pleasure you experience is modulated by important brain neurochemicals such as dopamine and serotonin. Dopamine and serotonin are the chemicals that can help you to feel good and even boost your self-confidence. Alas, some of these experiences of pleasure can be addictive so you may unconsciously want to keep offending or overpowering others to feel superior and respected. A dark aspect in you—the Abuser aspect—starts to come into being.

Once created, this aspect looks ugly and nasty so you may want to run from it, hide or ignore it. You may be afraid because it feels like the aspect carries such a dangerous or even 'demonic' force that if it were to return, it would cause you to hurt people again. Or, perhaps you are not afraid. You believe that you had a reason to 'punish' others. You were only defending yourself! You've managed to justify what you did, so you don't feel guilty for inflicting pain on those who disrespected or hurt you. Or you believe that because you simply couldn't control yourself, you are not responsible for what you have done.

There is a tendency in each of us to create a barrier between 'me who is okay' and those 'other parts of me who are not okay'. We tend to separate ourselves from our undesirable aspects, or to project the not-okay aspect onto others and blame them for the problems and the wrong things that are going on in our lives. So some people subjectively experience the Abuser aspect as 'other than themselves'. They say, 'I don't know what got into me!' or 'I lost control and didn't know what I was doing!' or 'That was completely out of my character'. But no matter what they say, they know that they have created an aspect that is still in a state of disgrace. They don't feel good about it and want to keep it suppressed or cut off from their conscious awareness. Or they may say, 'Of course I hit you! You deserve it!' Abusers need to keep rationalising and justifying why they do what they do; otherwise, they feel uncomfortable. They are like an alcoholic who rationalises their behaviour and always finds excuses for feeding their addiction. And even when they make the decision that they will resist the temptation and not react explosively, it's hard. The aspect that has become addicted to abusing is waiting for something to happen—something that would trigger their "explosion".

As well as the above, the Abuser aspect will mess with the mind, so perpetrators will be caught up in unconscious, automatic thought patterns. These thought patterns are products of various beliefs about ourselves ('I am offended! I must avenge myself!'); others ('She disrespected me! She must be punished'); and the world in general ('This is a dog-eat-dog world! I'm not going to allow anyone to abuse me!'). The problem with these patterns is that they trigger repetitive feelings such as being hurt, humiliated, frightened or ashamed, disrespected, inferior or ignored.

These feelings or emotions are unpleasant, so abusers want to get rid of them. They can change the unpleasant and disempowering emotional states if they quickly generate the empowering anger or rage. Explosions of rage can serve as a painkiller, or they can mask (at least temporarily) painful emotions. Like being on autopilot, anger then will be automatically channelled into abusive or physically violent behaviour, and this behaviour will cause their partner's distress. As the Abuser aspect has already been crystallised in their personality, perpetrators feel compelled to repeat the pattern of abusive behaviour. Why? Because they must 'feed' the Abuser. The 'food' is the thrill when two key components are mixed together: a nasty attack fuelled with anger and a partner's emotional reaction—her sense of degradation, pain and/or fear. Both components must be present for the full experience of the high. If an abuser is angry and abusive, for example, but the victim is indifferent or not hurting, the Abuser aspect cannot draw pleasure from the 'experience'.

The theory of energy vampirism

Psychopaths tend to see any social exchange as a "feeding" opportunity.[5] **Robert D. Hare, PhD**

Feeding on the life force of humans? Is this statement a gross exaggeration? Science fiction? Paranoia? Let's see.

Life force is the ability to assimilate and use energy. There are various forms of energy. Nutrients in food give the body's cells the energy they need to operate. Human energy is spent on the performance of various physical functions, but it is also radiated out into the surrounding space in the form of mental and emotional energy. Attention is, for example, focused mental energy. Recognition from others and human attention is food for the psyche. If you focus on me, you are giving me your mental energy. If you are freely giving me your attention, that's not stealing. When two people truly meet each other in a free exchange of mental/emotional energy, both benefit from the encounter and may feel more vitality than before they met. Conversation sparkles with stimulating thoughts and feelings.

144

The exchange becomes invigorating rather than draining, regardless of the content and even when people talk about unpleasant or painful things. This is not the case when we interact with the 'energy vampire'.

Once upon a time, someone had the idea that we could live off of the life force of others. Even when slavery was given up, exploitation remained a significant feature of man's relation to man, which is still the case today. Many people manipulate psychic energy, such as the energy of attention. If I am keeping you in the work corridor, telling you my story and not caring if you are interested in it or not—nor do I care that you may be in a hurry to do something urgent—then I am 'energetically feeding' on you.

In order to get attention, people can manipulate energy either aggressively, by directly forcing you to pay attention to them, or passively, by playing on your sympathy, guilt or your weaknesses such as not being able to say 'no'. There are numerous methods of 'energy draining'. The most aggressive type of 'vampire' is the intimidator with a gun pointed to your head. You will certainly pay attention to him and give him everything he wants from you. Those who play 'Poor me' may get your attention and sympathy using different strategies. For example, the people who play perpetual victims needing your attention, pity, sympathy or material support will provoke your sense of responsibility and remorse if you refuse to listen to them or rescue them. When you present with the solution for their problems they react with, 'Yes, but...', because they are not interested in solutions. They want your services or money, or they want your focused attention on them, perhaps your pity, kindness and sympathy because it feels like recognition and love to them.

Another type of 'energy vampire' is the Drama Queen/King. They function on a high level of energy derived from conflicts, chaos, conspiracy theories, dramas and problems, draining those around them, especially in their work environment or family. They need drama because it gives them a sense of aliveness and vitality. Constant talking is also a form of energy vampirism. People who demand centre stage or incessantly talk may like the vibration of their own voice, but they also need an audience to feed them with attention, recognition or admiration. After feeding, the energy vampire feels better, at least for a time, but the victim feels drained, exhausted, empty, or irritated.

A person usually becomes a 'psychic energy drainer' unconsciously. Throughout their life, they have noticed that there are situations that bring them satisfaction and a rush of energy, and then, without being aware of it, they attempt to repeat the experience. The majority of them are not fully aware that they drain you because their focus is on getting 'food' (attention) from you, not on damaging you. This does not apply to re-offending domestic violence perpetrators. Some of them are extremely dangerous energy vampires. What is energy food for them? Their partner's distress!

If they crave dominance, they'll do everything in their power to push their partner into the position of subordination and then feed on her submissiveness. Dominance could be defined as a personality trait that involves a motive to dominate other people, to have control over social or material resources, and the power to punish others (to inflict pain). The dominance—'I am the one who will tell you what to do! You will not tell me what to do!'—provides very pleasant feelings of pride, significance and status, but to generate that feeling it is necessary to have a submissive partner who can be 'punished'. If an abusive man gets addicted to the blend of 'her distress–his satisfaction', the distressed victim (drained of her life force and vitality through the repetitive patterns of abuse) is in serious trouble and sometimes even in mortal danger.

He can lift himself up if he pushes her down

Divorce lawyers claim that the most common reason women give for leaving their husbands is 'mental cruelty'. 'He hurts my feelings and never apologises. When I complain, he says I'm too sensitive. He ignores me except when he wants something from me. He rarely calls me to see how I'm doing; instead, he tells me what I should do. He feels entitled to openly express his unfavourable opinion and criticism, but he will not tolerate being criticised himself. He played on what he knew would hurt me. He would find his angle in and go on and on about it.'

There are many abusive men who are not physically violent, and, in fact, they do not appear to be abusive at all. Instead they are passive–aggressive. This type of behaviour is still a pattern of abuse, but it is played out in a way that protects the abuser from counterattacks. The patterns may have some of these characteristics: he 'forgets' to do what his partner has asked him to do, or he deliberately procrastinates to make her wait; he repeatedly postpones decisions that are important to her or he mismanages something important to her; he secretly frustrates and undermines her plans or her reputation; he sets her up to look foolish or he says offensive jokes about her in front of others, followed by the comment, 'It was just a joke, don't you have a sense of humour?'

Recognising her emotional needs and expectations—and denying them—is also a form of passive–aggressive abuse. For example, he does not praise the work she has done for him or does not make any appreciative remarks after something significant she has done. Or he (this one is particularly nasty!) finds her weak spot—something she agrees with him, at least partially, that is not 'perfect'—and then he keeps hitting her with that, with the rationale such as 'I'm only telling you this for your own good'. She is untidy; she is not a good cook; she is fat; not educated; she is irresponsible with money. It can be such a pleasure to remind her of her flaws.

The man who is an expert on his partner's 'weak spots' detects her vulnerabilities and weaknesses, and then feels it is his duty to let her know what's good for her and what's wrong with her. However, it is not always easy for the woman to see the hidden motivation behind his repetitive pattern of hurting her, so she may want to improve herself to avoid his shaming. 'He's right,' she may think. 'I should be more cautious with spending money; I should be a better cook, housewife, mother, partner...' Or he says something that hurts her, but she believes he is telling her that for her own good. 'I should really lose weight so I'll look more attractive.'

At some stage during this nasty game, many women realise that the man is actually not that interested in her wellbeing when he criticises her. He only rarely notices when she makes improvements or corrections in the things he is disgracing her about, and he may even secretly sabotage her. But even when the woman realises this, she may want to please her man. She hopes the grumpy, nervous and angry aspect of him will disappear and the nice man in him will come back again. Then they will be as happy as they used to be in the beginning of their relationship. 'If I fix things, he will see how much I am trying to improve our relationship; if I help him to solve the problems with his parents or siblings, and cope with his stresses at work, he will realise that I am worthy, a good person, lovely, pretty, everything that he used to tell me when we were in love.' But no matter how much she tries, she cannot get rid of that sarcastic, contemptuous, cynical aspect of him—the aspect that pops up in her space and directs offensive words to her. Why is he repeatedly doing that?

If we ask people with this passive–aggressive behaviour pattern, 'Why do you do that?' we might notice that many of them are as puzzled as we are. Such attitudes and tendencies may take the form of almost automatic behavioural reactivity. When they feel discomfort or distress, they turn to their partner and say something that will make her feel uncomfortable or distressed. Some clearly see that putting their partner down serves to help them feel better. They may also feel a sense of satisfaction when hurting her feelings or sabotaging her intentions, projects or goals.

Having the power to exert influence over another person's life can make the abuser feel good. He finds sweet pleasure in watching his victims' disappointments, their crest-fallen reactions when he smashes their hopes and expectations. Or, he feels *high* when the victims lose their aura of self-confidence after he pulls them down.

Many abusers are eaten up by envy and resentment. They feel incapable of creating something valuable, so their only pleasure is to bring the targeted 'superior' person down. Some like to do this secretly. For example, the abusive man's satisfaction may grow from his ability to control or undermine the woman behind her back, without her realising how she is being harmed or manipulated. When this type of abuser hurts their partner secretly, or erodes their confidence covertly, the pleasure is similar to the satisfaction of an anonymous phone caller who is disturbing you in the middle of the night.

Though it doesn't leave physical scars, this type of abuse can have a huge impact on a woman's confidence and self-esteem. In some cases, the hidden aim of emotional abuse is to damage the victim's sense of self-worth and independence. This then imprints the feeling that without him she is nothing, she will have nothing, and most importantly that there is no way out of the relationship (toxic bond) with him. But why does he want to keep her in the relationship?

The focus of emotional abusers is to find just the right insult to deflate their partner's energy and lift their own. If they have already discovered the pleasure of hurting her, of course they do not want to lose her—they want to keep her in the relationship so they can feed on her distress. Interestingly, similar to other substance or behavioural addictions, repetitive patterns of emotional abuse also tend to increase in frequency and severity.

A General Theory of Crime

Does the re-offending domestic violence perpetrator abuse his wife because he seeks pleasure and wants to avoid pain? Michael R. Gottfredson and Travis Hirschi's research revealed that criminal events are generally based on immediate gratification or removal of an irritant. 'Nature has placed mankind under the governance of two sovereign masters, pain and pleasure (Bentham 1970 [1789]:11). In this view, all human conduct can be understood as the self-interested pursuit of pleasure or avoidance of pain. By definition, therefore, crimes too are merely acts designed to satisfy some combination of these basic tendencies,' Gottfredson and Hirschi write in their book *A General Theory of Crime*.[6]

The offenders often appear to have little control over his or her own desires, the authors noted, and 'those lacking self-control opt for the desires of the moment, whereas those with greater self-control are governed by the restrains imposed by the consequences of acts displeasing to family, friends, and the law.'[7] At the heart of criminal events and criminals is one stable construct: low self-control. They define low self-control as the 'tendency of individuals to pursue short-term gratification without consideration of the long-term consequences of their acts.'[8]

The Abuser persona

Personality aspects—healthy or unhealthy, light or dark—are little psychic structures. They are 'entities' made up of emotions and attitudes that motivate or influence a person's behaviour. The Addict aspect of a heroin addict, for example, can be compared with a cunning little animal. It seemingly has a life of its own, led by a primitive intelligence focused on survival. In order to survive, it needs to feed through regular feeding cycles. And what is 'food' for the Addict aspect? The experience of pleasure when drugged with heroin.

There is a striking similarity between this aspect and the Abuser aspect. As though they were siblings from the same 'family of aspects', the Addict and the Abuser have been created in a similar way. The Addict has been created through feeding the habit of injecting heroin, for example. The Abuser has been created through feeding the habit of inflicting pain on an intimate partner. Similar to the Addict, the Abuser has been strengthened by accumulating particular experiences: experiences that generate a sense of satisfaction or a pleasant release of inner tension.

For example, a man acts abusively to reduce unpleasant tension or hide his pain, humiliation, degradation, shame, guilt, fear or neediness. He'd get a sense of satisfaction when the unpleasant tension had been discharged—or he'd experience the pleasant *high* (pride, a sense of being powerful, in control, etc.) when he used anger and violence to mask the *low* (unpleasant emotional states)—and this unconsciously motivated him to repeat the experience and develop a new aspect in his personality.

The more life energy a man invests in the habit of punishing his partner and gets satisfaction from it, the stronger his Abuser aspect becomes. As the Addict aspect influences the person addicted to heroin to repeat the pattern of addictive behaviour, so too the Abuser aspect influences a man to repeat the pattern of abusive behaviour.

Both types of behavioural patterns—addictive and abusive—tend to escalate over time. Indeed, the Addict aspect and the Abuser aspect look like they are twin brothers (or perhaps they are one and the same type of aspects?). They may even have the same function in the 'internal family system' of personality aspects—the function of masking painful emotional states.

Just as the people addicted to drugs may use drugs as a way to cover up unpleasant emotions, childhood trauma, family issues or socioeconomic distress, abusive men may use abusive behaviour to mask distress and hide vulnerable aspects, especially their weak and wounded Inner Child aspect. And just like the Addict aspect in the personality of the man who has become heavily addicted to heroin, the Abuser too can gradually take control in the man's everyday life and run the show. The 'show' is, of course, the frequent conflicts and dramas. The Abuser aspect thrives not on heroin but on negativity: the man's hostile, offensive or violent impulses and the woman's distress. Drama and conflicts are its food. The name of the Abuser's game is 'Inflict and suffer pain'.

Once created and strengthened, the Abuser aspect in the re-offending domestic violence perpetrator's personality has a dormant and an active stage. How long it remains dormant and in what situations it will be activated varies from person to person. If it has been already created in previous relationships, it is often clever enough to wait until a new couple starts living together or signs the marital contract. (If it shows up too early, before the relationship is securely established, the woman might get scared and leave, or lose interest in the man).

In some other relationships or circumstances, it needs to wait longer—perhaps until the woman gets trapped in the situation when it is difficult for her to leave the abuser. Circumstances such as the woman is pregnant or with a small child, she is financially dependent, she is ill, she is not welcomed back in her parents' home etc., are the right moments to begin with feeding cycles.

When ready to feed, the Abuser can be triggered by any event at any time. It can use the most insignificant little incidents, memories, or words someone says. When it finishes with feeding, it goes back into its dormant state like an animal that has just had a meal.

The 'evil eye'

Indigenous cultures respect the energy of the eyes. The energy can be healing, but also harmful, even dangerous. The stories and myths like the one about Medusa teach us that the transmission of certain mythical dark forces is possible through direct eye contact, and some people say there is a grain of truth in it. They believe the 'evil eye' is a gaze that can inflict injury or bad luck on its target, so direct eye contact with evil creatures (or evil people) should be strictly avoided. Many victims of domestic violence would agree. They say that they feel a soul-shattering chill when they look into their abuser's eyes at the time he attacks them.

If we listen to domestic violence horror stories, we may notice one detail the victims of abuse occasionally mention.

They say they have the impression that their assailants go through a dramatic personality change at the time of abuse. They even claim that they can clearly sense when the 'monster' is taking over. The 'switch into the Abuser', and sometimes a surprisingly sudden change in the man's behaviour, is most recognisable in the expression in his eyes. In such moments, the women know that if they don't grab the children and escape from the house immediately, 'there will be blood'

Indeed, if we observe the man's eyes in such moments, we may notice something peculiar—there is no usual light in them; it's as if the man, who was there just a few moments ago, had suddenly disappeared. Instead, something cold and revolting is gazing at us. Who is this creature that is staring through the man's eyes? Where is this hostility and hatred coming from? It is feeding time!

When a woman notices a dramatic personality change in her partner for the first time, this can be quite a shock for her. She may wonder whether this is her partner's 'real face' that she had never seen before because he was hiding it. 'I've made a terrible mistake marrying this man!' she might think. However, that 'real face' is just a hungry aspect that has temporarily taken control. He can be very dangerous, though.

Some domestic violence victims report that their violent husband's personality change has become permanent. It's as though he carries a particularly dark aspect that is never completely dormant and needs to feed frequently, so the man finds himself in a continuous need for enemies. He is angry and always ready to fight. As if he could never get enough, he must keep pulling others into his drama by getting them to react, thus feeding the Abuser. Very few people have such a heavy, dark Abuser aspect, but they do exist.

Problems with serious drug addictions can also lead to profound personality and behaviour changes. There are heavy drug addicts who are not in denial about the seriousness of their addiction. The lives of so many heroin addicts revolve around finding heroin and injecting heroin. Everything else is insignificant to them. They consciously identify themselves as addicts, they are aware of what they are doing and why they are doing it, and they openly say they will never quit. They will keep drugging themselves until they die naturally or from an overdose—whatever comes first.

There are also people with gambling addictions who will not stop gambling, and serial killers or rapists who will not stop raping and killing until they are caught. The cycle of feeding their addiction is a chain for life, and they become enslaved to it unless they break it. Yet, many drug addicts, gamblers, paedophiles, bullies and domestic violence perpetrators do not want to break it. Even if they were offered the easiest and most painless method to quit, they would continue with the habit until someone or something outside themselves prevented them from hurting others.

However, there are people suffering from addictions who would like to quit. There are also men who would like to quit abusing their partners. They say understanding what drives them would help them change the way they behave.

Chapter 10

DISSOLVING THE ABUSER

The basic assumption in some behaviour change programs for domestic abusers is that specific attitudes and emotions *precede* the abusive, problematic or detrimental behaviour. So if the perpetrator changed his mindset and core beliefs—mostly clustered around power and control; victim blaming ('She disrespected me! She hurts my feelings!'); and male privileges and entitlement or 'righteous anger' ('I have the right to defend myself! She deserves punishment!')—he would be able to correct or change his abusive behaviour.

There is nothing wrong with this assumption. One fundamental law in psychology is that our beliefs and the ways we perceive things determine our emotions and behaviours. We all know that stances can fuel emotions of anger and rage, and that cognitions—thoughts, perceptions, attitudes and convictions—govern actions, especially when they are charged with intense emotions. However, simply trying to change the beliefs and perceptions—to change the behaviour driven by them—does not always work. Even when we change attitudes and ways of thinking and feeling, we still might have problems with resisting the impulse to 'do something now that we will regret later'. We know such behaviour is detrimental, or there is no real reason to react in that particular way, but...

Some abusive men claim the mere understanding that specific thoughts, attitudes and emotions precede the problematic or harmful behaviour doesn't help much. The discernment of 'good and bad' is not enough to prevent them from doing what they shouldn't do, they say. Even when they are aware that their behaviour is abusive, dangerous to others, self-destructive or harmful to everyone involved, they still may have problems not engaging in it. They are consumed with guilt and shame; they do not want to control and dominate, yet they keep relapsing. Each time they abuse their partner, they hate themselves.

They may genuinely want to stop, but often find themselves in the same old repetitive cycle of verbal abuse or violence, triggered by the same old provocations. Obviously, there is something more, not just beliefs, attitudes or the desire to have power and control over the woman, which drives the re-offending abuser's behaviour. That 'something' must be taken into account as well, in addition to other relevant factors that motivate him to abuse his partner.

Why is abusing his partner good for him?

Instead of pointing to reasons why people should stop their detrimental or abusive behaviour, perhaps we should first focus on the reasons why they keep doing it.

Gamblers and drug addicts are aware of the ill-effects caused by their addiction, and they know all the reasons why they should quit. It does not help to keep reminding them of the effects of their habits. Tell a heroin addict that he should quit heroin 'because he is poisoning his body', and he would laugh at you. Heroin is more important than the health of his body. You cannot scare him out of addiction.

However, if you ask him why he keeps drugging himself despite the adverse and tragic consequences of his addiction, his honest answer is simple: 'Because it feels good!' The truth is that abusive behaviour can also make the perpetrator feel good.

Anything that works to create pleasure and remove stress is recorded in our nervous system. If the man's abusive behaviour has a strong connection with his sense of satisfaction, he may subconsciously resist changing it, no matter what. His need to remove stress and/or experience a sense of pleasure are momentarily fulfilled through his abusive behaviour, and without it, life would become even more challenging. Volumes of statistics and police reports have been written about the damage domestic violence does to everybody, including the abusers. The trouble is that until they clearly see what is good in it— what positives they get from their abusive behaviour and deal with these—they don't want to know about the statistics or the harm their abuse causes everybody, including themselves.

An honest intimate partner re-offender would admit that venting distress and discharging tension through abuse help him to feel better. It is a recognised fact that abusive behaviour can decrease unpleasant emotions and bodily sensations and produce a sense of pleasant relief. Angry outbursts shield people in situations when they feel threatened so they can feel safe and protected by their fury. Abusing an intimate partner can even give a perpetrator a sense of identity as strong and authoritative ('I will not allow anyone to abuse me!'). It can stimulate adrenaline production resulting in increased energy. Increased energy can give people a sense of power and 'being in control' so they won't feel controlled, disempowered, humiliated or hurt.

Serotonin may play a role in this as well. Serotonin is called 'the confidence neurochemical'—it flows freely when a person feels superior or significant. They enjoy the effects of serotonin when they feel respected or dominant, and their brain will seek more of the same by repeating behaviours that triggered its release in their past. Hence, the repetitive pattern of abusive behaviour. So how do you stop it?

Control yourself!

What triggers positive change in a person's abusive behaviour? Some believe that punishment, discomfort and suffering are the most important factors. If people suffer enough, they will change their detrimental behaviour—so punish undesired actions and withdraw the discomfort when the unwanted activity stops, and people will change their behaviour!

In this view, domestic violence perpetrators would be motivated to change if they feel enough discomfort, shame, guilt, threat, anxiety, pain or humiliation. If they don't change, that means that they haven't yet suffered enough. But many of us know things are not that easy. Just like we struggle with binge eating, problem drinking or pathological gambling, we often recognise the risk and harm involved in the behaviour and desperately want to stop it, yet we are also attracted to it. We are torn apart by intense internal conflicts and ambivalence. We want to change, but at the same time, we don't want to change.

Can the same internal conflict be the reason for a man's ambivalence about changing his abusive behaviour towards his partner? Indeed, his inability to deal with the state of tension caused by the 'internal war'—when one aspect of his personality does not allow him to do what another aspect wants him to do—could explain why the domestic violence perpetrator keeps relapsing. That is also one of the reasons why abusive men resist rehabilitation, treatments and behaviour change programs that do not support the tendency to seek pleasure through releasing tension. However, there are men who want to break the cycle.

> His inability to deal with the state of tension caused by the 'internal war'—when one aspect of his personality does not allow him to do what another aspect wants him to do— could explain why the domestic violence perpetrator keeps relapsing.

The man may want to break this cycle of abusive behaviour for a variety of reasons. Perhaps everyone around him, including himself, has noticed that even the smallest provocation sends him into a rampage, so he declares, 'It's time to stop!' Perhaps he wants to stop because of social pressures or for his partner and kids. Maybe he does not want his son to become an abusive man, or he wants to be a good person in the eyes of others as well as in his own. So he decides to control himself. But to be good does not mean he *feels* good. It usually means suppressing or controlling what is labelled as 'not good'.

Controlling what is not good is not easy. In clinical psychology programs, therapists teach clients techniques for moderating out-of-control emotions. However, physiologically, the attempt to suppress emotion is hard work, often resulting in unpleasant arousal and irritation. The domestic violence perpetrators who have managed to stop abusing their partners say they used to think their problem was a short fuse and a lack of control over their violent outbursts. Now they know the real problem was a strong sense of frustration when they *did* control themselves! Senad's experience clearly illustrates this.

When Senad believed that he was provoked, he tended to react instantly. As a typical Pit Bull-type of perpetrator, he had a short-fuse problem. He expressed his anger directly and frequently, especially in situations when he interpreted his wife's words as criticism or her behaviour as an attempt to manipulate, control or restrain him. He described the physical sensation in his body as a deep surge of anger that would start in the belly, rise upward and seek to be expressed externally—through words or actions, or both. He said he'd find himself in some kind of 'trance state' and described these feelings of arousal and intensity as akin to being in a 'fog'—not fully aware, or refusing to be aware, of what he was doing.

This automatic body-based reaction was his 'survival pattern'—a mode that he went into to protect himself from being overwhelmed by unpleasant emotions and sensations. He had a history of child abuse, and it was clear that his reaction had been conditioned and reinforced by his past experiences. This made the present threat much worse than it really was, as though the old experience of abuse was happening to him all over again, causing him to overreact to the current triggers. Over time, this response became so deeply entrenched in his body that it would automatically kick in whenever he felt distressed.

Nonetheless, he wanted to control himself. Some men wouldn't accept the challenge for their own sake but they are willing to do it for the sake of their children. Senad was one of them. But it wasn't easy. When he did not follow the impulse to explode, he experienced a very unpleasant sensation of discomfort. He was able to feel genuine remorse; he hated himself when he behaved like a bully or a tyrant and wanted to be a good person, but when he did control himself—when he was a good person—he didn't *feel* good. He found himself in the trap: Damned if I explode; damned if I control myself.

The typical problem with the 'control yourself' in dealing with harmful habits and addictions is that there is not enough power in this strategy to quit the habit. It sets offenders up for a relapse. The relapse usually starts with a sense of irritation and disappointment. After some time, the man gets tired of 'being good'. He believes that he has done the right thing and behaved correctly, yet it is other peoples' behaviour towards him that has not changed much. Yes, he wants to be a good person but . . .

But the problem is ambivalence. He still feels frustrated and provoked every now and then, and he would like to 'explode' because the explosion would help him to release unpleasant inner tension. He finds himself in the same situation as the smoker who has just recently decided to quit smoking: He keeps craving a cigarette and is desperately trying to control himself at the same time.

Controlling himself is the necessary first step, and passing through ambivalence is a natural transient phase in the process of changing bad habits. It is when people get stuck in the war within ('I want to stop this behaviour, but I don't want to') that the problem persists. Until the abuser can resolve this intrapsychic battle, change is likely to be short lived. And not just that. As long as he

163

doesn't want to acknowledge the fact that he is stuck in this internal conflict, 'I want to stop abusing you, but I want to keep abusing you', he will blame his partner for triggering his unresolved 'inner war' between the rational mind and addicted Abuser aspect who resists change. This is often a key issue that must be addressed first for a change in harmful behaviour to occur. But how do we help men who are motivated to stop abusing their partners release their ambivalence?

Resolving the war within: 'I want to change, and I don't want to change'

One motivation for breaking an addictive pattern of abusive behaviour is the determination to be a good person. Another is not only about being a good person but is also about feeling good. A drug addict may have started taking drugs because he wanted to feel good. If he is serious about healing his addiction, he will want to stop taking drugs for the same reasons he started—to quit in order to feel good. But, is that possible? Millions of people say yes, it is possible. They have managed to heal their alcohol, drug, smoking or gambling problems. They are now feeling good and do not miss the high, the tension-release type of behaviour and the pleasure they used to crave. Some say that understanding the mechanics behind the internal war of 'I want to quit, and I don't want to quit', and being aware that they were dealing with a nasty addiction, has helped them tremendously.

Many addicts don't realise that they are addicted to a substance or a behaviour until they try to stop. Trapped in the repetitive pattern of abusive behaviour, perpetrators also don't realise they are hooked on abusing their partners until they try to stop. Even then, many would not admit to it. Victims may have a problem recognising the danger, too. The escalation of abuse might be so gradual that it is difficult for the victim to see what is happening until the abuse has become quite severe. The woman may learn to cope with, tolerate and accept her partner's abusive or violent behaviour. This sends him a message that it is okay to abuse her and get away with it, so nothing motivates him to quit the habit.

However, there are men who are able to see through the nasty game they play with their partners, and they decide to stop the game. Yet, the key issue in every addiction is that they'll suffer if they stop. The sense that they are sacrificing themselves, that they are losing something, or that they are limited and deprived when restraining from smoking, drinking, gambling or abusing is what makes it difficult to stop. Quitting smoking feels like suffering because smokers believe they are sacrificing pleasure. However, the pleasure they experience doesn't come from the nicotine itself, but from relieving the withdrawal pangs. Smokers know that it is fear that keeps people smoking—the fear of the unpleasant feeling they get when they want to smoke but can't. Once addicts do not have the feeling that they will suffer if they quit, they are free.

Fear also prevents the re-offending perpetrators from breaking the cycle of abusing their partners. Fear of what? Fear of being in an unpleasant state of inner tension and discomfort when they want to react violently but restrain themselves from abusive behaviour. However, once they dismantle the Abuser, they too are free.

Breaking the pattern of abuse is a 3-step process

Problems need to be revealed before they can be healed. Changes in behaviour and true inner transformation come when we are ready to look inside. Using the light of awareness, with compassion for ourselves, we can penetrate the unconscious drives that motivate an undesirable behaviour, no matter how painful or embarrassing it may be. That's why the process of breaking an addictive pattern of abusive behaviour has three major components: awareness, dis-identifying from the Abuser aspect, and restraining from 'translating' thoughts, beliefs and emotions into abusive words, abusive behaviour or violent acts. In other words, not behaving abusively or violently, no matter what a person believes, thinks or feels.

1. Awareness

Abusive men often don't understand where their addictive pattern of abusive behaviour came from and don't know how to stop. Many of them are deeply ashamed of their violence and would like to be shown the way back to non-violence. It is much easier to dismantle the Abuser aspect once a man knows what he is dealing with. So the first step in this 'psychic operation' is to recognise the Abuser and name it. Why is it important to name aspects?

Emotional states can be overwhelming. For example, traumatised clients speak of being 'hijacked' by all-encompassing emotions and sensations in traumatic flashbacks. Some avoid describing their inner life or deny such emotions to protect themselves from being flooded by disturbing sensations of hyperarousal. However, sometimes identifying or just naming emotional states seems to calm down amygdala activity in the traumatised client's brain.

Other clients report feeling numb or 'flat'; their inability to verbalise their experiences leave them confused. In some cases, shame may block the recognition of emotions. The empathic counsellor who understands 'shameful' experiences, names them and conveys their meaning back to the client, can help the traumatised person to recognise, formulate and process the trauma. Putting feelings into words can help us to heal painful experiences or deal with problematic life situations. It's the same with dealing with 'problematic' aspects in our personality.

However, there are men who deny that they have such aspects in their personality simply because it would be totally devastating for them to realise it. Especially if they see that their Abuser is a copy of their parent's Abuser. Our client's experience clearly illustrates this:

Senad's marriage looked frighteningly similar to his parents' marriage, yet he refused to see it. He distanced himself from the overwhelming events in his childhood and disowned his wounded Inner Child aspect, of which he was ashamed. Nor was he willing to recognise the Abuser within him. The epiphany that he was like his abusive father was very unpleasant for Senad. He denied that he was repeating the same pattern of violent behaviour until the day he saw his terrified son watching him abuse the boy's mother. 'I have started to lose it in front of my son!' he said with despair in his voice. The revelation that he was channelling his father, painful as it was, strengthened his motivation to quit domestic abuse.

Once motivated to stop, Senad was open to hear the information about various aspects in our personality, including the Abuser aspect: how it has come into being, why it 'operates' through repetitive patterns of abuse, and why the pattern tends to escalate. He was curious about these aspects and even started feeling empathy for them. His treatment was then geared to learning to 'objectify' the Abuser and to distance himself from it. He learned to observe the Abuser, without identifying with it, as identification would invariably intensify his emotions or evoke shame.

2. Dis-identification

We are much more than the sum of our personality aspects. Besides, not all aspects are permanent. Some can be created and then un-created, yet inviting an abusive man to perceive the Abuser within as separate from him may seem a bizarre notion. 'What do you mean it is not me? Of course, it's me!' a man might claim. But ex-smokers have created and then dismantled their Smoker aspect; gamblers can be 'gamblers-no-more'; and ex-domestic violence perpetrators have created and then dismantled their Abuser aspect. How does someone dismantle their inner Abuser?

'We are dominated by everything with which our self becomes identified. We can dominate and control everything from which we dis-identify ourselves,' writes Roberto Assagioli, a famous Italian psychiatrist and pioneer in the fields of humanistic and transpersonal psychology, in his book *Psychosynthesis*.[1] When we identify ourselves with a weakness or an overwhelming emotion, we limit or paralyse ourselves. For example, if we say, 'I was enraged,' the feeling tone is very different than when we say, 'An impulse of anger was attempting to overpower me.' When we employ cold, impersonal observation as if it were mere natural phenomenon, occurring outside ourselves, we avoid feeling overwhelmed. That's why the essential step in the process of 'eliminating' the aspects such as the Abuser is to differentiate and distance oneself from these semi–conscious or unconscious contents (aspects) by personifying them.

Warning! This doesn't mean distancing oneself from the responsibility and accountability for abusive behaviour!

Instead of strongly identifying with it as 'me' and 'mine', the men motivated to stop abusing their partners start observing the Abuser as a seemingly separate psychic entity with its own identity and agenda. Why is it relevant to 'objectify' and then employ impersonal observation of the Abuser aspect, as if it were outside of the man's personality? Many abusive men are not fully aware what activates their abusive behaviour. They behave as though they are possessed by something (some kind of force) that operates from beyond their conscious awareness. They identify with 'it' so they feel compelled to act it out its agenda as if they were marionettes. But if they differentiate themselves from this unconscious content and objectify it—imagine it as a separate persona—it's easier to take it out of the unconscious and make it conscious.

Learning to describe the Abuser and the Abuser's agenda as though outside of oneself and without identifying with it, they can dispassionately notice the thoughts, beliefs, emotions and sensations in the body when the Abuser is activated, and above all, the Abuser's hidden intentions.

What is its agenda? Like a parasite, the Abuser uses a partner to feed off of. It feeds on the perpetrator's frustration or anger and the victim's anguish. When a man becomes the watcher who simply observes this inner aspect in his personality and starts to dis-identify from it, he no longer energises the Abuser through his identification with it. When the aspect is not energised, it can no longer replenish itself through the man because it cannot control his thinking. In what way does the Abuser control the man's thinking? It usually uses the narrative about the 'reasons' for the man's abusive behaviour. Consider this line of reasoning:

A) 'My father brutally beat me when I was a child,' a man says.

'Why?'

'Because he hated me. Even the most trivial things were triggers for him to beat me.'

B) 'My father brutally beat me when I was a child,' a man says.

'Why?'

'He craved it. He was hooked on it. The cycles would start with him blaming me for something, no matter how trivial it was, and his tension would gradually build. Then, when an explosive incident occurred, he'd bash me. After the beating, he would be okay for some time. Occasionally, even a calm, loving interval would follow. Or he would leave me alone for a couple of weeks, then it would start again . . .'

Under the Abuser's influence, the man may believe that he has a good reason to hurt the woman and that punishing her is justified, 'I didn't abuse her! I just wanted to punish her because she hurt me'. Another one is the belief that he *must* punish his partner if she says or does something hurtful or disrespectful. Why does he believe that he must punish (abuse) her? Because he is convinced that it is the only way he can discharge his unpleasant inner tension (and perhaps draw a sense of satisfaction from it). He perceives his distress as solely caused by the woman's words or her behaviour. He believes that he can't calm down unless she 'suffers the consequences' of her disrespectful or hurtful behaviour. So if the man is serious about deleting the repetitive pattern of domestic abuse, he'll need to see through these beliefs and to transform 'because of' ('I did it because you said...) into 'in order to' (I did it in order to punish you because when I hurt you I feel better) line of reasoning. He'll also have to erase the word 'punishment' from his vocabulary.

Self-Reflection in the Middle of a Duel With Your Partner

It is possible to practise the act of self-reflection even when caught in the middle of a duel with your partner. Instead of lashing out and falling back into old patterns—instead of immediately responding to what your partner says—you can pause for a moment, relax your shoulders and notice what you are experiencing. You ask the question, 'What are the thoughts, emotions and physical sensations that want my attention?' Watch the thoughts and emotions that are arising, without judging, justifying or acting on them. Give yourself a moment or two to not respond at all. See if you are blaming, interpreting or wanting to react to what the other person is saying. How do you want to reply? Do you want to explode or do you want to control yourself? Forget for the moment the reasons you would like to control yourself, and face the reasons why you would like to continue with fighting. Ask yourself the questions: 1) How does my partner's emotional responses to my anger outburst affect me? 2) If I punish her, will I feel better? 3) Do I actually enjoy it? 4) Even if I don't enjoy it, is it possible that I do this because it has become a habit?

You become aware of your typical patterns of relating simply by paying attention to how you are driven to react. That's how self-reflection can help you to recognise unwanted repetitive patterns of interpersonal communication. Some of them may be dysfunctional and harmful, so you want to eliminate them.

3. Restraining from abusive behaviour, no matter how you feel

The ultimate goal of operation *Dismantling the Abuser* is to starve it to death. This means that the man must go through the phase of abstinence or sobriety, like in alcohol and drug abuse recovery programs (Alcoholics Anonymous). This phase is about self-control. Regardless of how he feels, he refuses to feed the Abuser with his partner's distress, so even in the situations when he does feel anger, he chooses not to act out. He does not translate his irritability, anger and frustration into violent or abusive behaviour, nor say something offensive. This is easier said than done, however.

Like the drug or alcohol addicts who don't realise that they are addicted until they try to stop, the majority of abusive men don't realise that they have become hooked on abusing their partner until they try to control themselves. Yet, the awareness and the acknowledgement that a man finds it difficult to stop abusing his partner—even when he wants to stop—is an important first step in the healing process.

Healing starts from acknowledging that
it is difficult to stop abusing your partner.

Allen Carr claims that it takes three weeks to starve the 'little monster' in the smoker's gut to death: 'You have got to starve him for three weeks, and he is going to try to trick you into lighting a cigarette to keep him alive.'[2] The Abuser aspect is equally manipulative. One of its manipulative strategies is to influence a man into thinking he can solve his 'relationship problem' if he reduces the intensity of his angry outbursts and curbs his aggression, 'so he won't hurt his partner too much'. This does not work because with his abusive behaviour he'll generate the woman's distress, thus feed the Abuser aspect and keep it alive. As long as the Abuser is alive, the man will have to exercise self-control all the time. He cannot relax; he is anxious, tense and edgy even when having a good time with his partner. He cannot allow himself to relax out of fear that he could lose control over the 'Angry me' who would then start a fight.

Many people addicted to a substance or a behaviour go through cycles of temporary change and relapse simply because they continue to feed the Addict aspect ('I'll have only one drink...') thus keeping it alive. The real solution is to dissolve it. However, the period of 'waiting for the Addict/Abuser to die'—the period when the addicts have to control themselves and resist temptations—can be difficult. Not necessarily because it lasts long—you need twenty-one days without a cigarette to purge the 'nicotine monster' from your system. And if you have been clean and sober for ninety days, you get into the third of fourth stages of recovery from drug and alcohol.

That's why psychoeducation—knowing *what* you are going through and why you are going through it—is an important part of drug and alcohol rehabilitation programs. If you work with drug and alcohol specialists, they will teach you about treatment issues such as symptoms of withdrawal and how to handle cravings. They'll help you identify the triggers that prompt you to use drugs or alcohol and teach you the techniques of avoiding triggers. However, this stage of recovery—while you're waiting for the Addict to starve to death—can be challenging, even if you are in a professional treatment program and receive support and encouragement.

The man who is quitting intimate partner abuse faces similar challenges. The problem is that in most cases, the Abuser does not dismantle immediately. It will most probably have a certain momentum, like a spinning wheel that will keep turning for a while even when it is no longer being propelled. It will continue to operate for some time and will try to trigger a man into reacting abusively. Nevertheless, the moment the man sees through it and recognises its hidden agenda, the Abuser will begin to lose energy.

The trick is just not to translate the thoughts ('I am attacked; she is disrespectful; she is humiliating me...') and emotions (anger) into abusive behaviour. This is not about controlling thoughts and emotions. Although some people have control over their mental and emotional processes, the majority of us can't control what we think and feel. But we can control how we'll use our physical body or what we'll say or do. We can choose to channel our emotions of anger or rage into abusive behaviour (to act out emotions and impulses and hurt our partner), to go to the gym and punch the punching bag, or choose to do nothing. It's up to us.

However, it is not always easy to choose not to behave abusively because we don't give ourselves a moment or two to stop and decide what to do. The problem is that most of us tend to focus on the external circumstances that trigger our reactions and behaviours, not on our internal mental processes and psychological states. But we can develop a witnessing mind.

Three Themes That Often Preoccupy the Mind: *Relationships, Money* and *Conflicts*

Not many of us have been trained to observe our thoughts, emotions and actions, but we can train ourselves to track our reactions triggered by someone's words or behaviours. Practising mindfulness or self-awareness also helps us to see the connection between all three layers—mental, emotional and physical—in our inner mind-body temple. This can help us to better understand typical everyday themes that often preoccupy us: issues with intimate relationships, money and conflicts with other people.

Intimate Relationships: You find yourself thinking/stressing about your relationship with your partner. You might be at the mercy of *Grief*. Could grief be at the root of your current relationship problems? Initial, often hidden, feelings of grief may be related to a sense of abandonment, abuse, neglect or separation you experienced as a child. How did your parents communicate love to you? Did they meet your emotional needs to be loved, seen, acknowledged, appreciated or respected? Are there any similarities with your current relationship issues? Do you feel any tension or physical sensation in your chest area when you go through painful relationship issues and experience grief?

Money: You find yourself thinking/stressing about money. You might be at the mercy of *Fear*. Can you relate the current issue with money to issues of survival or a lack of support you experienced in childhood? Who was your father? Was he a man you could rely on, who supported you financially and emotionally, or the opposite? When you are worried about money do you also suffer with lower back pain? What is your back pain telling you about your financial, emotional and existential back-up, or lack of it? Are there any similarities between your life situation in the past and the here and now?

Conflict: Are you preoccupied with fantasies or thoughts about confrontational communications? Do you have arguments in your head with people who frustrate you? You might be at the mercy of *Anger*. Do you have unresolved issues with a sense of power? Did you experience an initial loss of personal power in the relationship with your parents? Are you replaying the same dramas you had with your parents or the people from your childhood who overpowered you? Do you believe that they took your power away? Did they leave you powerless and humiliated; did they invade your private space; did they want to dominate, take from you or control you? Do you want your power back?

Tracking an emotional reaction is a process of observing what triggered it; what type of emotion we are experiencing; where the emotional charge (the physical sensation) is in the body; and what we are trying to do. For example, we see that a person is behaving arrogantly, wanting us to acknowledge him or her as being right and therefore superior. We feel anger and sense tension in our jaw. The anger urges us to defend ourselves. Or, perhaps, we attempt to make the other person see us as right and superior and them as wrong and inferior. When we become interested, curious and focused on what we are observing—be it another person or our own thoughts, emotions and sensations in the body—we usually slow down our responses. This gives us time to consciously choose how to behave.

Instead of reacting as though we were 'possessed', we pause for a moment to observe our thoughts about the person or the situation we have found ourselves in. Or we observe our anger and the temptation to retaliate, or the urge to release the unpleasant tension and feel the pleasure of being right or superior. That is how we start to establish a relationship with various aspects in our personality. Once we know our aspects better, it's easier to distance ourselves from their agendas.

The witnessing mind can also help the man who wants to understand what drives his explosive or abusive behaviour and why he goes through repetitive patterns of abusing his partner, but he must recognise his inner Abuser first. How does he recognise the Abuser? He learns to catch the Abuser the moment it awakens from its dormant state and comes to the forefront. He watches out for any sign of discontent in himself—it can take the form of irritation, impatience, a gloomy mood, anger, rage, a desire to hurt, a need to have some drama in his relationship and so on.

The Abuser is usually triggered by what his partner has said or done. Once this aspect has taken him over, the man wants to punish or retaliate, which means to inflict pain. He may not be fully conscious of this or he may claim that he does not want to hurt his partner. He wants only to defend himself. But if he looks closely, he'll find that his words and actions tend to generate the woman's pain, a sense of degradation and/or fear of him. So he chooses not to hurt her, no matter what he thinks or feels.

Observing the Abuser's contamination and brainwashing strategies

When the Abuser becomes active, a man's entire thought processes and sense of self may be aligned with the Abuser's agenda. For example, a man is having a discussion with his partner. The Abuser aspect will prefer a violent argument over a civil discussion. It will prefer the battle between two self-referencing people who are so entrenched in their own position that they cannot see the value in another point of view, especially when it is hungry and craves the drama.

When the Abuser in him is hungry, a man will tend to attack his partner and he may also want his partner to be angry with him. To increase the level of tension in both of them, he will either make provocative comments about her or attract derisive comments from her. He will want war. His motto in such situations is 'Bring it on!' Or he may easily become opinionated during a peaceful conversation in order to stir up a heated debate. He wants to prove that he is right; however, it's not the truth he cares about but the negative energy generated from proving that his partner is wrong. When his partner is hurt and humiliated, she will generate and radiate pain. The Abuser will love it. The emotional charge that it reaps from the ensuing drama is precious food for their parasitic aspect to feed on.

Here is one typical scenario of the drama between He (the man) and She (his partner):

Scenario: He is doing (or not doing) something. She doesn't like what he is doing (or not doing). She complains or reacts with negative comments about him or his behaviour. He explodes in anger and punches her in the face. This is the third time he's hit her in the last four months. Every time he hits her, he feels terribly guilty and promises that he'll never hurt her again.

What is this story all about? Ever since his childhood, he had looked for similar injustices, received them with enthusiasm and exploited them to justify his rage. Perceived 'provocations' serve him to vent rage on someone and blame them for it. He has forgotten what the injustices or provocations were about but remembers in great detail the course of the battles with the 'provocateurs'.

He is secretly delighted in his partner's provocations. He often sets her up for a predictable 'fall' (he overtly or covertly provokes her criticism or complaining) to further the cycle of abuse and end the drama with his abusive behaviour and her pain/humiliation. The whole drama becomes a feeding frenzy. And that's what being addicted to abuse is all about.

The majority of domestic violence perpetrators are not psychopaths. They are capable of feeling guilt, remorse, empathy and compassion. They know the difference between right and wrong. They are aware of the consequences of their violent behaviour for everybody involved, including themselves.

However, at the time of the 'battle' the man won't know that he is hurting his partner. He will be preoccupied with his own sense of frustration or pain, and his pain will always be perceived as caused (not just triggered) by her. Why? In this game, the man's rational thinking is contaminated by the Abuser aspect so the distress is seen as the fault of the other and never the self. Again, the aspect in his personality who wants to continue with the abuse is responsible. That's why in the TA school of psychotherapy, decontamination of the Adult's rational thinking is an early therapeutic requirement in treating any kind of psychological problem.

Psychoeducation that includes decontaminating the man's rational thinking is crucial in preventing and treating domestic abuse, and it's an important first step in healing our relationships, too. But to decontaminate the rational thinking of a man who is motivated to stop abusing his partner, we must know how the Abuser aspect contaminates it.

Even if an abusive man decides to change, the Abuser aspect makes it difficult for him to stop his abusive behaviour by firmly cementing the set of beliefs about why he does what he does. Its contamination and brainwashing strategies are based on three premises: 'You have been attacked'; 'Your attack in return is justified'; 'You are in no way responsible for it.'

The first premise—'You have been attacked'—is about blaming their partner.

The definition of BLAMING: The practice of identifying a person or people responsible for creating a problem, rather than identifying ways of dealing with the problem.

If a man is serious about quitting intimate partner abuse, he should remove from his mind the myths, fallacies, beliefs and illusions about causes, reasons and rationales for the abuse. But his Abuser aspect will not allow it. It is not in the Abuser's interest that he stops abusing his partner. That's why the Abuser tends to contaminate his thinking with the narrative about being attacked; thus, he has a justified reason to defend himself or punish his attacker. Only if he has a real reason can he be angry or feel rage. Only if he feels rage can he be abusive. Only if he is abusive, the woman will react with fear/pain/hurt/degradation. Only then can the Abuser feed on her distress. Finding the reason is where the power of the Abuser's brainwashing is the greatest because it would starve if nothing is found to trigger the players in the domestic abuse horror drama.

The belief that there is a reason for abusive or violent behaviour is not the Abuser's creation. Such beliefs are usually brought about in our mind by the brainwashing we may have experienced long before we entered into our current relationship. We see other people being abusive or violent to their partners, and we copy not only their behaviour, but their 'reasons' as well. Nevertheless, the Abuser will use and misuse this rationale for abusive behaviour, especially in a situation when it is hungry (or bloodthirsty!).

When the Abuser is active, the man is like a 'rebel looking for a cause'—looking for a reason to attack. He feels compelled to feed the Abuser. The compulsion to feed the Abuser through the repetitive patterns of abuse is a sinister mental trap, and it makes the habit difficult to quit. On top of that, the pattern of the man's abusive behaviour tends to escalate. As the repetitive pattern of abuse tends to increase, so too does the mental contamination—the process of 'poisoning the mind'.

What was not accepted as a good enough reason for the man's violent behaviour in the beginning of their relationship is now perfectly tolerable. After years of family violence, any relatively plausible excuse can be used to justify the abuser's attacks. Like a junkie in crisis who takes whatever he finds on the market, the violent man takes anything as a rationale or provocation that justifies his abuse. Even if he feels guilty, even if he feels empathy and compassion for his partner, his compassion for the woman is blocked until the Abuser aspect gets enough of the 'drug' for the day.

When the feeding time is over, if the man feels shame and guilt for what he has done, the Abuser aspect will do his best to 'help' him by contaminating (again) his rational thinking with the narrative about it being 'her fault'. Why is it always her fault? It is imperative for the man who is not a psychopath to project blame onto his partner. Otherwise, he would feel remorseful. He doesn't want to see himself as someone who wishes to hurt his partner. He doesn't want to see that he feels compelled to inflict pain, so having a real reason and blaming her for his abuse give him a sense of self-righteousness. He brings in psychological artillery in the form of pseudo rationality: 'Everyone would agree with me that I shouldn't tolerate such behaviour...', and then he can keep hurting her and obtain guilt-free satisfaction from that. Being protected from a sense of guilt and shame, he can continue to feed the Abuser aspect indefinitely, which practically guarantees re-offending.

The victim too is often brainwashed into believing that the external factor is indeed the reason for her abuser's violent behaviour. She tends to rationalise his 'out-of-proportion reaction' to what she has said or done. She might think, 'He is too sensitive because he is experiencing stresses at work'; 'He has a problem with a short fuse'; or 'I shouldn't have said that', etc. However, the abusive man may start experiencing discomfort even before something external triggers him. He may not be fully aware that his unpleasant inner tension is not really caused by his partner's words or behaviour but by his hungry Abuser aspect, who is craving drama. Nevertheless, the sense of irritability or agitation the man feels prompts him to launch attacks on the woman to generate her distress, under the premise that he was attacked by her.

Another two premises—'Your attack in return is justified' and 'You are in no way responsible for it'— are based on the deep-seated belief that it is okay to perpetrate the abuse.

As a result of contamination and brain washing, the abuse in a domestic violence drama is skilfully presented as either a self-defence or a righteous punishment. Perpetrators, those who are not psychotic or psychopaths, justify their abuse with the rationale that it is okay to punish someone who they claim, has abused them. This core belief—that it is okay to abuse the woman who is your perpetrator—is shaped by social structures. It is embedded in patriarchal cultural institutions and settings, men's family-of-origin experiences and social norms. Peer influence is also an important factor in the process of contaminating the man's rational thinking when it comes to 'punishing his wife for her transgressions'.

Other abusive men would certainly encourage the perpetrator to keep 'defending' himself or continue with episodes of 'punishing' the woman ('It is her fault so she should be punished!') However, there is an additional reason, not just patriarchal values and norms, why abusive men encourage other men to keep up their abusive behaviour. If, for example, a man finds himself discussing domestic violence issues with other men who abuse their wives, he may notice an interesting dynamic in such groups: openly talking about giving up the habit is taboo. But talking about why he should continue is encouraged. All sorts of reasons as to why it is justified are welcomed:

'Isn't it normal to react in that way?'; 'If you don't do that, women will do to you . . .'

The man will certainly not be asked to stop his abusive behaviour. It is the same with other addictions. Addicts often instantly sense when someone who shares their addiction is moving away. Others want to make sure he doesn't. They fear that if he gets clean, he will leave the group. If he left, they wouldn't feel good about themselves. They would feel judged for the habit they still struggle with but that he was able to get rid of. So not only a drug addict, an alcoholic or a smoker, but also the man who wants to stop his abusive behaviour will have to deal with all sorts of sabotaging and self-sabotaging strategies invented to prevent the Abuser aspect's demise. One of such strategies is a threatening announcement: 'If you leave me, I'll kill you!'

The man addicted to abusing his partner is as desperate to keep her as the heroin addict is desperate to stay in touch with his heroin dealer. Some abusive men can instinctively sense a woman's hidden, unspoken intentions and wishes to run away from him.

Frightened that he might lose her, he proclaims, 'If you leave me, I'll kill you!' (and/or 'I'll kill myself'). The threat, of course, is the Abuser's manipulative strategy. It serves to prevent the woman from leaving the toxic bond, thus leaving the Abuser to starve to death.

As mentioned previously, the 'therapy' for the inner Abusers is to starve them. In treatment, this is referred to as 'showing them to the door'. These aspects are not amenable to change. You cannot reason with them. The solution is to stop feeding them! A man who has managed to free himself from the repetitive patterns of abusive behaviour is the man who has purged the Abuser aspect from his system. However, it will be difficult for the man to purge it unless he makes three conscious decisions: 'Not to hurt the woman'; 'Never again'; 'No matter what!' These decisions have nothing to do with promises.

The Abuser no more

Once a man recognises the repetitive pattern of his abusive behaviour, the questions are: 'Is he willing to get out of it?' And 'Will he keep making excuses to justify the abuse or will he make a conscious choice to stop it?' If he continues, it usually means he is still getting something from it. But if he decides to erase the pattern of abusive behaviour, two things will help him: the insight into what it makes difficult to stop and the power of intention to stop it.

There are men who'd like to quit their abusive behaviour. They are able to see through the nasty game they play with their partners and that the pattern of their behaviour is seriously escalating. However, the key issue in every addiction is that the addicts will suffer if they stop.

The sense that you must control (sacrifice) yourself, that is, restrain yourself from doing something you'd like to do, is what makes it difficult to quit an addiction. That's why even the men who genuinely want to stop abusive behaviours, and who manage to suppress their urge to abuse their partners for some time, relapse into a pattern of recurring violence. The thoughts: 'I am controlling myself... I am trying to be good... and yet she keeps provoking me...' are the thoughts that 're-activate' the Abuser and cause the man to relapse.

The unpleasant sensations in the body, combined with the belief that he sacrifices himself by restraining from discharging tension through verbal abuse or physical violence, is what makes it difficult to stop the repetitive patterns of abusive behaviour.

In such moments, becoming the Witness can help immensely. The Witness is aware of the inner tension, nervousness and unpleasant sensations in his body, while reminding himself of the decision he has made ('Not to hurt the woman'; 'Never again'; 'No matter what!'). This awareness and stance can help the man to dismantle the Abuser aspects in his personality and become harmless.

However, for the abusive man who has been the victim of abuse himself, being harmless doesn't necessarily mean that he has been totally transformed and healed. Starving the Abuser is only the beginning. If he is to heal the buried childhood trauma of his own abuse, the man must go deeper. So how do we help an abused man to step out of the path of his abusive father's footsteps and get rid of the problematic Abuser aspect in his personality?

There are three layers of the domestic abuse problem these men need to address. Dealing with the repetitive patterns of the man's abusive behaviour is only the surface layer.

The addictive defences—and not just alcohol or drugs, but also the repetitive patterns of abusive behaviour— should be confronted first. This means that the man's abusive behaviour must be stopped, allowing the underlying tension, discomfort or pain locked in the Inner Child to surface.

Second, the man's relationship not only to his wounded Inner Child but to the Warrior/ Tough Guy aspects must be attended to. The insights and integration of these personality aspects—the traumatised Inner Child and the Tough Guy who keeps the Child aspect suppressed—lie at the core of recovery and inner transformation. Finally, the buried early trauma of abuse (which has often set the whole 'Abuser process' in motion) must be resolved.

There are three layers of the problem. Dealing with the repetitive patterns of the man's abusive behaviour is only the surface layer.

Senad's healing journey

Senad behaved as though he was addicted to rage. Tolerance is a key element in every addiction, including 'rageholism', and gradually, the repetitive patterns of his abusive behaviour escalated and spiralled out of control. One day he slapped his wife in front of their six-year-old son. He didn't realise the boy was watching him. It was a wake-up call for Senad. 'I could have bashed my wife, sick as that is. But when I saw my son standing there watching what I did to his mother... this little boy...' He didn't want to lose his wife and he did not want to hurt his child; however, it took him a while to dismantle the Abuser aspect in his personality.

He needed his rage. Rage protected him from painful emotions and unpleasant body sensations. It also lifted him up and helped him with his depression. Nevertheless, he wanted to stop with the repetitive patterns of abusing his wife.

The essence of 'deleting' the repetitive pattern of abusive behaviour lies in the art of practising maturity through engaging 'functional reasoning'. In Transactional Analysis (TA), this is called the Adult ego state. The Adult observes and contains immature aspects and their impulses. Taught how to 'be in his Adult ego state', Senad learned to recognise when the Abuser was about to re-enact its usual pattern of abusive behaviour.

Once he recognised it, he found the way to prevent it. Each time he felt the physical flood of agitation or rage but didn't lash out, he'd congratulate himself. That's how he started giving himself functional parenting and support. He even started to feel compassion for himself. We say that change comes when a man is ready to look inside, with compassion for himself, and penetrate the unconscious drive that motivates his abusive behaviour with the light of awareness. Senad was ready. Once he resolved to take up his healing journey, real therapy could begin.

The most difficult part of his healing journey was to accept the fact that he was hurting and that he needed counselling help. Yes, he experienced difficult and perhaps even traumatic events in his childhood and during the war in Bosnia, but he didn't see himself as wounded in any way. In our culture, the wounded victim is 'feminine'. Senad wanted to see himself as a warrior, and the Warrior is 'masculine'. When hurt, the Warrior reacts not with fear, humiliation and helplessness but by lashing out. Such emotional states were firmly controlled by the Tough Guy persona in Senad's personality. He would rather get angry and blame others, or criticise himself for not having been tough enough to defeat his opponents, or smart enough to avoid being hurt than feel sadness, grief, fear or, even worse—acknowledge that he was a helpless victim.

Such acknowledgement could perhaps help him to go through the process of mourning, releasing pain and eventually healing the wound, but it would also confront him with his vulnerability, helplessness and powerlessness—the very things he was most afraid of. To protect himself from his 'weaknesses'—all those things he believed were wrong with him and was ashamed of—he had

had to harden his heart, choke off, deny, repress, dissociate and 'send into exile' the wounded Inner Child aspect in his personality.

Mindful curiosity and interest in the various aspects of his personality helped him to some extent tolerate intense emotions and sensations that he previously had felt overwhelming or uncontrollable, but that wasn't easy for Senad. He identified with his aggressive parents and learned *acting-out* —which provides temporary relief of inner tension or pain—from them. His father unknowingly taught him how to mask or disown vulnerable feelings while reinforcing the male entitlement to express anger. Senad 'inherited' his father's belief systems, too.

Strategies such as normalising the abuse, minimising the effect of abuse on women and children, and getting satisfaction when abusing, while blaming the victim in order to justify the abuse, are essential in maintaining the cycles and transmitting the violence from one generation to another. Senad internalised all of these stereotypes. He didn't see how he was damaged by his painful childhood experiences, so he normalised his abusive behaviour, discounted the damage he was doing to his wife, and even found pleasure in abusing her. Yes, he'd feel guilty, but he also found a way to justify his abuse as self-defence or revenge for her 'disrespect of him'.

And there were moments, he revealed, when he wasn't sure if he was punishing his wife or his mother. In such moments when he was 'in the fog', he said, his wife and his abusive mother were one and the same. It took him a while to realise that he was harbouring severe resentment towards women, especially his mother and wife. He attacked his wife because of what she said or did, but also because of his unresolved issues with his mother whom he saw as disrespectful, unloving, even cruel and sadistic.

However, he refused to see himself as the humiliated or powerless victim of his abusive mother.

Senad felt shame, not just because he had been repeatedly told by his mother that he was useless and worthless, but because he had been humiliated by a woman. In his culture, and in his mind, being humiliated by a woman means being emasculated. And if he is not a 'real man' he is a weakling, like a vulnerable, frightened girl. This type of shame—not for what the boy has done but what others have done to him and how they have made him feel about himself—is toxic, and it poisons the child's psyche. The greater the sense of humiliation, embarrassment and feeling that 'something is wrong with me' the greater the shame of 'losing face' (being emasculated).

The embarrassing experiences when abused by a woman, and the resulting unworthiness, rejection or helplessness had a powerful impact on Senad's sense of self, so much so that he started to believe that indeed he was hopelessly defective. His sense of shame for being 'weak'—unable to protect himself from his abusive mother—persisted long after the episodes of abuse, like an open wound that has never healed. Senad grew up, and other women in his life touched the wound, intentionally or unintentionally. If he was to heal the wound, he had to reconnect with the wounded boy within, but it was painful.

When the victims of abuse identify with their aggressors, they internalise the aggressors' beliefs and attitudes. They normalise their abusive behaviours, blame their victims and minimise the consequences of the abuse. They also disown their abused Inner Child aspects. Senad too, disowned his wounded Inner Boy. It was easier for him to recognise other aspects in his personality, such as the Tough Guy, who wouldn't tolerate anything that smacked of weakness or the 'feminine' in him. He learned how to observe the Tough Guy's instinctive response and intentions, and noticed that when this aspect was in control, he tended to immediately 'channel' the thoughts ('She is attacking me') and emotions (rage) into behaviour—hurtful words or abusive actions. He realised that he was giving himself licence to act abusively whenever he'd feel uncomfortable.

But how did this Tough Guy aspect in Senad's personality come into being in the first place?

If we have the wounded Inner Child aspect whose predominant emotional states are fear, humiliation, powerlessness and inferiority, we can create the Warrior aspect—the courageous, strong and powerful persona—to overcompensate for the Inner Child's weaknesses, vulnerabilities and neediness. Or we can create the Tough Guy aspect to combat the 'internal enemy'—the emotional states that we perceive as unacceptable, such as fears, dependence, sensitivities and flaws, especially when the flaws entail our softer, 'feminine' side.

Senad was conditioned to suppress his 'feminine' side from early childhood onwards. He vividly remembers an incident where both his father and mother treated him with contempt when he showed empathy, grief and compassion for his injured dog. 'Since then, I have never shown grief,' he admitted. He recalled the moment when he decided, 'I'm never going to be a weakling again!' This was the moment that he turned away from what he perceived as the vulnerable place within, unwilling to pay any attention to his feelings of grief and pain. Instead, he invested a lot of energy into his Tough Guy aspect. The Tough Guy in him dreaded what it sensed as weakness, loathed Senad's vulnerabilities and considered the wounded Inner Child as the source of all trouble. The fragile and frightened Child, without a sense of self-worth and self-respect, is Senad's most vulnerable soft spot and, as far as the Tough Guy is concerned, this 'worthless aspect' should be treated like unnecessary heavy baggage. In other words, Senad should refuse to feel like a victim, deny that he was abused and behave as a 'man' not a weakling.

Senad's Inner Child was wounded by numerous experiences of horrific abuse, but the Tough Guy in him had no empathy for it. Why not? The Tough Guy's task was to keep Senad's emotional wounds and painful sensations buried, making him tough and insensitive to his own pain, but also to the pain of others. And here is the reason the abuser who is not a psychopath has an issue with 'lack of empathy' for his victim. As the man has no empathy for his wounded Inner Child aspect, he can no longer feel the anguish of others—his wife's or children's.

To feel empathy, he needs to heal the trauma of his own abuse—to face whatever is painful, dissociated or denied, to re-member the split-off parts and integrate them. But this is difficult so many victims of domestic violence and childhood abuse prefer to avoid their painful and sometimes shameful past. Whenever Senad was triggered and his painful emotions would start surfacing, his rage and violent behaviour 'helped' him avoid or mask his unpleasant feelings. Often, he would feel guilty and ashamed of what he had done to his wife, but...

The first time he hit his wife was when he found himself in a conflict with another man. He expected his wife to be on his side, but his wife 'sided with the "enemy",' he said. Senad punched her hard in the face and kept calling her names. When he saw the blood on her face, he knew he had lost control, but he told himself that she deserved it. Yes, he admitted, for a moment he did feel remorse and even wanted to beg her forgiveness, but he also wanted to be 'strong' so he somehow managed to squelch that morsel of guilt.

His parents considered him a strong 'real man' only when he'd live up to the patriarchy's standards and rules—imposed mostly through control, fear and violence. His father also had the Tough Guy aspect in his personality. 'The old man never showed compassion or "weakness" in himself or to others,' Senad said.

One day Senad noticed that he was conditioning his son in the same way he was conditioned by his father. His young son had started showing an interest in art and had an 'emotional streak', and Senad didn't like it. It smacked of the feminine. He wanted to draw his son into sport, auto mechanics or 'men stuff' to counteract the strong pull of 'sensitivity' in the boy. The boy was also 'too needy' ('He craved his mother's attention too much') and Senad felt contempt for his son's 'neediness'. He was actually in contempt of his own craving for his mother's (and his wife's) attention and love. Senad couldn't tolerate his fear of abandonment, grief or any kind of 'unmanly' and 'shameful' emotional states, especially his so-called feminine traits like sadness, empathy and compassion for himself and others.

It took him a long time to recognise his wounded Inner Child aspect—the sensitive vulnerable boy within who was still hurting. This aspect bore the pain of being abused. It was waiting, metaphorically speaking, for the right timing: for Senad to grow up, become more mature and stronger enough to start unburdening the emotional charge. Healing Senad's childhood trauma, and the trauma he experienced during the war in Bosnia, involved releasing his terror, shame, humiliation and other painful feelings that were never fully recognised and metabolised.

The healing process also included addressing and correcting dysfunctional beliefs 'attached' to the emotional charge generated at the time of traumatic events, but Senad didn't want to be reminded of them. When triggered by his wife's words, and when his suppressed painful memories would start resurfacing (sometimes in the attempt to be released and eventually healed), Senad would feel rage. The Tough Guy in him who 'will not allow anyone to disrespect him or mess with him!' almost always reacted explosively in an unconscious attempt to mask the pain bottled up in the wounded Inner Boy part of his personality. That is how his anger outbursts served him to unleash his tension and frustration, cover his 'neediness', shame, pain, humiliation and fear. The weakness he simply couldn't tolerate and felt compelled to anesthetise with anger and explosions of rage. 'Once you suppress all other unpleasant feelings, you simply don't know how to react. The only thing you know is how to rage!' he said.

Senad also used to act out abusively when he felt *low* and craved *high*. Some people crave drugs, alcohol or gambling, but Senad played a hot potato game with his wife.

How did that game work? When triggered by his wife's words or her behaviour, which he perceived as disrespectful or abusive, he acted as if he had been traumatised by his parents all over again. But he wasn't aware of this, nor did he want to feel painful feelings. Instead, he would unconsciously stage the drama he experienced in his childhood. He would lash out and slap his wife like his father or mother used to slap him. Thus, his wife—his victim he used to despise in such moments—became the abused child he had learned to despise. Instead of him, his wife was cast in the role of a victim. She felt the pain, fear and degradation Senad didn't want to or couldn't *consciously* feel.

Being victimised themselves—and denying the impact the abuse from the past has on their current violent behaviour—perpetrators tend to 'do unto others as they have been done by'. Senad was indeed a victim in his childhood home and in the concentration camp during the war in Bosnia, but that is the type of experience he desperately tended to repress, deny or dis-associate himself from. His father did the same.

Senad's father was also the victim of an abusive father. The victims of abusive men—who have identified with their abusive fathers—are often their own sons. Many violent men disregard their history of being victims of abuse and turn their back on the past they no longer wish to be part of. When the unrecognised pain they have carried in their wounded Inner Child aspect tries to break through to the surface, the man may suppress the vulnerable boy inside and inflict pain on his own son instead—a version of what he himself has been through. That's how he winds up replaying the scene of childhood abuse with his own son. While the role of victim is visibly taken over by his son, the man can experience a pleasant boost of energy due to temporary 'freedom' from his wounded Inner Child aspect. He can even enjoy the sense of power to inflict pain, which is the same pleasant high his father sensed when he was abusing him. This is how the 'experience of abusing' can become addictive and is passed down through the generations.

Senad didn't abuse his son, however, but his wife. He manipulated his wife into feeling the painful emotions, bolted in his own Inner child, he didn't want to feel. Playing this hot potato game helped him to remain unconscious, but it didn't help him to get rid of his traumatic childhood memories. In a way, traumatic memory is not memory at all; it is a form of unconscious reliving or behavioural re-enactment, which is one of the symptoms of intrusion in posttraumatic stress disorder syndrome (PTSD). Senad wasn't remembering the painful experiences. Instead, he was unconsciously acting them out in (unsuccessful) attempts to release dissociated or repressed feelings of pain, terror, shame and humiliation. 'Those who cannot remember the past are condemned to repeat it,' the philosopher George Santayana wrote.[4]

We say that those who don't heal the painful past are condemned to repeat it, and often inflict it on others. Why would they inflict it on others? The unresolved pain of previous generations operates in families like an emotional debt. It will be transferred, like a hot potato, to the next generation, and if they haven't been able to deal with it and heal it, to the next generation. We either face it or we impact our children with it. The abusive fathers who were victims of abusive fathers will 'do the work' or not—they'll face the pain and heal it or pass it on to their children.

If Senad was to break the chain of violence from one generation to the next—if he was to stop conditioning his son to be a victim of domestic violence or an abuser (or both)—he'd have to heal his traumatic experiences. He decided to 'do the work'. In a safe space and supportive therapeutic environment, he experienced the pain of traumatic interactions with his perpetrators—both in the concentration camp and in his childhood home. In doing so, he learned to face and gradually metabolise his feelings of terror, shame, helplessness, degradation and anger.

Once he felt empathy for himself and identified with the injured child within, he could dis-identify with the aggressor (his internalised abusive parent). By acknowledging the trauma and renouncing his identification with the aggressor, the frozen state of his depression broke up, and simple, healing grief melted his heart. He made a conscious choice not to abuse his wife, and he even went so far to learn to ask her for comfort and support.

At the end of his healing journey, Senad integrated his wounded and traumatised aspects. There was no more unmetabolised pain attached to them, so there was no need to protect, suppress, repress or project anything that looked weak, vulnerable and feminine in him. 'I don't have to make my wife respect me because I am not ashamed of the wounded boy in me any longer,' he said. When he stopped believing that his feminine Inner Boy aspect was 'all about weaknesses and vulnerabilities' and thus should be repressed, he stopped pressing his son to develop a powerful, masculine Tough Guy aspect. That's how he managed to overcome the internal division between wounded boy versus tough guy, inferior versus superior, feminine versus masculine inside himself, in his relationship with his wife and with his son.

Fathers play an important role in the prevention of domestic violence. Senad didn't have a protective, caring father. For Senad's father, indulging his rage was more important to him than his son. Senad loved his son; he did care about his boy. He said he wanted to be a better father than he'd had.

How do people change?

Both Senad and his wife claimed that Senad changed during and after treatment. But what did that change look like? 'The day he could stop, restrain himself and think, *Am I going to be abusive or not?* instead of behaving as though he had been possessed by an evil spirit, that's the day I saw that he was a changed person,' his wife said.

But really, how will a man know that he has changed and broken the cycle of abuse? Is it because his repetitive pattern of abusive behaviour has stopped? Yes; but not just that. In general, feeling relaxed along with no longer being preoccupied with conflicts, frictions or fights with their partners are also good indicators of real change. And there is one more thing: Most abusers are skilled at minimising the severity of abuse ('I just pushed her a little bit'), denying that it has occurred ('I didn't touch you!') or blaming their partners and distorting responsibility for the abuse ('I was simply retaliating and standing up for myself, just like anyone would do'). When abusive men stop using these rationalisations, we think they are likely to eventually dismantle their Abuser aspect. 'Now, when our arguments progress and tend to escalate, I blame neither my wife nor myself. I just say, "Okay, we have to stop talking." That allows me to step aside and calm myself down,' Senad says.

How do people change? What was it about Senad's healing journey that caused him to change? The information about patterns of abusive behaviours, psychoeducation and decontamination of his Adult ego state (his rational thinking) were definitely powerful healing factors. The insights into the nature of his repetitive patters, and the reasons the abuse escalates, helped him to understand the nasty games he played with his wife (and their illicit gratifications), and thereby helped him stop playing them. However, the most important factor was: He was the one who requested treatment for his problem.

It's common for domestic violence abusers to seek counselling or attend Men's Behaviour Change Programs as a result of pressures applied by family or by the courts. They are not willingly involved, but instead feel coerced and even victimised in the situation. But there are also men who have recognised their Abuser aspect and the damage the abuse does to their partners and themselves. They want to quit.

The following bits of information can motivate a man who looks for the 'Dismantle the Abuser Program' button and help to kick-start an awakening in anyone who has a genuine intention to stop domestic or intimate partner abuse:

The mechanics behind the repetitive patterns of intimate partner abuse and the fact that domestic violence tends to escalate in frequency, intensity and diversity is an important argument for insisting on viewing these patterns of abuse within the addiction paradigm. Just like the patterns of addictive behaviour, the repetitive cycle of abuse will last a lifetime unless it is broken. The perpetrator is stuck with either a lifetime of domestic violence drama and misery, or he can break the cycle.

It is easier to quit any harmful habit when you know exactly why you feel compelled to keep doing it even when you want to stop. It is easier for a man to stop abusing his partner once he realises why he does it: to feed the Abuser aspect that thrives on the habit of abusing his partner. The 'therapy' for this type of problem is the same as therapy for quitting smoking, alcohol, drugs or gambling: dismantle the Aspect addicted to a substance or behaviour. These aspects are not amenable to change. You cannot reason with them. The solution is to stop feeding them!

A man who has managed to free himself from the repetitive pattern of abusing his partner is the man who has purged the 'hungry monster' from his system. It is easier to purge it from his system when he makes three conscious decisions: 'Not to hurt his partner'; 'Never again'; 'No matter what.'

PART THREE

The Way Out of the Domestic Abuse Trap

Chapter 11

IN THE TRAP

There are many women who would like to understand why their partners hurt them over and over again, no matter how disconcerting the insights are into the nature of repetitive cycles of abuse in their relationships. They want to look behind the patterns of abusive behaviour, the patterns that tend to increase in frequency or severity. They ask what causes them, how they can be altered or how to find the way out of the domestic violence trap and set themselves free. Unfortunately, not all victims ask such questions. There are many abused women who take personal responsibility for the abuse and blame themselves for what the abuser has done to them.

It's all my fault!

When children believe that something wrong has happened to them, they tend to blame themselves. Even when they are abused, they may think it is their fault. Why? They blame themselves if it is the explanation given to the child, either explicitly or implicitly, by the abusive parent. But self-blaming can also be a strategy to maintain a sense of control: 'Yes, I was disobedient and they punished me, but the next time I'll be good, so they won't beat me again.' This can serve the important purpose of preserving a child's primary attachment to its parents.

When brutally and repeatedly hurt by parents, the child has two choices: either to believe that the parent is unloving, dangerous and a bad person who gets his fix by inflicting pain and humiliating the child, or to internalise the blame and believe that the abuse is their fault. Unwilling to see the parents as malevolent, children prefer to idealise them as good and loving people who have the child's best interests in mind. But someone has to take the blame for the abuse, so if it can't be the parent, it must be the child. Thus, internalising blame becomes a typical child's strategy to avoid a sense of terrifying helplessness in situations where they have nowhere to go or when it is too risky to blame the parent they depend for their survival.

Such thinking is erroneous; moreover, the profound sense of inner badness often becomes the core around which the abused child's identity is formed. However, the self-identification 'I am bad'—imposed by abusive parents—preserves a relationship with the parent, so it is not readily given up even after the abuse has stopped. Such self-perception, 'I am a bad person', or the line of reasoning, 'It was all my fault!' can persist into adult life.

The victims of domestic abuse who were abused in childhood often keep the same belief system: 'It's my fault; if I change, the abuse will stop.' We may say that they are in denial, but denial is an important psychological defence mechanism.

We can face our distress only in proportion to our hope of recovery, so denial protects us from feeling more pain than we can handle. Besides, denying helplessness and blaming themselves give victims ensnared in the 'domestic violence trap' a sense that they are in control and that they can do something to change the situation. Not only denial but, paradoxically, *survivor's guilt* (or survivor guilt, also called *survivor syndrome*) can serve as a defence mechanism against highly distressing or traumatic experiences. It occurs when a person managed to survive a tragic event and others did not. The person feels guilty for not taking proper steps to avert the tragedy and believes he or she did something wrong, but also when people who survived torture, rape or abuse blame themselves for what happened to them. Why would victims blame themselves?

> Ironically, victims of rape who blame themselves have a better prognosis than those who do not assume this false responsibility: it allows the locus of control to remain internal and prevent helplessness.[1] **Bessel A. van der Kolk, MD**

There is a difference between stress and trauma. The keyword that can help us understand the difference is the word 'helplessness'. If you have experienced a dangerous situation but you managed to escape it, or fight back and defend yourself, the experience might have been very intense and disturbing; however, not necessarily traumatic. But if you are helpless—you try to activate an emergency flight-or-fight response, but neither 'fight as hard as you can' nor 'flee as fast as you can to get away from danger' is possible—the body and mind become overwhelmed. The built-up tension that cannot find resolution through the fight-or-flight response morphs into a 'chunk of frozen terror'. A 'breaking point' is reached: the point of transition from stress into trauma.

Being overwhelmed, the psyche uses the defence mechanism of dissociation to dissociate the fragments of the terrifying experience that couldn't be metabolised. Dissociation is a key characteristic of traumatic experience. This defence mechanism serves the purpose of protecting the psyche and buffering the central nervous system under conditions of extreme tension; however, you may end up feeling numb, disconnected or 'broken'.

Feeling broken is a painful feeling, so some victims of traumatic events tend to deny it or claim that they were not totally helpless. For example, the victims who feel survivor's guilt believe that there was something they could have done to help or prevent the misfortune or disaster. Yes, they made a mistake of some kind and feel guilty or responsible for the consequences of the mistake, but they were not helpless! It is easier to tolerate guilt than overwhelming grief or pain. Thus, the victims' preoccupations with the personal responsibility for the tragic events can help them, at least temporarily, not to feel intense grief. Or it may give them a sense of hope: They believe that they can learn from the experience and perhaps prevent negative consequences or avoid similar situations in the future. That's how survivor's guilt becomes a coping strategy and serves as a defence mechanism against highly distressing experiences. Some abused women also use this coping strategy.

Holding on to feelings of guilt and blaming themselves for what has happened may seem absurd, or totally delusional, yet victims may use it is a protective mechanism against sinking into deep despair. They prefer to feel guilty rather than feel totally helpless and broken.

However, victims who blame themselves for being abused—even if it was a functional survival strategy when they were a helpless child who couldn't leave their parents—is not a functional or empowering coping mechanism. If they are an adult and still believe they can't leave their abuser even if they can, that means their rational thinking is contaminated by old fears experienced in childhood. On top of that, the abuser's drops of psychic acid ('It's all your fault!') may have very corrosive effects on a victim's mental state and their sense of personal power. The longer they stay in a toxic love relationship the less self-confidence they have; the less self-confidence they have the more difficult it is to escape. Holding on to blame can be extremely detrimental because it keeps victims trapped in violent or abusive relationships. It fuels their decision to stay with their abusers, or to go back to abusive partners, time and time again.

However, trying to avoid a sense of helplessness or overwhelming emotional state is not the only reason why the victims—both children and adults—may blame themselves for the abuse they have experienced. There is another one: They unconsciously pick up the abuser's guilt!

When domestic violence perpetrators refuse to take responsibility for their abusive behaviour, they project the blame onto the woman or children they are abusing. The victims can unwittingly take on the perpetrators' guilt and shame, thus 'rescuing' them by owning and absorbing the feelings the perpetrators cannot or refuse to feel. Hence the guilt that the victim of abuse feels can be the very feeling the abuser is unwilling or unable to *consciously* feel.

A Hot Potato

Can emotions 'travel' from one person to another? Emotions are fluid carriers of information about our inner psychic states. Some sensitive and empathic people can indeed unconsciously 'pick up' the emotions of others and even feel them as if they were their very own.

There are beliefs in some Indigenous cultures that emotional energy and psychological conditions can be contagious. Vulnerable people can be 'infected' by another person's intense and harmful emotions, or they take on the disturbing conditions such as anxiety, depression or suicidal ideation from others. Some even believe that a potential 'donor' can become magically free of troublesome conditions by passing them on to the person who becomes a 'recipient'. Transactional analyst Fanita English refers to such 'transmissions' as 'passing on a hot potato'.[2]

When someone throws negative projections onto others in attempt to get rid of the undesirable parts of themselves, it is as if they are darting poisonous projectiles into these other people. In Jungian psychology, *shadow projection* is a psychological defence mechanism in which we split off our own shadow or darker aspects and project them onto others. Such projections can shape the people on whom they fall. When a parent, for example, is 'cursing' the child, telling him, 'You are so stupid! You'll never amount to anything!' these negative markers can seriously burden the child. The 'cursed child' might indeed keep exhibiting more and more of his 'stupidity'. The same may happen to the adult victims of abuse.

The domestic violence perpetrator who blames his partner with, 'It's all your fault!' and 'See what you've made me do!' often does it to manipulate his victim into feeling the painful emotions—guilt and shame—he doesn't want to feel. This defence mechanism is called *projective identification*. The mechanics behind it is similar to the hot potato game.

Melanie Klein, a psychoanalyst and pioneer in object-relations, described projective identification as a primitive defence mechanism in which one person (donor) alienates or disowns certain unwanted aspects of themselves and attributes the aspects to another person (recipient) who internalises and experiences them. Getting rid of the unwanted aspects by projecting them can lead to bolstering our self-view. Couples therapists spend considerable time on the recurring patterns of projective identification sequences. This occurs when one partner disowns disturbing thoughts and feelings of worthlessness, inferiority, shame or guilt, and unconsciously induces similar thoughts and feelings in the other partner by behaving in such a way as to stimulate them. For example, a husband is feeling humiliated because he has been criticised by his boss. He comes home and tells his wife that her dinner is disgusting. Now she is feeling hurt and humiliated, and he is miraculously feeling better!

Intimate partner abusers do the same thing. Using the familiar methods of shaming and blaming, they shove their uncomfortable emotions onto the woman.

Like in a hot potato game, 'I'll make you feel bad so I don't have to', the victim of domestic abuse is often made to feel worthless, ashamed, guilty, a failure, unattractive or whatever it is her abusive partner is trying to offload. Some women may really buy into it. They own his 'stuff' (his guilt, remorse or a sense of shame) believing that, 'It was my fault'. They may even start thinking that something is wrong with them. And the more the victim believes, 'Something is wrong with me' the more the abuser feels justified in labelling her with negative labels or 'righteously' attacking her because 'She deserves it'. 'It was my fault' and 'Something is wrong with me' are the lines of thinking that may pull a victim deeper and deeper in to the domestic violence trap.

Entrapped

The questions most often incredulously asked of intelligent women trapped in abusive relationships are, 'How did you get into something like this?' and 'Why did you stay so long?' The unspoken subtext seems to be, 'How could someone like you end up in an abusive relationship? There must have been something wrong with you.' Not understanding the true nature of long-term abusive relationships is the principal reason why women stay in them, and why others can't comprehend why these women stay with their abusers.

To understand how the woman has found herself entrapped in such relationship and to answer our research question 'Why do so many abused women return to their abusers who just abuse them again?' we must seek first to understand how the perpetrator 'influences' the victim to stay with him or return to him. As long as we 'psychoanalyse' the woman without clearly seeing what her abuser does to keep her in the toxic bond, we cannot see why she goes back to a partner who repeatedly hurts her. But not all abusers are the same. Different types of domestic violence perpetrators influence their victims to stay or return to them in different ways.

After decades studying violent marriages, professors Neil Jacobson and John Gottman concluded that Cobras' and Pit Bulls' 'styles of abusing' women differ. Pit Bulls are the stalkers and the jealous husbands and boyfriends who tend to see disrespect or betrayal at every turn, and it infuriates them. They may act out of dependence, a fear of abandonment, emotional oversensitivity and rage. And when their anger explodes into violence, they seem to lose control. Cobras, on the other hand, are often seen as cold and calculating con artists, relatively free of emotional dependence, but with a high incidence of antisocial, abusive or even sadistic behaviour.

While a Pit Bull type of re-offender may periodically hurt his partner to vent tension and gain satisfaction from it, a Cobra's hidden agenda (often hidden from himself as well) is not only to openly abuse her but to slowly drain the woman of her self-confidence and self-worth, leaving her feeling miserable and powerless to protect herself.

A Cobra man is not 'needy' but he needs to have his way, to be the boss and make sure that everyone, especially his partner and children, know it and act accordingly. He wants power and control over the woman because he enjoys the 'I dominant-You submissive' game and because the 'I dominant' position allows him to continue with abusing his partner. Although he may not easily lose control like the Pit Bulls, he can be seriously violent.

'He once killed the cat as a warning to me that if I decided to go back to my country of origin, this could happen to me,' Snežana said about her Cobra ex-husband.

His abuse never stopped. When his physical violence succeeded in intimidating her, it was replaced by a never-ending barrage of emotional abuse—he was in her face, demeaning, degrading, humiliating, harassing her...

That was sufficient to remind her that the threat of his physical violence was always present.

The researchers Jacobson and Gottman found that battered women are less likely to leave Cobras out of fear for

211

their safety. In many cases, when a woman attempts to leave the bond with a Cobra, he pursues her and intensifies his beatings. Even when the physical attacks abate, the emotional abuse continues and serves to keep the woman intimidated and afraid. The woman may find her life situation extremely difficult to deal with. She feels powerless to protect herself from being abused and helpless to escape from her toxic bond with the abuser. She is looking for the 'exit', but it's nowhere to be seen. She often askes herself how she has found herself in that nightmare. Indeed, how has she been trapped in the man's web in the first place?

If we compare an animal trap to the domestic violence trap, we can find many similarities. Like an animal trap, the domestic violence trap may be initially attractive and easy to get in to, but then turns out to be much harder to get out of. In order to understand human traps, let's first explore the well-known animal trapping strategies: alluring; keeping the animal in the trap; and using it for the trapper's purposes.

Alluring. The trapper sets up a trap for the prey. The trick is to encourage the animal to take a path leading to the trap. The trapper must consider the types of bait, the placement of the trap and where the animal is most likely to be caught. The success depends on the trapper's personal experience and familiarity with the needs and habits of the animal. The bear, for instance, the experienced bear trappers claim, is more likely to step into the trap when its attention is diverted upward, towards the bait.

Keeping the animal in the trap. The trapper makes it difficult or impossible for the animal to escape once it has been caught. Most wolf traps have drags with logs attached to the trap chain. The drag prevents the wolf from pulling its leg out of the trap.

Using the animal for the trapper's purposes. That is the reason the trap is set up. The trapper needs the animal for his own survival; he will eat the animal, use its fur, skin, etc.

How do the human victims wind up entrapped?

Alluring: Unlike an animal trap, human victims are caught with a psychological hook: unfulfilled needs. The usual allure is the promise that their needs will be met.

The alluring strategies in child sexual abuse, cults and intimate partner abuse are very similar. The bait for the child is loving attention, a sense that she/he is important and special to 'someone' (a paedophile) who sees the child's talents, specialness, goodness, beauty. The opening scene in this type of child-abuse horror story is about making the child feel good about themselves through fulfilling their needs for recognition, love, attention, sympathy, kindness, or whatever the child needs. This is called grooming. Similarly, recruiters who allure vulnerable people into a cults, as well as domestic violence perpetrators, especially those Cobra type coercive controllers, do the same. The primary message in grooming is: 'You should like what you are getting from me; I'll make you feel good about yourself.'

The definition of **GROOMING**: A predatory act of manoeuvring prey into a trap.

We all need loving attention, personal relationships and to live a purposeful and meaningful life. If these needs are not fulfilled, a void is created. Anything that comes from the outside world and promises to fill a void in us could be perceived as good. Hence, we might find ourselves wide open to various 'offerings' from sources with a hidden agenda and end up indoctrinated into a sect or cult with charismatic leaders or an abusive relationship with a charming man. Their 'front page' looks very attractive, and they promise to fulfil unfulfilled needs, but that is because they target vulnerable places in the potential victims. Their promises are the baits that serve to allure. In the same way that our need for spiritual development may lead us into the cult trap, our vulnerability and unfulfilled needs for personal relationships may lead us into the domestic violence trap.

'My marriage with him was like living in a cult. He took control over my entire life.' **A victim of domestic violence**

Many victims of domestic violence claim that their marriages have a lot in common with cults. When they recognise their abuser's manipulative tactics and understand how they work, it's easier to seek help and consider how to safely escape.

The well-established template, copied and applied throughout the history of humankind, is actually very simple and always the same: Prey upon women who look for a relationship, and when you find them use your secret weapon: love bombing!

The process of domestic violence entrapment usually starts with the development of trust and intimacy. If the future perpetrator claims that he loves the woman, she may believe him. We may believe him too. But if we scratch the surface, we may notice that his love is more about his desire to get the woman to devote her life to keeping him satisfied. Nevertheless, the woman is lulled into a sense of closeness, intimacy or security that he provides her. Once ensnared in the domestic violence trap, just like in the animal trap, it's very difficult to get out.

Keeping the victim in the trap. Just like the cult leader and the paedophile, the intimate partner abuser seeks 'relationships' with their victims that will last for an extended period of time. They will exercise a variety of tactics and strategies to make sure their victim does not escape. One of the strategies is known as the double bind: a sense of being stuck in internal conflict.

The Double Bind

The double bind is not just a simple contradiction or a 'one-off' circumstance where you find yourself trapped by two conflicting demands in a 'damned if I do and damned if I don't' kind of situation. It is usually a long-term psychological condition created by an unclear, overwhelming internal conflict. It occurs when a person cannot confront, but at the same time cannot avoid, an existing situation. The result of such intrapsychic conflict is a sense of being stuck. The internal conflict creates tension, but there is no possibility for tension release. The person can neither resolve the situation, nor opt out of it.

Here is an example of the double bind in a habitual pattern of self-sabotage: A parent feels threatened by their daughter's achievement (school or professional achievements, successful marriage, and so on). Not being fully aware, the parent sends the subliminal message 'I want you to fail'. But what the parent is aware of and what they are saying is, 'Work hard, I want you to succeed'. This means that the daughter receives two conflicting messages. One message denies the other, but neither of them can be ignored or escaped from. This leaves her torn both ways, so that whichever demand she tries to meet, the other demand cannot be met. She cannot do or gain something without sacrificing something else. She has difficulty in defining the exact nature of the paradoxical situation in which she is caught. She is getting more and more confused. She might feel intense anxiety; however, it is difficult to give up and leave the situation. She ends up feeling inadequate, guilty or 'bad'.

The combination of these two messages presents the daughter with a double bind. The quasi-solution is, 'to get my parent's love, I need to work hard but fail', so she unconsciously decides to work hard but sabotage herself. The problem may emerge especially when she is close to making some important achievement. For instance, she gets good marks, but fails at the final examination.

We can find a similar 'formula' that keeps devotees in the cult trap. The emphasis in some cults is on the spiritual path that is 'leading to something special' (for example, enlightenment). There is a carrot on the end of a stick, and the members will keep chasing it as long as they are 'on the path'. It is in the interest of the organisation that the members stay on the path. The organisation needs seekers, not finders. The leaders will condition the seekers to believe that they can achieve that 'special something' only if they commit to the system. The members must believe they cannot achieve it by themselves outside of the organisation, but only as active members and through the program of the leader. But if they are to stay in the program that leads to something desirable, they must endure exploitation and abuse. They also find themselves in a double bind.

The double bind is often a setup for traumatic bonding, and traumatic bonding is also one of the reasons for staying in abusive relationships.

What do long-term abusive relationships and animal traps have in common? The two key components used in constructing the animal trap: a) something that will lead the animal to get into the trap; and b) something that will keep the animal there, are also the key components in human traps. The purpose of the lure, such as love bombing, is to reel the victims into the trap by exploiting their needs and vulnerabilities.

Is it true that anybody can fall victim to these predators' manipulative tactics and strategies?

Just as the skilful trappers know how to set up animal traps, manipulative coercive controllers have mastered the art of attracting people, often at critically low points in their lives when they are lonely, confused, dissatisfied or lost. All of us, at various times, can fall into vulnerable states during which another person can wield more influence over us than at other times. We are all more vulnerable to flattery, deception, enticements and baits when we are at a major life crossroad, disenchanted, depressed, anxious or feeling needy. A charming man comes into our life and offers love that will last forever. However, if he is a dangerous coercive controller, at some stage in the course of the relationship he will 'introduce' a series of psychological processes like mind manipulation or well-packaged psychological control methods. These are all used to keep the victims entrapped in the abusive relationship.

It is devastating to observe how re-offending domestic violence perpetrators use various methods to undermine their victims' independence or their capacity to think critically, and seduce them into a state of physical, psychological and/or financial dependence. Especially financial dependence. Many domestic violence abusers want to control their wife's money and make her dependent on them, thus being unable to leave them.

Dependence is also fostered by isolating victims from other sources of support and emotional closeness. Just like cult leaders isolate members from others who could help them to escape or support them once they are out, an intimate partner abuser also tends to isolate his partner from her family and friends, particularly from 'those who don't like him'. Isolation includes controlling the woman's social activity: who she sees, who she talks to, where she goes... Or he may constantly accuse her of infidelity and demand that she could prove her loyalty to him by giving up her work (independent source of income). Isolation also helps confuse or disorientate the woman and make her more dependent on her abuser.

Power games and mental manipulations

As in all forms of abuse, domestic abuse involves the loss of a victim's sense of personal power.

What is power? We often define power as the ability to manipulate or control others. We don't recognise the many other ways to be powerful outside of the control sphere: We have power when we create something; when we bring about what we seek or prevent what we don't want. However, the capacity to control other people is also a manifestation of power. When power is expressed in the form of control, it is equivalent to oppression because it is based on disempowering others.

The coercive controller likes the 'I dominant' position, and when he wants to dominate the woman, he uses power games—like the repetitive transactional (relational) patterns of behaviour. This type of game is designed to cause the 'submissive' (his partner) to do something she would rather not do, or to stop her from doing what she wants to do. The ultimate manifestation of psychological oppression—the ultimate result of the abuser's 'I dominant-You submissive' game—is the 'slave mentality'. The slave mentality is a frame of mind in which the rationale for abuse is internalised. The victim accepts the oppressive circumstances of her life and even defends her oppressor against anyone who criticises him. The classic case can be found in the abused wife who will justify and defend her brutal husband, refusing to leave him even when it would be safe to do so.

The coercive controller plays the game because he wants to be recognised as someone who is powerful, in control and superior. He is hungry for that type of recognition. When he gets it—either in the form of compliments and praise or indirectly (the woman is obedient)—he feels good about himself. Being able to control his partner and the position 'I dominant' brings him a high, so he seeks power for power's sake. Hence the discourse: 'Domestic violence is all about power and control'.

This drive for recognition is what motivates his controlling and manipulative behaviour, but he can't feel superior—and gain the sense of satisfaction that comes from dominating her—unless the woman feels inferior. So he must take power away from her. How?

Many victims are unaware of how power games operate because they are immersed in and forced to accept abuse from early childhood. After spending her young years under the routine sway of other people's power (usually her parents'), the victim of intimate partner abuse tends to adopt the role of the oppressed. The acceptance of power imbalances and abuse of power may be drilled into her through her life-long experiences of male domination. So it may not be surprising for her to see that her male partner is abusive too.

And yet, it's not easy to understand these women. It doesn't make sense that an independent, intelligent woman would stay with a man who abuses her. It doesn't make sense that after she leaves him—for very good reason—she goes back to him. Is she under his spell? Is the mother who stays with a violent man, and puts her children in danger, brainwashed?

Indeed, the coercive controller uses various psychological power manoeuvres and thought-reform processes designed to produce changes in attitudes and the loss of a victim's sense of personal power.

This type of manipulation, which relies entirely on obedience on her part, tricks the woman into staying and tolerating abuse while giving an illusion of choice: 'Nobody is forcing the victim of domestic violence to stay with her abuser, so why doesn't she just get up and leave?' The answer to this perennial question is: Because she has become the perfect victim. The perfect victim, in this context, is someone who appears to be willing to stay and tolerate abuse of her own free will.

> The definition of **PERFECT VICTIM**: Someone who appears to be willing to stay and tolerate abuse of her own free will.

To morph her into the perfect victim, an abuser uses a range of tactics such as conditioning, indoctrinating, manipulating, double bind, emotional blackmail, brainwashing, contaminating rational thinking and gaslighting. For example, gaslighting or milieu control—controlling what a person sees, hears and experiences—is a systematic pattern of mental manipulation used to undermine the victim's belief in the validity of her own perception. How does it work?

When we invalidate or deny people's experiences, or the way they see things, we make mental invalids of them. When one's perception or intuition is repeatedly and thoroughly denied, the person can be made to feel crazy ('Something is wrong with me...'). That's why the abuser uses gaslighting when he wants to mess with the woman's sense of reality, causing her to distrust herself and trust him instead. He may manipulate factual information and play tricks on the victim, move or hide things, and when the victim asks him if he has moved the object, he denies it, saying he never saw it. Gradually the victim, unable to work out the game, finally begins to doubt herself. She begins to feel that she can't do anything right any more, and she doesn't feel that she can trust her own mind.

The tactic is often very subtle, and victims don't know it's happening to them. They don't know they are being subjected to mind-numbing treatments that block their critical and evaluative thinking. As a result, they may lose a sense of adult competence and feel disempowered to leave an abusive relationship even when they can leave.

Another typical example of gaslighting is when the abuser convinces the woman that she deserves 'punishment' or that the abuser's physical or verbal outbursts are the result of misbehaviour on her part. The goal is to make the victim question herself and continue to tolerate abuse, so he will portray all punishment as her fault: 'If you didn't do this, I wouldn't do that'.

If she believes this, she will excuse or forgive her partner's cruel behaviour. Or he'll explain that it is for her own good ('He only wants to help her to improve herself and become a better person'). She may believe that he is right when he attacks her because, after all, she *is* messy, irresponsible, selfish . . . she indeed misunderstood or misinterpreted something. She feels guilty for what she has done or said. Over time, her guilt becomes toxic shame—shame not because of what she has done, but because of who she believes she is. So she starts to feel bad about herself. She starts losing her self-esteem, confidence and sense of competence. Or she may hope that if she improves herself, or approaches him differently, he will stop his abusive behaviour towards her.

These mind control techniques are often used in combination with the specific 'training' of *intermittent punishment and reward* or the intermittent reinforcement of punishment (abuse) and reward in the form of love bombing, praise, flattery, kindness, gifts and attention etc.

Why all these manipulative tactics? The abuser may or may not be aware of this, but these tactics are used to carry out the re-offending abusers' intent (conscious or unconscious) to continue with the abuse.

Their main purpose is to condition the victim to tolerate abuse and stay in traumatic bonding.

Warning! As his abusive behaviour gets worse, so the victim may tolerate it better! The most striking characteristic of the repetitive patterns of abuse found in domestic violence is the victim's increased ability to tolerate abuse. As the violence escalates in frequency, intensity and diversity, the victim may become desensitised and tolerate increasing levels of violence. Gradually, the victim is able to endure more intense physical, emotional, or sexual trauma and pain.[3]

What does it mean to condition a victim to stay entrapped in an abusive relationship? First of all, it means to keep her ignorant of the pattern of abuse and purpose of the repetitive pattern of the abusive behaviour—often reframed or justified as punishment for something she did or didn't do.

It takes the victim time to realise that she is in an abusive relationship; especially when she finds herself in the toxic bond with the manipulative *coercive controller*.

Coercive control is the insidious pattern of behaviour and manipulative tactics that abusers use to dominate and entrap their victims, so he will do his best to monopolise the victim's perception. Perception about what? About herself, him and the nature of their relationship. The goal is to transform the woman into a 'submissive' so he can play the 'I dominant–You submissive' game. He wants her compliance. He may or may not reward her compliance but will always punish her for not complying. When he puts her down he lifts himself up—that's what the game 'I dominant–You submissive' is about. Once he introduces the game, he wants to continue with it.

The woman may try to explain his behaviour. Does he suffer from some kind of a personality disorder? Is he just stressed because he's lost his job? She turns excuses into reasons. She does that because it's impossible to comprehend that her partner could inflict such cruelty upon her just because he craves it. So she takes the blame or attempts to find the way to help him, fix him, show him how to love. She can't see through his desire to keep her submissive and hurt her because the abuser hides his pleasure when he abuses her and skilfully hides his strategies for generating her pain, humiliation and fear.

How exactly does the coercive controller manage to maintain power and control over the woman's life and extract her pain, degradation and dread?

Subjugation is usually a step-by-step process. It may start with isolating the woman from those who could help her out of the coercive controller's trap. At first it may appear that he has his partner's best interests in mind. He wants to support her and offers advice on how to deal with unpleasant situations or interpersonal problems with friends and family. The 'support' may slowly spiral into him being in total control over her relationships with other people. And once the abuse starts, she can expect to be 'discouraged' from speaking with outsiders (including the police) about her and her partner's 'internal affairs' (his abuse).

Most of the oppression or abuse that victims of coercive controllers experience is psychological in nature. However, physical violence may be 'under the surface', backing up psychological abuse. Just an occasional violent outburst by the Cobra-type abuser is usually sufficient to keep his partner terrified and in line for a longer period.

During that time, his menacing tones and looks are enough to remind her of the latest violence and keep her submissive.

The abuse usually starts gradually and slowly. In the beginning, even a malignant abuser can be very compelling. He is charming, loving and attentive. He cares about his partner, so the woman feels good about herself, about him and her relationship with him. On top of that, he may want to be the most important person in her life. To become the most important person in her life, he must eliminate those she can rely on. 'He is jealous because he wants me all to himself,' she may think.

He may isolate her geographically, moving her far away from family and close friends, or he may gradually discourage her to keep in contact with them. (Later in the course of the relationship, the victim may isolate herself, doesn't tell anyone about the abuse and stops socialising with friends because she feels shame, fear or the desire to protect her abusive partner).

The physical abuse usually starts gradually. It may not begin until after an engagement, marriage or pregnancy. Abusers typically begin subtly with an intimidating stance, a hand raised, a grab at her arm or a quick slap to get her attention. If she tolerates it out of fear that she might aggravate him if she reacts, or perhaps hopes that his attack is just an accident, the abuse usually escalates into harsher physical slaps, chokes, grabs or even punches. After the episode of abuse, he may apologise, promise he won't do it again, make love to her...

'The first time he became enraged by something I said, I couldn't help but feel guilty,' Snežana said. The man who loved and admired me so much suddenly became so enraged by my words. It was such a shift in his personality; he was so angry that

224

I assumed I must have deeply offended him. I apologised, but he kept verbally abusing me anyway.

He became angry and abusive more and more often. Every time we fought, I found myself swept into a silly debate. His arguments would leap from topic to topic, wild accusations were thrown at me because of something I couldn't even remember, or he would deny my memory of an experience or interpretation of the event we were arguing about.

The first time he hit me, he apologised and acted nice. Naively, I hoped that it wouldn't happen again. He abused me again. I was crying, I said I'd leave him. But his mood shifted, and he gently and charmingly drew me back in. I had the good moments with him again. A few weeks later, he hit me again... I was desperate. I called my friend and asked her to lend me some money so I could return to my country, but he threatened that he would come after me and also threatened suicide. He wasn't abusive for some time.

On the contrary, he was very gentle and loving...

Over time, I lost a sense of clear thinking. Being loved and hurt were episodes of that same ever-turning wheel, round and round and round. I was punished, adored, then punished again.

It's a toxic, scary mix but I felt pleasant relief when the abuse stopped, and especially when he was kind and loving after the episodes of abuse.'

Humiliation and belittling—the most common types of emotional abuse—may start out as subtle jabs or embarrassments, which then turn into full-blown yelling matches or serious insults. Or he treats her like a misbehaving child, yelling, disciplining, demeaning and pointing out her every fault. However, if she tries to correct him, she should get ready for a seriously defensive or violent backlash.

One of the most effective ways to degrade the woman is through sex, so he may rape her. Many victims report being raped by their abusive partners, or coerced into sexual acts they find humiliating, sadistic and painful. However, after the 'incident', he may show remorse, regret and guilt. He'll try to make it up to her . . . give her gifts.

Rules and regulations

We know from social psychology that we can control people by administering a system of: a) Rules and Regulations, and b) Rewards and Punishments using the 'carrot-and-stick' method. The subordinates will feel fear of punishment if they do not obey the rules and proscribed regulations—that is the stick. But they hope that they will be rewarded if they follow the instructions, rules and regulations—that is the carrot.

Rules and regulations are not effective unless people either obey or disobey them. The man who wants to be the boss holds both the stick and the carrot, and he insists that others have to obey the rules; otherwise, they will be punished.

Some of the rules are explicit and some of them are implicit nonverbal requests such as 'Don't disturb him while he is taking a nap!' When the woman wants to please him, she tip-toes around him, trying not to provoke his anger. Or she self-edits what she says or does because she wants to prevent herself from 'pushing his buttons'; she wants to obey the rules he has imposed on her. As long as she follows the rules and fulfils his demands (and neglects her own needs and wants), he can draw satisfaction from it; he feels respected, he is dominant and she is submissive. Thus, the purpose of the rules and demands is to extract her continual obedience. She must follow his directions and instructions about what is proper and what is not, what she should and shouldn't do so he can feel good about himself. But the abusive man also needs rules to justify his abuse.

Yes, the rules the coercive controller imposes on his partner are about respecting him as superior, or he may impose rules and regulations to secure his needs and privileges that involve her services to him, access to sex, etc., but there is more to it. One of his needs . . . or better to say his secret desires . . . may be to occasionally 'punish' (abuse) his partner. Introducing the rules and regulations will then give him an excellent opportunity to blame the woman for breaking his rules. He will feel righteous in punishing her for her incorrect behaviour when she misbehaves or disobeys explicit or implicit 'guidelines' and 'codes of conducts' in his house. In some cases, the rules are constantly being revised as this will give him an opportunity to punish her more frequently.

He may also indirectly or unconsciously set up situations where he can feel let down or betrayed (she didn't do what he expected her to do), reinforcing the drive to punish her. This feeds his Abuser aspect addicted to abusing his partner. This doesn't mean that he is always aware of the game he plays! He may be totally unconscious of what he is doing and why he is doing it.

In her ground-breaking book *Rape in Marriage*, Diana Russell presented two lists side by side: Biderman's Chart of Coercion, and the common techniques of domestic perpetrators. The lists were virtually identical. The only difference was that whereas captors in North Korea deployed the techniques tactically, husbands appeared to be replicating the system of coercive control unconsciously.[4] **Jess Hill**

If we ask him why he is playing this 'control game' with his partner, we may find out that one of his ingrained beliefs is: 'If you don't control her, she will control you!' He is most sensitive and feels easily triggered when he interprets his partner's criticism or requests as 'her attempts to control him with her agenda' or 'her attempts to impose her rules on him'. If his partner wants to leave him, he can also interpret it as her attempt to control him with her decisions that affect his life too. To be controlled means to be exploited and misused. This is a dog-eat-dog world; you either control or you are controlled. Thus, from his perspective, his controlling her life—through imposing his rules and regulations on her and not vice versa—can be seen as a defence mechanism: 'As long as I control you, I am protected'. So he needs to make sure that he will not be coerced into obedience ('You try to tell me what to do and how I should behave and see what will happen!').

In addition to that, the control struggle can infuse an abuser with vital energy. He finds pleasure in controlling and imposing his rules because the 'game' is exciting. If his partner submits too soon, he may get bored. When boredom sets in, he feels that his life and relationship is depressing, but anger and the 'control or be controlled' game and style of relating can be a way to lift his mood. And, of course, the best part of the game is about punishing his partner for disrespecting him or not obeying his rules and regulations.

The Purpose of Entrapping the Victim: The reason the trapper sets up the animal trap is because he needs the animal—he will eat the animal, use it for his purposes, use its fur, skin, etc. What is the purpose of entrapping a human victim?

The cult leader and his people, as an example, will do their best to manipulate and control the members to keep them in the cult trap. Why? The organisation cannot survive without the members, so the purpose of overpowering and controlling them is to prevent them from leaving. Once they are locked in the system, the members will be gradually transformed into the batteries that keep the organisation going. They become suppliers of the human life force—they supply labour, money and/or various other services that will continuously stream from them to the cult leader and his organisation. On top of that, they may be used for the cult leader's pleasure. Yes, cult leaders may be power and adoration addicts, but many of them are sex addicts, too. They can be addicted to physical abuse, dabbed as punishment, as well. Exactly the same as some intimate partner abusers.

The domestic violence perpetrator does not break down the victims' self-esteem, isolate the victims, induce the victims' paralysing dependence on him or abuse them *in order to* control them. It's the other way around. In many cases, controllers control the victims *in order to* keep them in the trap. Why do they want to keep the victims in the trap? So they can continue with exploiting and abusing them. If they depend on what the trapped woman supplies, of course they will want to keep their victims entrapped.

We say that domestic violence stems from a desire to gain and maintain power and control over an intimate partner. Undoubtedly, there may be pleasure in the mere act of controlling and overpowering the woman and/or securing male privileges. However, this control game in the domestic violence drama is not only about gaining and maintaining power and control over a partner. It can be about feeding an addiction of abusing the victim as well, and the abused woman should know that.

The 'drug' for addicts who are addicted to the *high* of abusing their partners is an 'emotional cocktail'. This cocktail is generated by the perpetrator's abusive behaviour and the victim's suffering, pain, humiliation and fear. Therefore, the perpetrator's abuse must be provocative enough to spark a specific reaction from the woman. He needs her response. He may or may not be aware of that, but he feels compelled to inflict pain because he can't release his tension, or gain a sense of pleasure, unless she suffers.

Why does the pattern of his abusive behaviour escalate? He rationalises his abusive behaviour as punishment for what the victim says or does, but he may also become addicted to the 'experience of punishing'. Over time, he develops a tolerance, just like with any other addiction. To gain the same level of satisfaction, he must inflict more pain to generate a stronger emotional response from his victim, or he must inflict the same pain more often.

Some domestic violence perpetrators are psychopaths. The victims who understand the nature of these predators have a much better chance of escaping the trap.

Who are Psychopaths?

The behaviour of psychopaths is so strange that normal, ordinary people simply do not understand it. Are they aliens? In order to harm someone intentionally, most of us would have to be either seriously threatened by the person we were hurting, or we do that under the influence of intense rage. But inflicting pain calmly or for fun and thrills has no place in the emotional repertoire of normal, mainstream and 'good' people. Are they mad?

The concept of psychopathy is very important in the legal and judicial world. Are psychopaths mad, or simply bad? Psychopaths do meet current legal and psychiatric standards for sanity. They understand the rules of society and the conventional meanings of right and wrong. They are capable of controlling their behaviour and are aware of the consequences of their acts. The problem is that this knowledge often fails to deter them from abusive or antisocial behaviour.

How can we protect ourselves from them? Can we learn the art of psychopath-spotting?

There are many ways to describe them, but there is one particular theme that runs through the case history of psychopaths: a lack of empathy. Their inability to care about the pain and suffering of others is well known. The other personality traits that psychopaths possess are manipulativeness; irresponsibility and parasitic lifestyle; narcissism and grandiose sense of self-worth; superficial charm; lack of remorse; pathological lying; proneness to boredom and looking for excitement and thrill (some psychopaths describe 'doing crime' simply for excitement, thrills and the adrenaline rush); tendency to bully fragile people and suckers for power—they like to exercise power and control over others. They are often unfazed by the possibility of being found out. Most people would be devastated and humiliated by public exposure as liars and cheats, but not the psychopath. They are different from other people, but they do not see how they differ from others. As far as they are concerned, they are not different at all; they experience the same anger, frustration, rage, boredom as everyone else.

Warning! Psychopathy is not just about personality traits; it is a syndrome—a cluster of related symptoms. People who are not psychopaths may have some of these personality traits, too.

Here is how renowned expert in psychopathy, Professor Dr Robert D. Hare, describes the world of psychopaths in his book *Without Conscience*:

1. Many clinicians have commented that the emotions of psychopaths are so shallow as to be little more than proto-emotions: primitive responses to immediate needs.[5]

2. Their statements often reveal their belief that the world is made up of 'givers and takers', predators and prey, and that it would be very foolish not to exploit the weaknesses of others.[6]

3. They love to have power and control over others and seem unable to believe that other people have valid opinions different from theirs. They appear charismatic or "electrifying" to some people.[7]

4. Psychopaths tend to see any social exchange as a feeding opportunity. A good-looking, fast-talking psychopath and a victim who has "weak spots" is a devastating combination.[8]

What are the causes for this personality disorder? Is it nature, nurture or both? Some theories outline the position that a failure of the parent-child bond to form at the proper developmental stage (from birth to age two) is a major factor in the development of psychopathological problems, including psychopathy. Professor Hare disagrees and claims that there is little evidence that early attachment difficulties have anything to do with the development of psychopathy: 'While some assert that psychopathy is the result of attachment difficulties in infancy, I turn the argument around: In some children, the very failure to bond is a symptom of psychopathy.'[9] But this doesn't mean that parents and the environment are completely off the hook, he warns. Psychopathy emerges from a complex, and often poorly understood interplay between biological and social factors—genetic factors contribute to a basic personality structure, which in turn influences the way the individual responds to life experiences and social environment, he explained in *Without Conscience*.[10]

It is a well-known fact that some of the men who continually assault their partners are psychopaths. This fact has serious ramifications for the prevention of domestic violence and treatment programs. Psychotherapy, counselling or anger management programs, behaviour change programs for domestic violence perpetrators. Nothing seems to work with psychopaths! Why? A basic assumption of counselling is that you are able to recognise that you have a problem and need help. Another important component of effective counselling or behaviour change programs is that you actively participate with a counsellor, psychotherapist or group facilitator in the search for relief of your symptoms and emotional difficulties.

None of this has any relevance for psychopaths. They do not want counselling because their abusive behaviour towards others doesn't concern them. 'There is nothing wrong with me,' they believe. They can even be quite pleased with themselves and find their behaviour satisfying and rewarding. Besides, many psychopaths have an inflated view of their self-worth and importance and some simply don't see what is wrong with their behaviour. They have a sense of entitlement and see themselves as superior beings who have the right to live according to their own rules. If their behaviour is maladaptive and problematic, it is problematic for others or society, not for them. So, why would they seek help?

The psychopaths who abuse their partners may be pushed into behaviour change program for domestic violence perpetrators by family members, or because of a court order, or when they want to apply for parole. However, the majority of them will re-offend. This is because the abusive behaviour of psychopaths is notoriously resistant to change.

Most people are perplexed whenever a convicted killer, paroled from prison, promptly commits another violent offense. They are incredulous, "Why was such a person released?"

Their puzzlement would no doubt turn to outrage if they knew that in many cases the offender was a psychopath whose violent recidivism could have been predicted if the authorities – including the parole board – had only done their homework.[11] **Robert D. Hare**

But perhaps the most disturbing consequence of sending a psychopath into behaviour change programs for domestic violence abusers is the false sense of security or hope it can engender in the abuser's partner. 'He's been treated. He is now rehabilitated. He will not abuse me anymore', she might conclude, thus missing the chance to end her abusive relationship with a psychopath.

Alas, there are many women who manage to escape the domestic violence trap, only to come back to it again. Or they manage to break the relationship with a pathological narcissist, only to find themselves entangled in the toxic bond with another guy with a narcissistic need for grandiosity, entitlement, power or specialness. By the way, why are these pathological narcissists so abusive?

Many of them didn't have proper care in childhood, whether it was being under-protected or over-protected. A disregard of the child's basic needs disturbed their development of self-esteem and the ability to function effectively. In order to protect themselves, they invested a lot of energy building up the personality aspect 'I am special'. The aspect serves as a mask for character flaws and weaknesses. But to maintain the illusion about their specialness, the narcissists demand that they continuously receive mirroring and stroking from others. The attention, admiration, fear, respect or similar responses from 'admirers' is known as narcissistic supply; it can be anything that shields the narcissist from feeling a sense of shame or abandonment.

The narcissists need a narcissistic supply on a regular basis—they can be addicted to praise, or they need a submissive partner who confirms their beliefs around their omnipotence (aka power and control) in order to preserve their fragile ego. The partner is merely an object to serve their needs and provide narcissistic supply, and the pathological narcissists will use every form of abuse in order to make sure that their needs are met.

If the abused partner severs all contact, the narcissist can no longer feed on the victim, so his hoovering and baiting efforts will intensify. If his partner finds herself in a situation where she must be in contact with him (e.g. she shares parenting responsibilities with him) but she is trying not to react emotionally to his provocations, he will seek to trigger her by targeting her vulnerabilities. Why? He must. As with any addiction, being without a satisfying 'supply' has significant repercussions for the afflicted. It's therefore no surprise that faced with being unable to feed off of his partner, the very darkest aspects of the intimate partner abuser take over.

When the pathological narcissist feels disrespected, unappreciated or exposed (when his weaknesses are unmasked) he reacts with narcissistic rage. This fury and vitriol can be seriously dangerous. In the moment of narcissistic rage, he can be completely out of control. This does not mean 'out of control' with respect to intentionality, awareness of his actions or behaviours, nor consequently of legal responsibility. What makes his cruelty 'out of control' is that he is aware of what he is doing, but he doesn't care about the consequences of his abusive behaviour. What makes him mortally dangerous is his belief that: a) he is entitled to do so (to inflict pain or even kill the victim); and b) the victim deserves it.

There is a body of evidence suggesting that once a woman has become the victim of an abusive narcissist (especially if it happened in childhood) she is already unconsciously primed to enter the nasty 'game' that opens her up to further abuse. Having been victimised in childhood, she often internalises that there is something wrong with her or that she deserves this kind of abuse, and resigns herself to that fate. What makes her vulnerable is her inability to discern what's going on in the toxic bond with her abusers.

Indeed, in many cases, the abuse is very insidious, covert, cunning and often indirect. This form of intimate partner abuse is often carried out in a subtle and clandestine manner because narcissists go to great extent to avoid being observed publicly as being abusive. They inflict much harm, and on top of that the Dr Jekyll and Mr Hyde behaviour of the narcissist (loving one minute and totally enraged the next) can be very confusing for the victim. For example, a woman who is abused by her narcissistic spouse may hate the conditions she is living in: her unhealthy relationship and all the abuse that goes with it. On the other hand, she fears being lonely, or she is scared of a violent reprisal from her narcissistic captor, so she may choose to stay put. She experiences the cognitive dissonance—an aversive state when there is a conflict between two beliefs or opinions—but she tells herself that he only fights with her because he loves and cares for her. Such a line of thinking will reduce her anxiety, allowing her to bond with her abuser, to the point that she will even protect him from others. Or she may refuse the help when people attempt to rescue her or encourage her to leave the abusive man. She may become so enmeshed in the relationship with him that she feels that her world would fall apart if her marriage ended.

One more woman killed by her partner, this week

Why do so many abused women return to their abusers? Experienced caseworkers who work in family violence services can help us answer this question. They explain that as long as we focus exclusively on the woman and 'analyse' her, without clearly seeing what her abuser does to get her back, we cannot see why she goes back to a partner who repeatedly hurts her. The caseworkers know very well that such a woman's decision is often a result of the abuser's appeals to her sympathy, through descriptions of his own pain and suffering. Her abusive partner gives her an emotional account of his personal distress, and thus instils in her a sense of pity and guilt. Here is the typical domestic violence story from a caseworker's everyday practice:

You meet her at the hospital. She has been beaten by her partner. What's happened? The victim explains: 'He punched me in my stomach a few times, he strangled me to the point I could not breathe, and I fell on the floor. He spat in my face and held me down, strangling me again. I have two broken fingers and have pain in the chest and ribs. I have been totally abused; I really hate him!'

You are told that the guy is very remorseful for what he has done; he is standing in front of the hospital, crying. A few minutes later, the police arrive and arrest him. The victim is not feeling sorry for him at all. She is absolutely determined that she doesn't want to see him ever again!

Sometime later, you learn that she dropped the charges. That didn't surprise the caseworkers who were working with her. As many as seventy percent of the victims recant.

Seventy percent? Even half of that is a staggering figure! But why do the women do that? Exploring the abovementioned example of the woman who said, 'Never again!' but dropped the charges against her abuser nevertheless, you realise that she has gone through her own inner emotional cycle that consists of several stages:

The beginning: She intended on following through with prosecution. She experienced fear, pain, degradation and anger for being abused. She decided that she would not tolerate it any more.

The middle stage: She moved from anger to sadness, guilt and regret. She genuinely wanted to leave him, but she also felt confused and turned her attention inward, looking for what she had said or done to set him off. She felt partially responsible and blamed herself for causing the abuse. Besides, he called her all the time, promising that he'd never do it again. He was very remorseful, and she wanted to believe his promises that he would change, so she gave him one more chance.

The end of the cycle: She finished by helping *him* out. The roles in their relationship have been reversed—with him becoming a victim of distress and suffering, and her becoming his caretaker. Amazing! How did he manage to turn her into his caretaker? The Men's Behaviour Change Program group facilitators who work with domestic violence perpetrators will tell you that he has used the standard guidelines for winning over a woman. The guidelines are as follows:

1. Initially, she'll refuse to help you. She will stand up for herself and resist you. She might even threaten to talk to the police about some other, even nastier, incidents. You express regret, you apologise. You promise it won't happen again, but minimise the abuse through denial and convince her it didn't happen like she remembers. Then you shift the blame and explain that she was actually at fault. If she reminds you about what you did to her, respond with: 'But do you remember that before anything happened, you did (this and that...) to me!' Clearly indicate that she initiated the conflict. If her stance about what happened does not change—and the probability is that it won't even when you express regret, say 'sorry' and promise that it won't happen again—keep portraying yourself as a victim and proceed to the next step.

2. If you are separated, when you see her or call her, always describe your suffering, pain and depression. Give details about the terrible psychological condition you are in. If you are in jail, clearly describe the jail conditions as intolerable, or how lonely and miserable your current life is, how much you miss her, how much you are hurting without her love. You mustn't lose contact with her! When you call her or send her text messages, always say something positive about her and your relationship. Remind her that you share a unique bond not understood by others, and that you are soul mates. Invoke images of the happy life you had together, your dreams, your songs

. . . depict special places you visited, or the events and the place where you met and shared romantic moments. Use poetry, roses and chocolates or other objects and imagery to solidify the pleasant moments you've spent together . . . but don't forget to mention how much you suffer. If even that is not enough, and probably it isn't, proceed to the next step.

3. Her stance will soften when you become increasingly depressed, anxious and threaten suicide. You must move her from resolve and anger to pity, guilt and regret. Appealing to her pity and getting her to soothe and take care of you are your best strategies. Use them!

4. Maintain contact with her. Keep reminding her of your lonely life or that you're sinking into serious depression. Tell her about your preoccupations with suicidal ideation and that your life has no meaning without her. Plead that your fate is in her hands now. The key is to convince her that if you did something 'harmful' to yourself (or to someone else), she would be to blame because she didn't prevent it although she could. Remember, the key words are pity and guilt. Keep pushing until you get this 'guilt response' from her.

5. When the conversation starts revolving around her trying to help you prevent your suicide attempts, assuage your suffering and depression, or get out of jail... gradually guide her through the legal process to the point where she'll drop the charges. Give her clear instructions what she should say or do.

The sad end of this story

Six months later, you are reading two articles on the same page in the local newspapers. One is about the bashed woman from the caseworker's story. She returned to her abusive partner, and the man killed her this time. She died of multiple injuries and strangulation. Another article is about a heroin addict who died of a drug overdose. 'What a coincidence,' you think while noticing the commonalities in these two stories. If only you could have persuaded the woman not to go back to her abuser. He is addicted to abusing his intimate partner, and the death from his 'overdose' will be hers!

Strangulation Trauma in Domestic Violence

Strangulation has been recognised as one of the most severe forms of domestic violence. It is also recognised as a marker for future violence. It is not only inherently dangerous but is predictive of an escalation in domestic violence offences, including homicides.[12]

However, strangulation is a relatively under-reported, under-prosecuted, and under-treated situation in both the law enforcement and medical communities alike. In the past, strangulation in domestic violence was not aggressively prosecuted. The general feeling was that if it left no marks or did not immediately kill the victim, then it was not a serious incident. However, some governments have passed laws to make non-fatal strangulation a separate offence under the Criminal Code.

It is exasperating to see how many women unknowingly participate in their own defeat, simply because they do not understand the mechanics behind the patterns of abuse in toxic relationships. So what can we do about it? How can we protect our sisters and daughters from abusive men who manipulate women's needs or insecurities to lure them into abusive relationships? Knowledge is power. Once the woman gains insight into the re-offending perpetrator's underlying motivation, and the addictive nature of the repetitive patterns of abuse are made more widely known, it will be easier for women to defend and protect themselves from intimate partner abuse. But that's not enough. She needs to know herself, too.

There are many women who have managed to escape one coercive controller's spider web only to fall prey to another's. How to prevent it? This type of intimate partner abuser is skilled at detecting and ruthlessly exploiting the woman's weak spots. Her best defence and 'prevention strategy' are to understand what her weak spots are and to be wary of the men who zoom in on them. And yet even that is not enough.

The professionals who work with the victims of domestic violence claim that in a number of cases the answer to the question, 'Why are so many women repeatedly abused and killed by their partners and ex-partners?' is very simple: 'Because the justice system has failed miserably in protecting them from the abusers.' Weak justice responses make the victim feel incapable of seeking and getting help. In addition to it, the existing legal system makes victims responsible for themselves. If the abused woman doesn't provide a formal statement or doesn't want to continue with prosecution (perhaps because she is afraid, or she wants to get past the violent event and do not want to relive the incident by talking about it), the chances of the abuser being convicted are very slim.

The police dismiss the case and it's over with. Even when they are charged, domestic violence re-offenders often receive only minor consequences for their offenses. They would have their court dates, give their sob stories to the judge, and get back out on unsecured bonds. They can be charged many times and still there is no efficient system of tracking them. The domestic violence offenders continue with their violence; their behaviour escalates over time, which could result in serious injury or even death for victims.

David Kennedy, a New York criminologist who developed the Offender Focused Domestic Violence Initiative (OFDVI)—a novel approach to combatting domestic violence based on the strategy 'focused deterrence' (or 'pulling levers')—revolutionised domestic violence prevention and intervention.[13] When he was asked about his overall goal of the OFDVI strategy, he stated: 'We wanted to keep these women from being killed. Domestic violence has been growing in the extent to which society and agencies take it seriously for several decades now, but when you look at the steps that have been taken, almost all of those steps have been about the victims and the situation of the victims. And a lot of it has put additional burdens on victims to take action, protect themselves and extend themselves. And very, very little has been done that is even aimed at changing the behaviour of the abusers, and none of that has been very effective whether its enforcement or treatment or programs or fill in the blank... The most fundamental thing that we were about here was to try to fix that in some meaningful way.'[14]

The successes and benefits of applying OFDVI—the intervention model that was first introduced in Boston in the 1990s to reduce youth gun violence and was later used to curb domestic abuse and homicide in the city of High Point in North Carolina—have been extremely promising. The strategy wasn't designed to change a few offenders, but to change their attitude towards domestic violence, the creators of OFDVI claim.[15] 'This is in stark contrast to the current approach being taken against men who use domestic violence in Australia,' said Jess Hill, author of *See What You Made Me Do* and a fierce advocate for OFDVI.[16]

Chapter 12

THE VICTIMS WHO HAVE DIFFICULTY LEAVING

There are many ways of saying, 'It's the victim's fault; she should have left him earlier,' and there are many labels that implicitly blame victims for the effects of domestic violence on both themselves and their children. Some say that co-dependency is one of those labels. However, we can't disregard it. Co-dependency indeed can keep women entrapped in a snare of chronic misery and distress or pull them back again and again into the dangerous cycles of intimate partner abuse.

The definition of co-dependency—also known as *relationship addiction*—has evolved over the last few decades to describe a type of dysfunctional relationship pattern. A co-dependent is a person who can't function from his or her innate self, but instead organises life around another person(s) and has difficulties leaving a relationship with an abusive, controlling, selfish, narcissistic individual or an addict addicted to drugs, alcohol, gambling, etc.

The keywords that can help us to understand this concept are the words *personal boundaries* and *responsibility*. Co-dependents' problems with intimacy and communication in many cases arise due to confusion about personal boundaries and a sense of responsibility to others. They may have a warped sense of obligation and feel guilty even though they are not responsible for the problems created by their partners or family members. An abusive man then can easily take advantage of a woman who has a problem with boundaries. He can exploit her need to be in a close relationship or exploit her inability to stop feeling responsible for him and thus find the exit from her toxic bond with him.

Co-dependency usually begins by becoming attached to someone and ends with dependency on that person. 'Once attachment bonds take hold, dependency on the relationship turns into addiction,' Darlene Lancer explained in her book *Codependency for Dummies*.[1] Co-dependent people often define themselves by their efforts to take care of someone else because they 'need to be needed'. One's own needs and wants become secondary to those of the other person, and some women stay in dysfunctional relationships with men because they are, paradoxically, dependent on their partner's dependence on them. That is one of the reasons why co-dependency is described as relationship addiction.

Indeed, many women who fall victim to co-dependency have a strong Giver aspect in their personality. Relationships are their priority, and the best way to stay in a relationship is to be needed. Different people pride themselves for different personal qualities or achievements in life, but this type of a woman prides herself for being helpful, available, empathic and sensitive to other people's needs. 'People depend on my help. I can't leave them,' she says.

However, the hidden motives for being a selfless Giver can be hidden even from herself. She acts as if she is giving freely but she may secretly keep track of every act of kindness she gives and resent those who fail to return the favour or those who do not show appreciation for her gifts of love, attention or care. Nevertheless, she moulds herself to please others or adjusts her life to take care of other people. What about her needs? She, of course, needs love, respect and acknowledgement, yet she does not openly disclose that. Why not? Isn't that what a relationship is all about: mutual support, giving and receiving? Isn't it natural to depend upon others, and to expect them to return the favour or affection? Yes, it is, but co-dependence is not the same as healthy interdependence.

Nobody is totally free from the tendency to give in order to receive. We don't always give freely of our services or affection to others without expecting some emotional or material return. Often, when packets of affection are given to another, a debit note is handed over: 'I am giving you love, so you owe me...' In some marriages, the 'love' is given in exchange for something else, whether it be material possessions or returned emotion, a sense of recognition, satisfaction or a sense of security.

The woman with a strong Giver personality aspect secretly expects to receive in return for her giving, but there are usually two hidden beliefs (or two 'rules of conduct') attached to it. The first one is: You don't openly ask others to meet your needs—that's egocentrism and selfishness! The second one is: You have no right to expect your partner to meet your needs before you meet his.

She doesn't ask others to meet her emotional needs because the most frightening words in her vocabulary are the words *egocentrism* and *selfishness*. The internalised childhood programming reminds her that to be accepted by others she has to make her own needs subordinate to others; in other words, she mustn't be selfish. As a child, she would be praised for being helpful and selfless even when she simply attempted to coerce someone into appreciating or loving her, and that is usually how she has been trained to be a Giver—which means to fulfil her own needs indirectly, through giving and caring for others.

If she harbours the belief that she has to meet other people's needs first, she tends to assume responsibility for meeting her partner's needs, and even feel guilty for his distress or misbehaviour. If he is distressed, that means that she hasn't been able to do her job properly. She is not a good partner, and she deserves to be punished! Or she may believe that her partner's misdeeds are her fault, so she feels guilty or takes responsibility for his behaviour.

On the other side, she can easily get hooked on positive strokes and the kind of attention she receives when her partner expresses his adoration, reverence and love for her: 'What would I be without you?'; 'No one can do what you can do'; 'I can't live without you!' His loving attention is like oxygen she can't live without as she desperately needs his love, protection or appreciation.

The Giver and the Abuser

Some women with a dominant Giver aspect in their personalities report painful childhood experiences with their fathers or father figures. They describe their fathers as punitive, demanding or controlling, or they felt they had to meet rigid expectations in terms of how they appeared or behaved, otherwise they felt unworthy of their father's love. To get acknowledgement and appreciation, or fulfil their needs for closeness, they have unconsciously created a pleasing personality so that their father would notice them, love them or at least respect and appreciate what they have been doing for others. Even if their father did not reciprocate with giving back, the girl would hide a sense of disappointment or frustration that she was not getting much in return and keep giving and giving. When she grows up, she finds herself in a relationship with a man who resembles her father—she keeps giving but doesn't get much in return—and ends up as a victim of exploitation or abuse.

However, when she feels abused and misused, even the woman with a strong Giver aspect can react explosively, attempt to sever her connections with the abuser and fight for her freedom. Feeling deeply hurt, disrespected and humiliated, she may react with rage, or find herself caught up in intense conflicts and fantasies about revenge. The conflict can escalate into a full-scale war, but no matter how determined she is to stand up for herself, she still may have difficulties leaving her partner for good. She may leave him, come back and leave him again. Why is it difficult for her to make up her mind and leave the re-offending abuser? There may be several reasons for that. One of them is the issue of identity. Her abusive or violent partner may find his identity in being a strong Tough Guy ('No one is going to mess with me!'), but she finds her identity in relationship, so she may experience the loss of a relationship as the loss of her identity ('Who will I be without my partner?').

There are other reasons she may find it difficult to leave him for good. Being lonely and losing her partner's loving attention can be very difficult and depressing for the woman with this type of personality ('I feel miserable when I am single'). Or she may blame herself for his abusive or violent behaviour and may fear what might happen to him if she 'abandoned' him ('He won't be able to survive if I left him. He might kill himself!').

If her abusive partner was a victim of abuse in his childhood, her compassion for him may do away with her decision to protect herself. Some women tolerate their partner's abuse because they see him as a damaged little boy, but if she supports, takes care of him and heals him with her love, he will become the good husband she is sure he could become. This is her dream, and until she gives up that dream, she is not ready to leave him, no matter how abusive he is. Or she may believe, 'If I hold on long enough, he will realise that I don't deserve to be mistreated and he will change.'

Some victims believe that the good times they have together will make the bad times insignificant and easily forgettable. The 'good time' is powerful glue. Her need for love can be so strong that she craves moments of closeness with her abusive partner even at the expense of her own safety and security. Even when she finds the courage to leave, press charges or stand up for herself, the craving for closeness and attention will pull her back to him. Moreover, we can hear her saying that the 'conflict' (his hostility or abuse) between her and him is not always bad for their relationship because it can serve the 'constructive purpose of drawing them closer together'.

Warning! This belief that an episode of hostility or violence can serve the purpose of drawing them closer together can cost the woman her life!

Where does that idea come from? From the cycle of abuse.

The cycle of abuse

There are a number of factors that can influence the woman's decision not to leave her abuser: self-blame; denial; loyalty to the institution and sanctity of marriage; financial situation; feeling responsible for the partner's and/or children's wellbeing; fear of the perpetrator, etc. But the cycle of violence theory has significantly contributed to our understanding why the abused woman who, even when she can safely leave her abusive partner, still chooses to stay with him or come back to him.

The theory that domestic abuse has a pattern and occurs in a predictable cycle was originally developed by Dr Lenore E. Walker. 'In 1979, Walker interviewed 1,500 battered women and found that each of them described a similar pattern of spousal abuse. In her research, Walker identified this pattern as the "cycle of violence," which contains three distinct phases'.[2]

The cycle begins with a period of positive or close relations. The abuser may behave in a charming, caring, gentle, and affectionate way with the victim, and make the victim feel accepted and loved. Over time, tension develops. During this 'tension-building' phase, the tension can be generated or triggered by anything. 'The battering incident occurs in the second stage of the cycle. This phase is sometimes called the "acting out phase" or "acute battering phase", which may or may not include physical contact; it may involve verbal, emotional, and/or psychological abuse.'[3]

This phase typically ends when the batterer stops and his physiological tension declines. The third and final stage of the cycle is the 'honeymoon phase' when the batterer tries to reunite with his partner. The batterer may feel remorseful but will minimise, normalise or justify the abuse by claiming that it was the victim's fault. He may shower the victim with gifts, compliments, promises, demonstrations of love and acts of affection necessary for the victim to remain in the relationship. However, something will soon trigger him again...

But, let's forget about the perpetrator for the moment and go back to the woman who stays with him (and even claims that the episodes of his abuse can draw them closer) or comes back to him despite her prior decision to leave him for good. What is it in this triangular cycle (1.Tension-Building Phase; 2. Explosion Phase; and 3. Calm or Honeymoon Phase) that sucks the victim back in to the status quo? Hoovering?

'Hoovering' is a very suitable concept for understanding not only the cycle of abuse in abusive relationships, but also what happens in the mind of the victims as they are moved from one phase to the next. The metaphor, taken from the popular brand of vacuum cleaners, is used to describe how the female victim gets 'sucked back' in to the relationship with her abuser.

Hoovering is a tactic that ensures the abusers do not lose their partners. It is most likely to happen at the point where the perpetrator realises the victim wants to leave him or pull away from the relationship; wants to report about the abuse, retaliate or seek help from others; or tries to establish firmer boundaries within the relationship. The abuser fears the consequences of his abusive behaviour and/or the loss of his abused partner so he may shower her with gifts, compliments, promises, demonstrations of love and acts of affection to win back her trust and therefore maintain the status quo.

During the pursuit or honeymoon phase, the perpetrator may promise to never be violent again. He may himself believe this. He asks for forgiveness, may offer to go to counselling, is charming and may do anything to get things back to normal. Intimacy can increase during this period. They make up and perhaps have passionate sex. This phase marks an apparent end of violence, with assurances that it will never happen again, or that the abuser will do his best to change.

The perpetrator may be very attentive to the partner's needs, including buying gifts and helping around the house. The abused partner may insist on a list of demands and conditions that the perpetrator must meet in order to be forgiven and allowed back in from the cold. He is willing to comply and may even be grateful to be given concrete demands that can serve as reassurance the relationship is not over. She usually receives his loving attention and a lot of positive signs that she is important to him. Finally, he is meeting her needs!

Warning! His 'meeting her needs' after the episodes of abuse can be the most seductive lure that keeps a woman in the domestic violence trap!

And just as dust gets caught up in the vacuum cleaner, many victims get sucked back in to the bond when the abusive partner exhibits 'improved' (desirable) behaviour. What is in this tactic that makes it so efficient? Hoovering feels good for the victim—and that's the point! When you are being hoovered, your warm-and-fuzzy buttons are pushed, your feelings are validated, your needs are met, your dreams about love come true, your opinions matter, you are needed, you are the most important person in the world to that certain person. You might find yourself thinking, 'Finally! My message is getting through!' or 'He really does love me!' But watch out. Slave-owners know they have to feed slaves to keep them alive and productive, and abusers are often adept at giving their victims enough of what they want to keep them where they want them.

During the calm period, it could seem as though the abuser has changed. Both partners drift back towards their initial or default state when they turn their energy to mundane matters such as work, family, paying bills and taking care of everyday responsibilities. They are less vigilant in policing and controlling his anger outbursts. They communicate again; however, he may begin to feel resentful of the imposed 'control-yourself' attitude and frustrated by the limitations placed on him. It's just a matter of time before he'll get to the 'tension-building' phase.

This cycle can occur hundreds of times in abusive relationships. The violence may become more intense and the cycles more frequent. In some cases of severe domestic violence, the length of the cycle diminishes over time so that the 'reconciliation' and 'calm' stages disappear. Walker argues that 'each phase becomes shorter and shorter in duration and distance from the previous incident and phase, until the victim either escapes or is killed.'[4]

Each phase becomes shorter and shorter until the victim either escapes or is killed. **Lenore E. A. Walker**

How do we help a woman to find the exit from the domestic abuse trap? Of course, psycho-educating her about *what* she is going through is an important first step. She certainly needs to hear the information about the cycle of abuse or the pattern that tends to escalate. She needs to know that hoovering can easily contaminate the victim's clear thinking so she, for example, can't see the pattern or she believes the last episode of his abuse is just one more isolated event. However, understanding *what* she is going through is not enough. Many abused women ask *why* their abusive partner repeatedly abuses them.

Lenore E. Walker's theory of cyclic abuse does not explain the cause but rather the dynamic of abuse. Neither does this theory explain why the violence becomes more serious as time moves on.' Furthermore 'research is critical to our understanding of the etiology of violence and aggression,' Walker writes in the second edition of her ground-breaking book *The Battered Woman Syndrome*.[5]

And yet, if the victim of domestic violence ponders the question 'Why is my abusive husband repeating the cycles of violence?' this is the typical answer she may hear: 'Partner violence is considered a learned behaviour that is used to obtain and maintain power and control over a woman. The reason the perpetrator chooses to use violent behaviour is because violence wins; it works and the abuser gets what he wants in the relationship.' This theoretical approach is widely used in current domestic violence programs.

However, explaining domestic violence as a 'controlling patriarchal behaviour pattern of men who feel entitled to abuse their wives to maintain control over them', may not be good enough to answer the question: 'Why does my partner *repeatedly* abuse me and why does the pattern of abuse escalate?'

We argue that the re-offending abuser goes through the phases in the cycle of abuse strikingly similar to the phases in the cycle of addiction—and, in fact, in some cases, the cycle of abuse *is* a cycle of behavioural addiction. The re-offending domestic violence perpetrator's abusive behaviour may escalate because of tolerance, and the victim needs to know it.

Why didn't she leave him earlier?

Why didn't she escape immediately when she saw that he was abusive? There is no straightforward answer to that question. The reasons she didn't leave him for good the first time he abused her are multiple and often include the list of various rationales for her staying: 'It's not him! It's his 'problem' (alcohol, drugs, unemployment, his mother's influence), and once the problem is fixed, he'll stop abusing me'.

Other rationales include 'I simply refused to acknowledge that he hurt me intentionally; I'd try to forgive and forget'; 'It's me, I provoked him'; 'It's just not possible to leave. I have no money, nowhere to go'; 'He promised me that he'd do whatever it takes to change and not hurt me anymore'; 'The prospect of being alone looked too awful'; Even an abusive relationship is better than no relationship'; 'I was worried about finding someone else; I thought I wouldn't be able to find a better partner. This worry deterred me from leaving sooner'; 'I was determined to endure the relationship, no matter what, because I saw it as my duty because I didn't have a father and I wanted my child to have a father.'

As long as victims' fear of leaving him is stronger than the fear of staying, they will refuse help and resist efforts from professionals, friends or family. They may look stubborn, irrational or naïve, but the reason they stay is simply because the fear of leaving—whatever the reason is: 'He'll kill me if I leave him!'; 'It's too painful to be without him. I don't want to live without him'; 'I have nowhere to go, I can't survive without him', etc.—is stronger than the fear of staying.

It is a well-known fact that on average a woman will leave her violent partner a few times before she leaves for good. It's not easy to leave an abusive relationship, especially when you have been conditioned to stay or you crave the closeness with the man when he is not abusive.

Traumatic bonding

'No ordinary relationship offers the same degree of intensity as the pathological bond with the abuser,' writes Judith Herman in her book *Trauma and Recovery*.[6] A typical abusive relationship is by definition a rollercoaster. When the abuser starts exhibiting abusive behaviour, he usually switches back and forth between abuse and remorse. After the episode of abuse, he may plea for forgiveness and is attentive and loving again. This can be very confusing for the victim. Why does he do that?

The situation of alternating unpleasant and pleasant emotional states is known in learning theory as *intermittent reinforcement*. This type of conditioning can be highly effective in producing a desirable behaviour. The victim of intimate partner abuse can find herself in a similar situation. She is conditioned to stay in a toxic bond through the specific combination of intermittent *punishment* (abuse) and *reward* in the form of praises, gifts, loving attention and affection ('I love you so much, I can't live without you...').

Another important factor in this type of conditioning is unpredictability. The moments of closeness and tenderness are unpredictable, but they are so intense and fulfilling that the woman winds up staying with the abuser in the hope that moments like that will happen again.

The conditioning can sometimes look like this: The person first rewards you with a shower of affection. Nobody has ever met your needs for closeness, friendship, affection, like this before. Being with that person is pure joy! He sees something deep and valuable inside of you or tells you how lovely you are. You feel great when you are with him, and you want to tell him everything about yourself. Sometime later, you get the cold shoulder. He doesn't reciprocate your love this time. You believe, consciously or unconsciously, if you keep giving him more of your attention, money, services or power over your life, things will once again feel like they did before. If you invest more time, energy and affection into him, he'll get that amazing, loving feeling for you again. Indeed, every once in a while, your interest, love or affection for him is reciprocated. So, you try harder.

The alternating 'reward and punishment' in an abusive relationship conditions the victim to tolerate the abuse and stay in the traumatic bond. Traumatic bonding acts as the superglue and cements the relationship. It is resistant to change. Many women stay in abusive relationships because they have formed this type of attachment with their abusers. They may become emotionally dependent on their abusive partner because he occasionally shows kindness, love, attention and praise.

Again, traumatic bonding is created as a result of the ongoing cycles of abuse. The woman is subjected to unpleasant arousal during the incident of abuse, but she may also experience pleasant relief or release of tension when the incident is over. She feels good when he is attentive and kind, and his loving behaviour induces her to stay in the relationship.

The more invested (emotionally, financially, etc.) the woman is in the relationship, the more compelled she feels to stay. The more driven to stay, the more she will defend her abuser or justify her staying with him. She may escape during the episodes of abuse but come back to him later. 'He has abused me so many times; everything in my mind tells me to leave him for good, but the thought of leaving him makes me panicky. When I am separated from him, I find myself "craving" him and wanting to do whatever it takes to get at least crumbs of his kindness, attention, or affection... So I go back to him. Am I addicted to abuse? What's wrong with me?' asked the client who believed she was a 'masochist'.

No doubt, some abused women may indeed appear to be addicted to their abusers, but abuse is not what they are addicted to. It is love, closeness and intimacy that they need. We all have a need to form attachments with others, but the women with strong need for intimacy, affection and attention, praise or recognition—especially those who have the 'dependency dream'—seem to be the most vulnerable to the abuser's manipulative strategies to keep them entrapped in toxic relationships.

The dependency dream

In psychology, the wish to be taken care of (to have a caring parent) is called dependency. We adults are supposed to be autonomous and self-sustaining. We shouldn't rely on another as a child relies on a parent. Of course, we do recognise that we need each other for emotional support, intimacy, love, validation, for giving and receiving affection, and that is perfectly acceptable. However, underlying the mature interdependency is often the hidden longing of our Inner Child and its infantile yearning that is never completely outgrown.

This covert dependency—the wish to be taken care of or sheltered by a parental figure—is dabbed the 'dependency dream'. It can impair our clear thinking. If we recognise these suppressed wishes for what they are, we can decontaminate our rational thinking. Our rational thinking can be contaminated by a mixture of the abuser's manipulations and our Inner Child's delusions. But we usually don't recognise it or, even worse, we deny it. This denial makes us vulnerable to exploitation or abuse. How? For example, a woman ensnared in the domestic violence trap may believe that she will not be able to survive without her partner. What she really means is that it would be very difficult for her Inner Child aspect to emotionally starve again, without the closeness to the man and his loving attention, or his support and protection.

Field of intimacy

'Unlike other crimes, domestic violence is complicated by the not-infrequent complicity of victims who love their abusers,' some say. They are confused because they do not see that the victim does not love her abuser. So why does she stay with him, then?

We may think that a victim of abuse misses her abuser. But she doesn't miss the Abuser aspect in the man's personality. Sometimes she doesn't even miss the man. It is the emotional state that she craves—those moments in the field of intimacy, in between episodes of abuse, as though these moments have their own existence, independent of him.

What is it about intimacy that we often so desperately crave? Intimacy is a field, much like an energy field in physics.[7] It's like a magnetic force that pulls people together. This heightened emotional state can be so powerful that once experienced, it is never forgotten and is sought ever after. Like the hero in the movie *Shangri-La*, we are unable to find happiness again in the ordinary world after returning from Shangri-La.

If we have felt love and intimacy with someone, and then we are cut off from it, there is a tremendous motivation to get back to it—a strong desire to reconnect with that person even when he or she is abusive towards us. That's why some people with bad experiences with the field of intimacy avoid the pull out of fear that they will end up hurt again. But if we know that the 'pull' doesn't come *from* the abusive man but *through* him (what we yearn for is a state of consciousness, not the abuser), it's much easier to resist the urge to get back into the toxic bond with an abusive man.

However, in some cases, it is not the need for love and intimacy but a sense of powerlessness that keeps the woman in the toxic bond.

Learned helplessness

'It's heartbreaking, but there's not much that a free society can do if women insist on making bad choices (going back to the domestic violence perpetrator). Why can't she see the pattern and what might happen to her?' We often hear this question from judges, police officers, friends and relatives of the victim. Before we attempt to answer it, we need to understand the concept of powerlessness and the impact of repeated violence on the victim.

The fight-or-flight-response is the psycho-physiological reaction to a stressful situation. When we experience stress, the fight-or-flight response is activated, and we are usually very active (either fighting or fleeing) because we want to deal with the stressful situation. But the reaction to trauma—when we can't fight back nor escape from the situation—is different. We feel helpless because we can't do anything to protect ourselves. However, unless trauma is repeated, this feeling of helplessness will usually dissipate over time. But if we are exposed to repeated overwhelming experiences within a certain period of time, and we believe we are powerless to change the situation, we may easily become *passive*. We give up resisting and accept whatever situation we are in. That's how we may become conditioned to stay, even when we can leave.

The scientist Martin Seligman clearly demonstrated this in his experiment with dogs.[8] After being conditioned, the dogs refused to escape electric shocks even when they could. The same is with humans. If, over the course of our lifetime, we have experienced abuse and loss of control in the incidents of abuse, we become a pessimist. We create the belief system that there is no escape, and even when escape is offered, we may not act. We don't act because we have 'learned helplessness'.

This phenomenon called learned helplessness can help us to understand the impact of repeated abuse on a victim's behaviour. The abuser has power over the victim, so he maintains control of the situation. The victim learns that she is helpless to do anything about the circumstances.

The additional problem is that many victims don't only feel helpless to escape, but they also feel helpless to prevent the abuse. The abuse in domestic violence is a repetitious pattern; the abuser simply needs 'his dosage of her distress', just as a drug addict needs his drug, and whatever the woman does to prevent his abuse, it doesn't work.

Repeated abuse or physical violence diminishes the abused woman's motivation to react, so she becomes passive. A chronic feeling of powerlessness takes over because she has accepted the futility of her attempts to break free from the situation. Her cognitive ability to perceive the situation she has found herself in is now changed. She believes that she cannot do anything to protect herself, even when she can. As a result, her emotional well-being becomes precarious; she is more prone to sink into depression.

Some abusers indeed succeed in overpowering us because they have mastered the cruel art of exploiting our vulnerabilities and weakness, or our needs for love and intimacy. The longer we stay with them, the more we delay doing the important inner work we need to do. The inner work is to heal our wounds, expand our limiting beliefs, and ask ourselves, 'How can I grow from this experience so it doesn't become a painful pattern?'

Chapter 13

THE ANATOMY OF EMOTIONS

Emotions are messengers from our inner worlds that demand to be honoured and attended to. They are a complex information-processing system, designed to organise behaviour rapidly (e.g. flight-or-fight response), so they perform a vital function that helps us to survive and thrive. As the Latin word for emotion, *emovere* (move) suggests, emotions literally move us—psychologically and physiologically—into new response modes: to act, to avoid, to approach. They also shape and organise our experiences, help us to understand ourselves and others, and to discern what is going on in the external world as well. Emotions guide the decision-making process. Without emotion to guide us, we are bereft of preferences and have nothing to move us in one or another direction.

Emotions have been seen traditionally as part of our primitive animal nature, as something 'irrational'; therefore, not to be trusted. Reason, by contrast, has been thought to reflect our higher evolutionary self. However, both emotions and sensations, gut feelings included, are

necessary for rational thinking. To make a rational decision, we must feel the consequences of that decision, and
emotions help us with that. How thinking, emotions and
physical sensations are interconnected is best illustrated
by the kind of choices people make based on 'gut' feelings
when they are able to hear the message from the gut.

Unfortunately, we are not always able to hear these
messages. Everyday human life is based on the assumption that there is something wrong with us if we feel
certain emotions, so we decide not to 'hear' them. We
tend to 'fix' ourselves by accepting some of them and re-
jecting others. Never admit, even to yourself, that you feel
envious! Out of the seven deadly sins, five of them are
emotions: pride, envy, anger, greed and lust. An additional problem is gender stereotypes. Gender stereotypes
define who should feel what: Males should not feel fear,
but it is okay if they feel anger; females need to be soft
and gentle, they should not feel anger, but it is okay if
they feel fear.

There are many prejudices about emotions. One of
them is that if we allow ourselves to feel 'improper' emotions, we may lose control, act upon them and behave
inappropriately; we may 'translate' emotions into hurtful,
destructive and/or self-destructive behaviour, so it's better not to feel them!

We also tend to label emotions as positive or negative.
Such labels indirectly indicate that some aspects of our
psyche or certain life experiences charged with negative
emotions are not acceptable; therefore, they should be
suppressed or rejected. We then tend to mask unacceptable feelings with others that are less threatening or more
tolerable. Fear, for example, wears countless masks, many
of which are not immediately recognised. The mask that
hides the fear of abandonment could be not only anger

('Of course I am angry! You just walk away like I don't matter!'), but the need to control, or continuous dramas and conflicts with others. Such conflicts are often the result of our inability to recognise and accept fear (the fear of losing someone, for example), or not allowing ourselves to experience it.

Another complication with masking or misusing an emotion is that the emotion may become dysfunctional. For example, authentic anger helps solve a problem in the moment when we need to protect ourselves. Dysfunctional anger, on the other hand, is often nothing but a manipulation to get a particular response from others. In addition, some children learned that by showing one specific emotion such as anger or rage, they could get what they wanted or they got the attention they were seeking. Or they learned that they would not get the reaction they craved without using abusive behaviour. Showing a particular emotion helped them to get their needs met, so they re-play the same emotional and behavioural pattern in their adult relationships. They repeat the pattern of feeling angry, for example, and then justify their 'favourite emotion'—and the abusive behaviour fuelled by it—by blaming the victim.

Every genuinely experienced emotion is an opportunity to learn something about ourselves, understand what is happening to us or to resolve a problem. When we are not able, or not willing, to deal with life situations charged with unpleasant emotions, we tend to resist them or suppress, deny and fight against them. We resist them because we tend to seek pleasure and avoid pain, but if we block awareness of so-called 'negative emotional states', we do not receive the message the emotions convey.

Emotions as messengers

It's no coincidence that the word emotion is derived from the Latin verb meaning 'to move'. Although different emotions 'move' us in different ways, each one of them carries information and provides insights into our inner world, life situations and circumstances:

Fear

Fear informs us that we might be in danger or that there is a threat to our body, our personal integrity or social status, or that there is a threat to what we believe in or love. This emotion helps us to mobilise the physical and mental energy needed to run away or deal with precarious situations.

Grief and sadness

Grief indicates that we have lost someone or something important, so we need to re-orient or re-structure our way of living or relating and adapt to new circumstances. Grieving and allowing ourselves to experience sadness helps us to let go of what is perceived as lost, including lost hopes, or the things that do not support our growth and personal development. If employment arrangements or relationships do not work anymore (or do not serve us any longer), going through the experience of mourning can clear the space for something new and better.

Guilt and Shame

Guilt protects the integrity of the other; we feel guilty for what we have done to them, so we don't want to do that again. Shame, on the other hand, protects the integrity of our sense of self. We feel shame for what we have said or done, but we will correct ourselves and not repeat it.

Shame helps us to admit to our mistakes, especially when we deliberately set out to hurt someone, and in doing so, shame helps us to learn from our mistakes. We need to recognise and experience this feeling because shame supports us to grow into non-violent and caring people. That's understandable because guilt and shame serve to prevent us from harming others or ourselves. If we want to prevent or stop incorrect behaviour, we will need our guilt and shame.

These emotions also protect our sense of dignity and self-respect. The problem is that if we do not want to experience the emotions of shame and guilt, we do not welcome them when they naturally arise after we have done something harmful and erroneous. Instead of welcoming the guilt, we suppress it and project it onto others, blaming them. Hence, we cannot correct or moderate our behaviour. We will keep offending and hurting others because nothing will wake us up to the devastating consequences of our violent or abusive behaviours.

Apathy
Apathy is the feeling based on the belief that we can't do anything about our situation and no one else can either. The message from apathy is: *'You are feeling trapped'*. It can also be a detached emotional state, usually related to being stuck or imprisoned in a toxic environment. Apathy is a state of powerlessness—you long for change, but are not in a position to effect change. You don't have the emotional agility to make a conscious move happen. There is also a special alliance between anger and apathy. Apathy and the 'I don't care anymore' attitude is often a mask for anger. Many abused women know that. If you find yourself overwhelmed and stuck in this emotional state, ask the questions: 'What am I feeling, and what am

I avoiding feeling?'; 'Is something or someone draining my energy?'; 'Am I losing energy through suppressing emotions that would supply me with enough strength to do something constructive about this situation?'

Anger and Rage

Anger warns us that someone is threatening to penetrate our personal boundaries, or that we have been violated or blocked. The body becomes tense, stare fixed, eyes widen, the brows contract and the lips compress. The impulse is to move towards the person or the object, so as to take control or eliminate the obstacle. Ignoring this emotion or seeing it as 'bad' is a big mistake. Anger's basic message is one of protection, and that message must be heard and respected. We need to restore our boundaries, defend what is ours, and protect our sense of honour, if necessary. Anger also comes forward when we witness others being hurt through injustice or cruelty. Whether we are hurt or someone else, anger will alert and help us to shield, defend and prevent further harm.

However, this emotion is often misused. Anger is empowering. It is very physical; it makes you feel strong and has an energy to it that is pleasurable. On top of that, it can help you with various unpleasant situations in life. People use anger to lift themselves up or cover up other more unpleasant or disempowering emotions such as fear, sadness or a sense of neediness, for instance. Some abusive men cannot tolerate their neediness or the fear of abandonment common to the Pit Bull-type of abusers. Being needy or fearful is perceived as a weakness, and these men would feel intense shame if their vulnerability or dependence would be brought into the light.

Such 'shameful' emotional states, including so-called 'feminine' traits, are pushed down and locked into the Inner Boy aspect, firmly controlled by the angry Warrior aspect—the front persona in their personality. That is how the man's anger can serve not only to unleash his tension and frustration, but to cover his soft or feminine side—the weakness he simply cannot tolerate and must anesthetise with anger and explosions of rage.

What is the difference between healthy and unhealthy anger? Natural anger arises only in response to a real threat. Healthy anger, like any other emotion, comes up, addresses the issue and then moves on. Does that mean that we should always express anger instead of burying it down into the subconscious?

There has been much debate about 'expressing versus suppressing' anger and the use of 'emotional discharge' to reduce unpleasant emotions, especially anger. Many of us believe that we should openly express anger—act it out through some kind of a behaviour—instead of suppressing it or bottling it up until we can no longer keep it inside, and we explode. Why do we believe that? Because we assume that expression, either verbal or physical, has the effect of releasing, purifying and dissolving emotions. But has it?

Venting strong emotions—often erroneously called catharsis—or expressing emotions without deeper insights into what has triggered us does not always help us. The reason behind this is that overt emotional expression carries self-defining information: If you see yourself shaking in fear or anger, you will be convinced that you are frightened or enraged, and you may start shaking or raging even more. Screaming might have the same effect, and that is how people can work themselves into a frenzy. Obviously, the effects of discharging emotions are not always beneficial and do not necessarily support the healing process. Expressing emotions can even enhance their strength and keep them in focus.

The discharge of rage may also act as a reward mechanism. The 'blowing off steam' may reduce unpleasant inner tension and physiological stress in the short term, but reinforce the behaviour and promote future outbursts of aggression. Indeed, for some people, raging is a never-ending thrill. It lifts them up because it is fuelled by adrenaline—the exciting, pleasurable effect is produced when the adrenal glands dump a large dose of adrenaline into the bloodstream.

This works like magic and gives the body extra strength, so they don't feel fearful or vulnerable anymore. Disempowering emotional states such as feeling mistreated, devalued or betrayed also disappear. The feeling of rage can be pleasant and uplifting, and people behave as though they are addicted to rage. Life with their partner becomes nothing but warfare.

Some victims of abuse are also constantly angry. While the majority of abused women oscillate between expressing rage and sinking into grim despair or pain, others don't exhibit signs of feeling 'down'. Their chronic anger often serves as a permanent cover for the underlying depression, and they can even take their anger as an invitation to act violently towards their kids.

On the opposite side of the spectrum are the victims of domestic violence who suppress this emotion. Even when they need to restore their sense of self and heal their traumatic grief with the help of healthy anger, they still don't give themselves permission to experience it. This noble emotion can help them to release what needs to be released and free them from the bondage of toxic relationships. But they are afraid they'd be too overwhelmed and wouldn't be able to control their fury. Besides, rage begets rage, and if the abusive partner is physically stronger than the victim, the victim's own fiery outbursts might put her in serious danger. However, if she represses her fury and does not deal with it even when she should, she isn't doing herself any favours. So what should we do when we feel angry?

A way of dealing with emotions is neither to suppress nor to express (ventilate; act-out) them, but to fully experience them. There are situations in life when instead of either suppressing anger or expressing it and harming others by lashing out, it is better to allow yourself to experience this emotion first, and then dare to make others aware of it. How do we experience emotions? The experience of emotions such as anger doesn't mean that we must act upon them.

Emotions are energy-in-motion throughout the body. A current of emotional energy is like the flow of water. If we are not afraid of emotions—if we don't interfere with their natural flow by blocking, denying, judging, acting them out or somatising them ('transferring' them from the psychological sphere into the biological domain), emotions will arise, convey their message, help us understand the situation and activate an appropriate response, and the flow will recede. The emotional charge is then ready to be discharged—usually gradually through tolerable increments— and eventually dissolved. That's how we fully experience emotions.

Why is experiencing (instead of expressing-or-suppressing) emotions important? The experience of emotions often creates a shift in the mind-body system. For example, the tense muscles that were blocking the free emotional energy flow throughout the body are now relaxed, and the emotional charge is released. Now we are in a different place than we were before. Sometimes, the experience of emotions provides deeper insights and creates a shift in perspective as well: We perceive the same situation from a different angle—so we say that the experience was 'cathartic'.

Catharsis: Is it Just About the Release of Emotions?

The ancient notion of catharsis—which literally translated from the Greek word 'katharsis' means cleansing or purging—was revived in modern psychology by Sigmund Freud and his associates. But is catharsis only about releasing the emotional charge?

Scholars claim that Aristotle defined Greek tragedy in part by the effect it has on its audience. If the audience experiences catharsis—a release of tension or cleansing of disturbing emotions such as fear and pity through watching the tragic story—then it is a good tragedy because the audience members leave the theatre as morally purified, better people.

Those who assume that catharsis is a release of pent-up emotions may believe that the mere expression of emotions has a healing aspect to it. They claim that tragedies give a free outlet for the painful emotions, including pity and fear. The audiences feel pity for the characters in the play who are suffering, and fear is derived from the feeling that a similar suffering might befall them as well.

Once these emotions are expressed, the audiences feel better. However, catharsis is not only about the release of emotions. The interpretation that the mere purging of emotions is a cure for psychological conditions, and that watching tragic stories helps us to expel or get rid of unhealthy pent-up feelings or noxious emotional charge, might be too simplistic.

Another view of catharsis is the idea that the most important element in the Greek tragedy is about self-knowledge. The fallen protagonist gains self-knowledge—a deeper insight into their internal emotional states and personality, and the tragic consequences of their actions. They experience a moment of truth in which they recognise and acknowledge their hidden or suppressed drives, mistakes or failures. Now they know themselves better; and experiential self-knowledge is what really matters. Such introspection and awareness create a shift in self-perception. What was hidden has now been raised into consciousness, and both the protagonists and the audience experience catharsis—the shift in consciousness that goes beyond mental processing, discharging emotions or accumulating information about ourselves.

The shift in consciousness promotes a psychological change in the heroes of the Greek tragedy, as well as in the audience. This change renews and restores the personality structure. Thus, catharsis has a corrective and restorative function that adds to the traditional meaning of the term 'a mere expression of emotions'. That is why catharsis is often discussed along with Aristotle's concept of anagnorisis: self-knowledge.

However, if the free flow of emotions is not allowed, for one reason or another, a stagnant energy blockage can be created. This is usually the point that sets the particular emotional–behavioural pattern into motion. That pattern—imprinted in the subconscious like some kind of mental programming—might start spiralling time after time in our life, often manifesting as repetitive relationship conflicts or problems.

What to Do When You Are Angry

Imagine that a conflict has presented itself for healing. By refusing to honour conflict with a partner—the conflict that has presented itself for healing—you may either try to suppress your anger and avoid the conflict, or go on a rampage. Not knowing how to protect yourself and the dignity of your partner at the same time, you may descend into abusive behaviour or you may get stuck in the role of Victim. This is a clear sign that you have not mastered the skill.

When you are abusive or violent, you dishonour others, including yourself, and you are misusing the noble energy of anger. You are out of balance, sucked into the role of Perpetrator. You don't understand that anger comes forward not only to help you protect yourself, but also to give you the strength you need to meet the opponent honourably during the conflict. If you were to personify anger, it would be clear that its essence is honourable; it needs to be used as a conflict mediator and noble protector. Genuine anger doesn't want to see anyone get hurt unnecessarily. You must set your boundaries mercifully!

An additional problem is that when you act with rage—when you misuse the energy of anger—you'll invest more of this energy-in-motion into the conflict than is necessary. For example, if you choose to use rage as a weapon to damage a person who offended you, you'll have to pore more anger into the situation than is needed for protecting yourself. You'll break your offender's boundaries and unnecessarily hurt them. In return, they might react with rage towards you and break your boundaries again. Then you'll have to react with a stronger force, and they will counteract with even stronger force. This is how personal wars with escalating rage get started. So, what to do?

Teachings of great martial arts masters can help us. They say if someone emotionally abuses you, the first step in dealing with fury is to welcome it without throwing it onto others. When you give yourself permission to radiate the energy of anger, your opponent will sense it, and his response might be different than when you radiate the emotion of fear. A surge of anger can help you to set your personal boundaries on fire and let people know not to mess with you.

Allow your anger to arise when attacked, but don't embark upon a 'search-and-destroy mission'. Instead, get grounded and solidify your boundaries. When you are centred and grounded, you won't have to lash out and explode like a street hooligan, nor will you implode into yourself like a weakling.

How do you set your personal boundaries on fire? Your arm's-length space around, above and below your body is your territory. It's helpful if you imagine adding the intensity of anger to your territory. In your imagination, pour the heat, colour, sound or sensation of rage into it. This quick mental action honours your anger, helps you to focus on the attacker and ground yourself at the same time. Take some additional mental actions, if you choose. You can populate your personal space with totem animals, protective ancestors, benevolent beings or a white light power. Any symbolism that works for you could be called upon and invited into your space to make you feel more secure.

It's important to know why and how to pour this e-motion (energy in motion) into your own personal space. Rage releases a huge amount of red-hot energy into the body, and the intensity of its physical energy can be danger-ous for others but can also affect your body if you try to repress it. Whenever possible, project this powerful emotion into your personal space. You are protecting your body from damage when you are projecting the rage onto your bounda-ries, instead of keeping it in the body. No one will be endangered because you are not discharging it through vio-lent behaviour—you are only channelling the energy of rage into your territory.

However, if you are fuming with rage, and you are afraid that you might hurt someone, especially a child, find a way to excuse yourself and go somewhere when you can be by yourself. Clear out the tension in the muscles and let loose through fierce body movements of shaking, stomping and kicking, squeezing a towel, punching a pillow or a punching bag in the gym. Yell and imagine that you are yelling at the person who has hurt you...

It's not necessarily bad to have aggressive thoughts and emotions towards those who abuse you. You don't have to play a saint who can always forgive and forget and never fan-tasises about revenge. Simply do not act upon these fantasies, but acknowledge and accept them with compas-sion for yourself. When you acknowledge your aggressive impulses, and perhaps release the tension in your body without hurting yourself or someone else, you no longer have to pretend that you think and feel what you don't think and feel. Just experience the feelings and move on. When there is negativity, sometimes the best bet is to not interact but to move out of the way. You don't have to go in every fight you are 'invited to'.

However, sometimes you can't ignore bullies and abusers. You must stay and deal with them.

When offenders are tolerated by others, or not punished for their wrongdoings, they will continue to offend, and even increase the frequency of their offences. Besides, if you choose to stifle and suppress the anger that comes forward, you ignore the uncomfortable truth that you have been abused. Certainly, you own dignity will be injured in the at-tack. It is difficult to heal the wound or repair the damage done to your dignity when you refuse to address your genuine emotions and the important messages they carry. On the other hand, if you choose to react violently, you'll most probably respond in a similarly offensive manner. Your counterattack may help you restore your sense of dignity temporarily, but it may ignite the opponent's counterattack that will increase the conflict, which might further endanger you. So how to respond if someone verbally attacks you?

The most instinctive way to respond is to attempt to reason with the person who offended you. Your natural reaction is to attempt to convince the attacker that they are mistaken; you want them to listen to reasons and arguments. But the fact is that it is difficult to reason with someone who wants to hurt you. There are better ways to stop verbal abuse. For example, your abuser has called you an idiot because he wanted to push you down in order to lift himself up. If possible, defuse the situation through 'surprise questions': 'Why are you picking a fight?'; 'Why did you say that?; 'Is there a particular reason you need a conflict between us?' Or state an observation: 'You seem to like putting me down'. Or reduce the tension by bringing some jokes or self-effacing humour: 'Oh, yes, I know I can be a silly guy, but "idiot" sounds awfully cruel, don't you think?'

What else can you do if someone verbally attacks you or perhaps blames you for something you have no control over? A good strategy in such situation is to ignore the actual content of what's been said. Instead, you identify the type of abuse employed. Then you name it and calmly ask the abuser to stop it. Let's say that your wife blames you for not planning the road trip in advance, and ending up in heavy traffic. Instead of attempting to convince her that you could not have envisioned the unexpected traffic, it's more effective to firmly state, 'Stop blaming me for something I have no control over.'

Or, for example, she is using a label such as 'irresponsible' or 'lazy' to describe you. Trying to convince her that you are not irresponsible or lazy is not going to have any effect on her. Firmly stating, 'Stop using offensive labels to define me,' or simply, 'Stop the name-calling,' (or 'Stop the character assassination') is more powerful.

If this calm approach does not work, the only meaningful response to verbal abuse is to 'leave the scene'. By refusing to engage with the verbal abuser and refraining from attempts to reason with them, you are showing that you are not going to put up with their behaviour.

There is one more thing that you need to remember: Some abusers will learn to correct themselves through repeated exposure to this approach; others will not. There will always be bullies and abusers. You'll be hurt no matter what you do. Your self-esteem will be de-stabilised and you may end up feeling wounded after a serious attack. Your healthy anger will not always prevent you from falling, but the understanding what has happened (and why it has happened) will give you the strength to recover and rise again. Remember the Taoist saying: The glory isn't in never falling, but in rising when you fall.

Substitute emotional states

It is important to learn to identify the emotions that are cooking beneath the surface and what they have to do with our current state of affairs. Counsellors know how difficult is to work with clients who are inexpressive or unaware of their feelings. Emotion takes us to the heart of the matter, and we can create an integrated emotional experience by identifying and naming implicit core emotions.

At the age of 2–6 years, children start learning words that correspond to feelings. Adults teach them to identify and correctly name their emotional states: I'm scared, sad, angry, disappointed, jealous.

Sadly, some families suffer from alexithymia: the inability to identify and describe emotions (from the Greek *a*-for 'lack', *lexis*-for 'words' and *thymos*-for 'emotions'). Instead of experiencing differentiated emotional states like grief, disappointment, envy, resentment and so on, they feel 'nervousness' or 'tension', which is actually not an emotional state but rather sensorial, physiological response to a situation. Some people who suffer from alexithymia tend to act out violently or react with primitive rage whenever they feel the urge to discharge unpleasant tension. Their angry, abusive or offensive behaviours have become almost an automatic reaction to any kind of stress. The impulse to rage in order to release tension is so quickly translated into harsh words or violent actions that the impulse and the action have become one and the same.

In some other families, only specific emotional states are mislabelled or discounted so children may grow up either without the ability to recognise them, or believe that certain emotions such as fear or sadness are not okay, and they learn how to 'keep a stiff upper lip'. These children grow up showing sugary happiness even at times of severe loss, or they exercise self-restraint in expressing emotions whenever grief, frustration or anger tries to surface. This is how they learn to substitute anger, fear or sadness with stoicism, or greed and jealousy with generosity. People around them sense that there is something phony when they exhibit their not-so-authentic feelings, and yet it is hard not to display them because acknowledging disallowed feelings, such as anger, for example, can be frightening. In their belief system, experiencing anger means to automatically act on it, so they may believe, 'If I allow myself to feel enraged, I might do something terrible!'

On the opposite side are those who come from families in which rage and abuse were the norm. That's because raging can serve not only to get rid of unpleasant tension and frustration, but as a substitute for other unpleasant emotions. When these people feel hurt, they get angry; when they feel disappointed, they get angry. When they are afraid, they will switch immediately into anger because fear is disempowering while anger empowers them.

If they feel rejected by their partners, they may experience shame or a sense of humiliation, but raging and abusive behaviour can help them to mask or avoid these 'unacceptable' emotions. This shift of emotions—from the initial feeling of shame, humiliation and vulnerability to the abusive reaction—can happen in a split-second. That's how they manage the intense, painful feelings.

Indeed, anger and raging can serve as an excellent anaesthetic, but people may not be fully aware of it. For instance, the abuser who perceives certain situations as humiliating—when others do something that hurt his pride, or others fail to do what his pride requires of them ('She disrespected me!')—does not necessarily feel humiliation or hurt directly. Instead, he is angry at someone who has hurt him. His angry response masks other unpleasant emotions and helps him not to feel them. Those who have provoked his rage should feel these emotions instead! That is why the repetitive pattern of abuse—reacting with angry outbursts whenever he feels hurt or upset—becomes a conditioned reflex. Unwilling or unable to stay in contact with his internal psychological states, the abuser is determined to avoid them.

> The repetitive pattern of abuse—reacting with angry outbursts whenever he feels hurt or upset—has become a conditioned reflex.

In some cases, the 'substitution process' is completely unconscious, especially when it is developed at very early age. Even when children are vaguely aware how they substituted painful emotions (being humiliated, for example) with more tolerable emotional states (being enraged), by the time they reach adulthood, they have repressed from awareness the 'process' of lifting themselves from lower, disempowering states (shame, guilt, fear) to higher, more empowering emotional states (anger).

They usually learn this strategy of uplifting themselves from others who have already mastered the skill, or through identifying with their aggressors. If a child, for instance, is criticised, he or she feels resentment and pain. To combat the emotional pain of criticism, the child identifies with the person who criticised him and treats others as incompetent. Why? It helps him to feel better.

Unfinished emotional business

So many of our current life problems are nothing but the repetition of the same old problems and troubles we have already gone through. Why can't we let go of the past?

We cannot let go of the past because we cannot come to terms with what happened. The experience was not understood and metabolised. This unfinished emotional business can manifest today as patterns of unconsciously replaying old family dramas. The repetitive patterns of conflict and friction with others often have their origin in childhood.

The old conflicts might be replayed with different people, in different places and under different circumstances, but if we look at them closely, we see that they share a lot of commonalities. For example, a woman's job environment mimics the emotional atmosphere of her childhood home. She is working with a group of bossy and bitchy characters who resemble her family members and make her life miserable. Or she moves from one relationship to another only to find similar problems, issues and personalities that 'drive her crazy'.

Others may create in their marriage a relationship dynamic that resembles the one they witnessed between their parents. The life script of many abused women is a copy of their mothers' or grandmothers' tragic life stories with their tyrannical husbands. A mother stayed entrapped in a marriage with her violent husband and endured abuse, and her daughter finds herself in a similar abusive relationship with her husband. Or the woman finds herself in relationship with a man who mimics the characteristics of her father who physically and emotionally abused her.

Many victims of domestic violence unconsciously reenact the same tragic experiences of abuse by their violent father with other abusive men. The blind obedience of a girl to her violent father's rules and directives of 'Endure the pain', 'Don't even try to escape', and 'Accept that the beating is all your fault' can be transferred into her relationship with violent men later in her adult life. And not just that. If she internalised her father's image of herself as a worthless, unattractive girl, then most of her adult life can be propelled by a self-defeating quest for the appreciation and love she longed for as a young girl.

Snežana's childhood experiences with her father clearly illustrate this. 'I used to think that my father was a sophisticated man who wanted everything in his and his family's life to be perfect. Now I understand that he was a tyrannical narcissist,' she said. She described her father as a man who wanted to impress everybody. For him, his image was essential. He demanded perfection from Snežana and her younger sister. The girls felt intense pressure to be perfect and ramp up their talents, looks, intellect and giving, caring personalities to please their dad. Snežana wanted to succeed in fulfilling her father's wishes to be the best at school, to look good, to be a great cook. But somehow, she would always fail, and her father would punish her with derogatory comments.

When she was a young girl, her father commented on how beautiful she was. But as she grew older, he would rarely miss an opportunity to comment on her weight. With deep resentment she described her life in the family ruled by her tyrannical, narcissistic father. Her mother did not protect her. Snežana's mother simply echoed her father as she felt uncertain of herself and wanted to please her husband. This pattern of pleasing men by playing 'I submissive' was the result of Snežana's mother's own childhood.

Repeating this psychological pattern was common in their family lineage. The women would marry a man similar to their abusive parent and raise a family in an abusive environment like the one they were raised in. Their children were in danger, too. It is a well-known fact that many adult survivors of child abuse show an inability to protect their children or to detect when the child is suffering abuse at the hands of the woman's violent partners or someone else. Snežana's mother didn't know how to protect herself and her daughters, so Snežana was exposed to the same painful experiences with abusive men as her mother.

Feeling powerless to protect herself and not being aware of the dynamics of pathological narcissism, Snežana went from a narcissistic, tyrannical father to a brutal, domineering husband. Nothing was ever good enough for her father, and nothing was good enough for her husband. In the beginning of their relationship, she was perfect! The moment she arrived in Australia—financially dependent and far from the people who could help her—things started to change in her marriage. Her husband wouldn't miss an opportunity to say something demeaning about her. She'd feel embarrassed, but the more she disclosed how she felt the more he'd hit her with humiliating comments and draw satisfaction from it as though he was feeding on her embarrassment.

Soon her relationship with him became clouded by his sadistic pleasure of hurting her. He enjoyed her feelings of vulnerability too; he knew that she worried that he could dump her for someone else and leave her alone in a country where she didn't know anyone. Her fears kept her in the toxic bond with a man who enjoyed abusing her. Only when her fear of staying with him (he started brutally beating her) was stronger than her fear of leaving, was she ready to look for the exit from the domestic violence trap. 'I think I ended up in this situation, in a shelter for the victims of domestic violence, without a home, without a job and money, because I wanted to get that man to love me the way my father never did,' she said in our counselling session when we explored her repetitive patterns of relating—first with her father and later with other men—and the beliefs that maintained them.

Snežana's first marriage and a few other relationships were also painful experiences for her. She would get into relationships with insensitive or abusive men, like her father was, only to confirm her old beliefs about herself as a victim of abusive males, and beliefs about men as cruel creatures. How did that belief crystallise in her mind in the first place?

When a girl's self-image has been ruined by her father's abuse, it usually means that the image of her father has been damaged as well. When a father image is damaged, the image of men in general is under threat, and the girl may create a strong opinion about all men ('Men are cruel').

Later in life, her convictions about men may become reinforced as she goes through traumatic re-enactments.

She unconsciously looks for love and appreciation from men who look like her father and ends up with cruel men (like her father). Thus, her beliefs that 'Men are cruel' become self-fulfilling prophecies. Often times, even when she tries, she cannot seem to free herself. Or she manages to free herself from one violent man, only to get entangled with another one.

That was the pattern that played out in Snežana's relationship with men. She was conditioned to give up her power to men and operate out of her weaknesses and passivity. Her view of herself in relationship with men—based on her experiences with an abusive father and a submissive mother—was that she was the dependent one, thus she must stay 'submissive'. Being submissive means that you are a victim at the mercy of the powerful, dominant male. That's how she was conditioned from her early childhood, so she kept seeing herself as a helpless victim, even when she could escape.

The Inner Tyrant

Evidence suggests that while some people who have been abused as children become abusive, the majority of victims of childhood abuse do not go on to abuse others. However, some victims who do not abuse others are self-destructive. They behave as though they have an inner Abuser aspect in their personality.

Many have internalised their abusive parent's distorted picture of them. A father told his daughter that she was stupid and fat, so now she labels herself with the same derogatory terms. The External Tyrant from her childhood now exists and attacks her from the inside—the abusive parent continues to live as the Inner Tyrant.

Oftentimes internalised psychological oppression occurs when people come to feel responsible for the abuse they endure. For instance, a wife quietly suffers her husband's endless offenses and indignities, and accepts them, even though, in her heart, she knows better. She does so because her Inner Tyrant (her Critical Parent ego state) constantly reminds her, literally whispering in her ear that a good wife obeys and does not contradict her husband. Any hints of complaint or self-pity are countered by her Tyrant's message: 'Don't be a complainer; be a good wife'. Those who internalise abuse in this way may display tendencies towards self-blame, self-hatred and self-harm. They may also end up as victims of other people's offenses or become victims of domestic violence. They do not abuse others, but they may find themselves on the other side of the spectrum as repeat targets of abuse.

Snežana's younger sister's life story is different. Sick and tired of being a victim of men, starting from her strict, authoritarian and dominant father, she became a misfit who rebelled against social conventions but in a self-destructive way. She appeared to be a powerful woman who fought against 'male tyranny', but the force she used in conflicts with men didn't bring any positive or constructive changes in her life. She would find herself in a never-ending war with men (occasionally interrupted with her episodes of binge drinking), and yet the rage she felt, the fantasies about revenge or the desire to have power over men didn't really empower her. On the contrary, every fight with her partner would end up in the same way as fights with her father—with her feeling disempowered or humiliated, while the man would feel empowered and in control.

Why do we replay the same old tragic dramas from our past, and how do we stop re-enacting our painful experiences with tyrannical parents? It is not easy to dismiss, ignore or escape the tyranny. Once the strong emotional pattern of relating—such as the one between a cruel parent and a helpless child—has been imprinted in the subconscious, it can be triggered again by anything associated with the original trauma. There are many examples of this. The abused women who behave as competent professionals or mature women in all other areas of life seem to be conditioned to react like helpless and terrified girls when exposed to their husbands' abuse. The girl could not leave her father's house and now, twenty, thirty or forty years later, she—an intelligent adult woman—is experiencing the same sense of helplessness or fear of abandonment. Belma's story clearly illustrates how the Inner Child's fear of abandonment can impact adult relationships.

Belma's violent partner, who wreaked havoc in her life for years, was gone at last. After years of emotional and even physical abuse, he had left to live with a friend. But instead of relief, she felt as though she was 'crushed'. Finally, there was an opportunity to live free of abuse, free of the daily criticism and insults, but Belma, an attractive woman and successful architect, was absolutely devastated. Why? She grew up with parents who often neglected her and occasionally abused her, but the idea of losing them was even more frightening than staying with them. As an adult woman, she was re-experiencing her old feelings of helplessness and dread when left alone. Staying even with an abusive man was less frightening than not having anyone.

The pain of unfulfilled needs

The most detrimental belief that keeps a woman trapped in an abusive relationship is the belief 'I need him (for this or that reason) so I mustn't lose him!' There is a huge difference between 'I need him' and 'I love him, and I like to be with him, but I am not dependent on him like a child dependent on a parent'. Once that dysfunctional belief ('I need him so I must stay with him no matter what!') has been corrected—and the woman's Adult ego state decontaminated—it becomes much easier to find the exit from the domestic violence trap. How has that 'I need him, so I can't leave him' belief been created? The crux of the problem is unfulfilled basic human need.

As children we need a safe environment free from abuse. We also need a parent who will turn and talk to us with genuine interest. If this did not happen, unfulfilled basic needs may convert into pain and chronic suffering. This pain will be stored in our subconscious until we are strong enough to face it. We will never get the old need met, but we can get over the pain! However, the pain will not let go until the basic need is acknowledged. It is the pain of an unfulfilled need that ultimately must be recognised and released if we are to heal childhood emotional wounds.

> We will never get the old need met, but we can get over the pain of unfulfilled needs! However, the pain will not let go until the basic need is acknowledged.

These wounds are one of the main reasons we replay unhealed traumas from the past through behavioural re-enactment. That's why we often repeat the same painful patterns of relating in childhood with abusive adult partners. What are the mechanics behind this?

The painful experience carries a strong emotional imprint and if the pain hasn't been released, the imprint can become the primer for the conditions of that painful experience to repeat throughout life. Like fractals—patterns that repeat their general features—the similar relational conditions of our childhood can be recreated in adult life. This unconscious compulsion (deeply hidden from our conscious understanding) wants to reproduce the past conditions. It does this as though trying to win in the end, discharge painful emotional charges, meet unfulfilled needs and finally master the traumatic situations. These are important contributors to our numerous problems in life.

One such problem is that we reproduce a childhood situation by unintentionally 'choosing' (or better to say, unintentionally attracting) a partner with personality aspects that will make it almost impossible to create a healthy and mature relationship. We will end up feeling hurt again. How can we stop this pattern from being repeated?

The first step is to notice the similarity between the pain in the here-and-now situation with the pain experienced in childhood. Observing the similarities between the current and the past problematic or conflictual situations will help us to start dissolving the repetitive pattern of conflicts or problems. For example, by perceiving the repetitive pattern in various life situations or interpersonal issues, we learn to recognise the similarities between our parental figures and the people who are causing us pain now. If we re-evaluate the present hurt and compare it with the childhood hurt, we will clearly see how it is one and the same.

The next step is to feel (not only think about it) the old pain *and* the pain triggered in our current situation until they become one. Why is that relevant? Experiencing the pain of now and the pain of then will provide deeper insights and better understanding of the distressing situations and our responses to them. As children, we could not fully experience nor understand what was really going on at the time of the distress. We simply could not cope with the intensity of the emotions or face what we perceived as hurt, loss or defeat. But now we can!

It is the pain of an unfulfilled basic need—underneath the hurt—that ultimately must be recognised and released if we are to heal childhood emotional wounds.

Emotional experience is crucial in this healing process. Mere intellectual evaluation, endless mental processing—or just talking about it—will not yield much benefit. In order to heal the pain, we need to feel it so the dissociated, repressed or never-fully experienced pain can be acknowledged and released. This means that the emotional charge attached to the childhood trauma has been discharged. Once released, we are no longer driven by it. We are not compelled to unconsciously act it out or re-enact it through repetitive patterns of dysfunctional behaviour. We don't compulsively repeat our old family dramas by projecting the offending parent onto our partners or other people. And, interestingly, when we release the childhood pain of not having our basic needs met, we also 'release' our parents.

In cases where our upbringing had been abusive or neglectful, we may experience unease and even disgust when we interact with our parents. We find ourselves easily triggered by them even when they are old, live far away from us, and can no longer influence our lives. Even when we have successfully built a life outside of our childhood home, when in contact with abusive parents we can immediately revert back to feeling powerless and frustrated like we are six years old again, or we start acting out anger and behaving like a raging, uncontrollable teenager. Or the interest that they may now show in our lives feels phoney, so we react with irritation and spite.

But when we allow ourselves to go through the process of mourning—releasing old pain and letting go of our hopes or yearnings for their love—we get to the other side of the 'bridge of grief'. We no longer feel pain, resentment or despair. We realise that it is in our human potential to take care of ourselves in a way that we haven't been cared for before. We can then start a new type of mature relating—both with our parents and partners—and this relating is much more rewarding and satisfying.

Chapter 14

HEALING THE TRAUMA OF ABUSE

Many victims of domestic violence experience intrusive thoughts about what has happened to them or they re-live the scenes of abuse through traumatic nightmares and flashbacks. These symptoms of intrusion are often accompanied by increased emotional and physiological arousal so the victims tend to avoid thoughts, people or places that remind them of traumatic events.

Some abused women also report a feeling of 'not being there' during a beating. They seemingly 'withdraw from the scene of violence' as though they were observing their partner's abuse from a distance, detached from their emotions and physical sensations. They learn how to move out of the body so they do not feel the horror of what's happening. The terrifying experience continues, but it is not happening to 'me'. By dissociating, the victim is able to endure the highly traumatic event without having to fully experience it.

Dissociation is a crucial strategy in dealing with trauma. Unfortunately, trauma survivors often rely too heavily on dissociation whenever they feel stressed; the freeze response can be their automatic response even to everyday stresses. Another problem is that traumatised people may try to repress or avoid remembering what has happened to them, or they may disconnect from the intolerable reality of the abuse. However, the painful experiences that could not be metabolised at the time of the trauma do not disappear. They may be just temporarily removed from conscious awareness, but they will find a way to intrude into the person's everyday life.

Trauma and The Symptoms of Intrusion

Trauma is not a story about something that happened in the past. Being traumatised means that the imprints of the trauma on the mind—the images, emotions and physical sensations—continue to be experienced in the present. Trauma survivors may relive traumatic experiences through 1) intrusive thoughts and images; 2) traumatic nightmares; 3) flashbacks; and/or 4) behavioural re-enactments.

These symptoms of intrusion can be understood as unconscious attempts at healing trauma through discharging the intense emotions associated with the real traumatic events. However, they can be unsuccessful attempts at healing, or even re-traumatising. Today we know that such spontaneous re-experiencing of painful events may be useful in gradually discharging and processing everyday stresses or releasing the pain of losing loved one, but they are often unsuccessful strategies for coping with trauma.

Recurrent, involuntary, and intrusive images: Some trauma survivors find themselves caught in re-experiencing the mental 'snapshots' of the traumatic events that intrude into awareness. The traumatic memory can be charged with intense emotion of terror and physical sensations of hyperarousal.

Traumatic nightmares: Victims of trauma may have recurring post-traumatic nightmares—the dreams about the frightening experience that happened in real life events.

Flashbacks: Flashbacks are similar to traumatic nightmares, but experienced while awake. A package of sensory impressions—the image, the smell, the sound—gets imprinted in the mind. When something triggers them, traumatised people may react as if the past events were occurring in the present. Instead of remembering, they re-experience sensations, emotions and cognitions related to the particular past event as though they were occurring now. They may relive the traumatic events through all five senses. They 'see' the people and the scenes of the event; they 'hear' screams and voices; they 'smell' blood and sweat, etc. Trauma survivors may confuse flashbacks with hallucinations and believe that they are 'going crazy'.

Behavioural re-enactment: The painful past can also be recreated and relived through what Sigmund Freud called *repetition compulsion*. He noticed that some people seemed caught in a compulsive repetition of destructive and self-destructive behaviour—re-enacting the traumatic event or putting themselves in situations where the event is likely to happen again. He described repetition compulsion as follows: '...the victim who did not integrate the trauma was doomed to "repeat the repressed material" as a contemporary experience instead of . . . remembering it as something belonging to the past.'[1] He and his associates believed that such re-enactment—the compulsion to relive past traumas—was an unconscious attempt to get control over a disturbing emotional state, as though the traumatised person unconsciously wants to find a resolution for the psychic tension accumulated in past traumatic events. These behavioural repetitions of old traumatic experiences are in modern psychology known as behavioural re-enactments (or traumatic re-enactment). Traumatic re-enactment is an unconscious process and is most noticeable in relationships.

These dissociated parts of the psyche can also create little aspects that tend to form their own seemingly independent identity. The wounded aspects hold the terror and shock from painful events as though patiently waiting for the person to become strong enough to get back to it, 'unfreeze' and release the emotional charge attached to the traumatic memory. They will stay dissociated until the time when they can be re-connected. When the traumatised person feels safe and ready to heal, the trauma from the past may start coming to the surface, and the emotional charge can start gradually discharging. The exiled parts—the aspects that hold the imprint of trauma—are finally re-collected (re-membered), and the healing process can begin.

Two Pillars of Light

How do we heal the pain of being abused? How do we lessen the impact these highly stressful or even traumatic experiences have over us?

When we start remembering them, the first impulse is to avoid, ignore or suppress the memory and emotions triggered by thinking about the painful events. We also tend to put something into the body, like food, drinks, cigarettes or drugs to soothe the painful emotions and unpleasant physical sensations that parallel these emotions. But no matter what we do, disturbing thoughts and feelings may keep coming back. The sensory, emotional and mental fragments about the experiences from the past may intrude into the present. They may appear as intrusive thoughts and images about the events, or as traumatic nightmares and flashbacks. The intrusions can be very unpleasant; however, understanding these symptoms and inner experiences can help in recovering from trauma. What does the healing process look like?

Emotional healing occurs when our wounded state of being is recognised, understood and transmuted. As long as the trauma remains hidden, it operates in the background. When we bring it out into the open, the observing self illuminates what was hidden. We facilitate healing when we become present to these packets of 'undigested' experiences, when we open them up and gradually metabolise them. As we do that, we transmute the lumps of suppressed memories and painful feelings attached to them.

The process is not easy but the *Witness* and *Compassion*—the two powerful 'forces' symbolically represented in eastern tradition as the two Pillars of Light—are in service to anyone who chooses to heal their emotional wounds. In many healing traditions, eastern as well as western, awareness and compassion are considered the key components that facilitate the psychological healing process.

Cultivating the Witness

At the core of recovery and transformation are self-awareness and self-reflection. If we are to heal our emotional wounds, it's important to cultivate the 'witness consciousness'—to become a neutral observer of our inner experiences. 'The witness place inside you is simple awareness, the part of you that is aware of everything— just noticing, watching, not judging, just being present, being here now,' Ram Dass writes in the book *Polishing the Mirror*.[2] What we call the Witness is actually another level of consciousness; we humans have this unique ability to be in two states of consciousness at once, Ram Dass explains.

It is interesting to note that the mere act of observing can facilitate the process of inner transformation and healing. Witnessing our thoughts, emotions, sensations in the body and behaviour is indeed like directing the beam of a flashlight at ourselves so we can face all our wounds and painful emotions, weaknesses and vulnerabilities. If we allow ourselves to investigate them with compassion for ourselves and without judgement, denial or any other defences, we can confront amazingly deep and painful memories. We do not have to like our inner experiences. Just allow them to come up and be aware of them. Emotions ebb and flow. No matter how painful, they will pass. But resisting them can make them persist. They can get stuck in the body, cause physical illnesses and more suffering.

Self-reflection can also help us to disentangle from who we were at the time of the assault (a helpless victim of abuse) from who we are now (not a victim anymore). How does that work? Our Inner Witness aspect—a non-judgmental observer —builds the platform from which we can look at our painful experiences and become aware of our past as well as present thoughts, emotions and current life situation. If we experienced abuse, for example, we observe and understand what happened at the time of the abuse, and what is happening in our mind and physical body now when we are safe. This is called *dual awareness*—being in two states of consciousness at once, as Ram Dass put it. It allows for exploring the painful past but without the risk of re-traumatisation because we are aware that we are in a safe space now. When we observe what happened 'there and then' from a place of 'here and now' we can experience and release the intense emotions we could not deal with at the time of the abuse.

Compassion

Self-reflection is one important component that facilitates psychological healing; compassion for oneself is another. This pillar radiates powerful but gentle, protective light. It has the feminine energy of Quan Yin, the Goddess of Compassion.[3] Quan Yin is portrayed in various forms, yet each of them demonstrates a unique aspect of her compassion and mercy. She is sometimes depicted as the divine mother who envelops her sick child in a blanket of love while absorbing and transmuting the child's pain. Her protective and healing energy is always present, but it is up to us when and how we want to evoke the Goddess of Compassion within.

How does Quan Yin (the compassion for ourselves) help us to heal? She helps us to feel the pain or distress (metaphorically speaking) when we re-member the traumatic event while feeling compassion for ourselves at the same time. And what is compassion? We could define it as unconditional acceptance of our inner experiences. When repressed memories of painful events return and come up to the surface—so we can re-member what was previously dis-membered and release the emotional charge from the wounds—we allow ourselves to experience emotions no matter how painful they are.

We may have uncontrollable episodes of crying but if we allow it instead of suppressing or avoiding it, a sense of relief often results, and the process of healing intensifies. It is not about allowing ourselves to cry but allowing ourselves to feel the pain. If the painful emotional experience is accompanied by tears, so be it. 'I've been thinking a lot about the little girl I used to be, and crying,' Snežana said in the counselling session when we were talking about her wounded Inner Child aspect. 'I never thought of what she had been through and how lonely she was. But I've been taking good care of her this week, holding her close to my heart, and it seems to me that she is feeling better'.

Instead of identifying solely with the wounded aspect in her personality, Snežana evoked the mature and compassionate aspects of her being. She was able to experience her mindful observer self—the Witness who observed the girl's thoughts and beliefs about herself and 'cruel men', her emotions and the body sensations that accompanied the painful emotions—while also feeling compassion for the little girl. Enveloped in unconditional acceptance, her Inner Girl could release the accumulated and never-metabolised pain, while Snežana's Wise Woman within took a mindful dual awareness stance, being present in the 'here and now' (safe space) and 'then and there', helping the Inner Child aspect to release the pain from her past traumatic experiences. That's how the Wise Woman or Man—the synergy of two pillars of light (awareness and compassion), metaphorically speaking— can help us to heal.

Once the pain is released and melts away, we can move on, free from habits of blame, self-blame or self-hatred. We can then feel compassion for others too, often born from understanding our own suffering. That is how insights and compassion will help us to heal—through plunging into our inner emotional states and unconditionally accepting and allowing everything we are going through. There is no place for judgement, denial or suppressing anything in this protected space filled with compassion. We resist nothing, and we fully allow the contents of our mind—whether it is a belief, an emotion, a sense of frustration, a desire for something or awareness of contraction in the body—while being present to it with an openness that takes no position about it. Through this process of healing our psyche matures. Trauma can then be even an opportunity for psychological development and growth.

Ruminating versus Reflecting

Some people are convinced that their repetitive problems or current conflicts with partners have nothing to do with old unhealed wounds. Some are not even aware of any problem or pain, past or present. They push it out of sight. However, ignoring the pain from past traumatic experiences does not make it disappear. It will intrude in everyday life, in one or another way.

On the other side of the continuum are those for whom the past is more 'real' than the present because something constantly triggers them and reminds them of the traumatic past. They relive, over and over, the abuse, neglect, abandonment...

**Playing Tetris Helps Reduce
the Impact of Emotional Trauma**

It's a well-known fact that policemen, lawyers and judges who deal with family and criminal cases are more prone to vicarious trauma—the trauma suffered by professionals who must listen to accounts, watch videos or crime scene photos of torture, rape, abuse and murder. Playing Tetris after watching videos or horrific crime scene photos could help them.

Who would have thought that a computer puzzle game called Tetris has a medical value? Researchers have recommended playing the video game Tetris as a 'cognitive vaccine' against flashbacks from traumatic events because playing the game after being exposed to trauma can reduce the number of subsequent intrusive images and flashbacks.

After any event, there is a window of about six hours where memories are consolidated and cemented in the mind. Sleeping on the memory strengthens it further, explained Emily Holmes at the Medical Research Council Cognition and Brain Sciences Unit in Cambridge, UK.[4] Instead of going to sleep after the exposure to highly stressful events, we should play Tetris, Holmes and her colleagues recommend. In 2009, they showed that playing the game four hours after being exposed to trauma reduced the number of subsequent flashbacks. But getting the game into a person's hands immediately after they have been raped, for example, won't always be practical, so the team tested whether it could still work a day later—after the memory had been consolidated and slept on.[5] It worked. Over the following week, the group that had played the game experienced 51 per cent fewer intrusive memories of the traumatising video than the group that hadn't played Tetris.

The rationale for playing Tetris—an approach to reduce intrusions—is as follows: Trauma flashbacks are sensory-perceptual, visuospatial mental images. Visuospatial cognitive tasks selectively compete for resources required to generate mental images. Thus, a visuospatial computer game (e.g. Tetris) will interfere with flashbacks. So, the researchers reasoned that an intensive mental task such as playing the game Tetris might be able to compete successfully with traumatic experiences, and thereby prevent the development of traumatic flashbacks.

Playing Tetris can also weaken cravings for drugs, activities and food. Scientists from Plymouth University and Queensland University of Technology, Australia, believe that playing Tetris to block flashbacks of traumatic events and reduce the risk of developing Posttraumatic stress disorder (PTSD) is only one benefit from the game. Professor Jackie Andrade, from the School of Psychology and the Cognition Institute at Plymouth University, said: 'Playing Tetris decreased craving strength for drugs, food, and activities from 70% to 56%.'[6]

Perpetually thinking or ruminating over past painful situations or about an ex-partner will not help the healing process. 'I finally managed to divorce him, but I am still crying, thinking, dreaming about him. I am desperately trying not to think, I am fantasising about the future to avoid thinking about what has happened in the past, then I am crying, thinking, dreaming about him again,' our client Belma disclosed.

Reflecting on past experiences, evaluating possible outcomes or making plans can be helpful in problem-solving and overcoming dilemmas. But rumination such as replaying the same conversation in the mind, obsessing over distressing past experiences and brooding on painful memories long after a course of action has been decided on, can become detrimental. It rarely offers new insights into the problematic situation and only serves to intensify unpleasant feelings. How to stop brooding and ruminating about past?

Rumination is defined as an obsessive thinking about an idea, situation or choice, especially when it interferes with normal mental functioning. Ruminative thoughts can keep us up late at night over-analysing what led to that awful conflict, relationship breakup or stressful family drama. The problem with the thoughts, 'I should have told him...'; 'If only I didn't...'; 'He shouldn't say that...' is that we, like a broken record, replay in our mind the same scenes that generate the same emotional responses, with no positive benefits from it. This type of rumination can lead to more rumination, and constant preoccupation with what happened can even prolong the distress. Changing the focus, or being involved in anything that could engage us, would help to break this vicious cycle.

One strategy for dealing with rumination is re-writing the story of what has happened. The aim is to finish the story with a happy ending, similar to the happy ending in fairy tales.

Fairy Tales Help Children Overcome Developmental Fears

Are frightening stories good for kids? Many parents have stopped reading fairy tales to their young children because they believe the stories are too scary. Indeed, the fairy tales of the brothers Grimm—Cinderella, Hänsel and Gretel, Snow White, Rapunzel, Little Red Riding Hood and many others—are nothing but horror stories in which little heroines and heroes experience terrifying events directed by evil queens, nasty stepmothers and witches, or they are abandoned by their own parents or are in grave danger when separated from them. Yet, children love them. Why? What's the pleasure in being scared by such stories?

Children have to deal with so-called normal developmental fears in their everyday life such as separation anxiety, fears that their parents might forget them or fears that they will be exposed to threat by malevolent people or 'creepy beings'. Storytelling can help them overcome these fears, but important requirements must be met: 1. The story must have a happy ending; 2. The story must be told several times in the same way, without changing the sequence of events; 3. The characters in the story are simple—they are either good or bad. There are no complex characters that the young child can't relate to or understand. 4. The story must be told by a trusting adult and in a safe environment.

Happy ending: When children listen to fairy tales, their own separation anxiety and other normal developmental fears may easily be triggered by the exposure to the frightening events in the story plot. However, the story has a happy ending so the tension—and unpleasant sensations of hyperarousal that accompany the emotion of fear—will find a pleasant resolution. The fears will be released thanks to the happy ending. Why is a happy ending so important?

When you find yourself in a dangerous situation—you are by yourself and you meet monsters, witches, ogres and people who mean harm—you must deal with it. Your fight-or-flight stress response is activated and you either overcome the danger, find a solution for the stressful situation, or you successfully escape it. Fairy tales are not complicated. Oftentimes they are simply a question of fighting with the bad guys or running for your life if you can't win the battle with the dangerous creature. This is how we learn to deal with evil and violence: Do something about it and solve the problem if you can or run away from it if you can't. Either way is okay, as long as you're not caught up in the freeze-or-collapse trauma response: total helplessness without a happy ending.

When you've managed the situation through fight or escape—when your dramatic experience has a happy ending— you're done. You don't feel fear any longer. On the contrary, you feel better, stronger, more competent and confident to deal with similar situations in the future.

Re-telling the same story: The same story needs to be told a few times, not just once, with the same line of events—rising action, climax, and successful resolution of unpleasant tension thanks to happy ending—to provide for the full emotional discharge through a gradual process of metabolising smaller 'increments' of fears. Thus, the stress or normal developmental fears will be gradually dissolved through the repetitive cycle of tension and relaxation. That's why you are not allowed to change the sequence of events. When you tell the story to a child, and you start improvising and changing the plot (just because you are bored with telling the same story so many times!), the child will immediately correct you: 'No, no, it wasn't like that! It was like....'

The repetition compulsion mechanism (insisting to be told the same story with the same plot line, many times) installed in the 'story-telling method' for dealing with overwhelming emotions is similar to the mechanics behind the symptoms of intrusion after traumatic events. However, this time the child manages to discharge the unpleasant emotional charge triggered by the fairy tale. The distress will successfully be released because the story, no matter how frightening it is, has a happy ending. Besides, it's much easier to allow the fear to arise—so it can be consciously experienced and released—when you know that everything will end up well.

When children lose interest in a particular story and say, 'Don't tell me that story, tell me something else,' this is usually a sign that they have managed to overcome the specific developmental fear triggered by the fairy tale and are ready to deal with other themes. Different fairy tales activate different emotional states, and some more complex stories, like Alice in Wonderland, can trigger several fears and unresolved psychological issues.

Good and bad characters: Small children cannot yet understand complex personality structures, so the characters in the story have simple 'good or bad' personality aspects. Of course, good always must triumph over evil. The children empathise and identify with their heroes and heroines who find themselves in trouble. By empathising with the hero figure in the story, it is possible to experience vicariously high-felt arousal without the real distress that the

303

hero or heroine may be experiencing. However, the child's own fears will be triggered. Their hearts beat faster, eyes widen as adrenaline pumps, but the hero triumphs, the happy ending provides resolution and the unpleasant tension activated by the scary dramatic plot is over, leaving an afterglow of satisfaction and well-being.

Safe space: A safe external environment is also an important prerequisite for dealing with frightening emotional issues. (It's not a good idea to tell the child a scary story in the shelter as the family seeks protection from shelling). The story must be told by an adult the child trusts. Just as the little heroines and heroes in the stories have those who comfort and protect them during their various dangerous situations, the children need to be accompanied by loving parents, grandparents or adults who care about their well-being while they listen to fairy tales.

It is not just fairy tales that help children to overcome their fears. Watching cartoons and playing repetitive scary games with a happy ending—kids can't get enough of games like 'hide and seek'—can also play an important role in dealing with normal, developmental fears.

Re-write your (hi)story: A creative writing exercise, if you feel inspired

You have been treated unfairly, or perhaps you have been abused. Rumination, constant mental preoccupation with what has happened, charged with painful emotions are the usual responses to such painful experiences. The 're-write your (hi)story' technique can help with minimising rumination after distressing events. The goal is to create the pleasant outcome that you will place alongside the unpleasant memory. You are looking to resolve the emotional tension by creating in your imagination a happy ending to the painful experience. Why? The ending of our life stories and experiences is very important. The ending will determine to a great extent how we will remember what has happened to us. An event makes its mark in our memories more by what happens at its end than at any prior point. That's why you want to rewrite your 'unhappy' story and create a happy ending that empowers you. Even if this new happy ending never happens in real life, it is real to the subconscious mind simply because you are able to imagine it.

To re-write your (hi)story, begin by imagining one emotionally heavy-charged scene:

1. Begin by being present and aware of your body in this moment.

2. Bring kindness and openness to your experience, and evoke a sense of interest and curiosity.

3. Recall one moment, or one unpleasant scene, perhaps an interaction between you and another person that went awry, and you ended up not feeling good about yourself, about that person or both, or not feeling good about relationships or life in general.

4. Stay anchored in compassion for yourself as you evoke this memory.

5. Notice how you feel, or remember how you felt, and see if you can locate where you feel or sense that in your body. Notice any beliefs or thoughts you may have about yourself, others or your life *now* because of what you experienced *then*.

6. Now begin to imagine something different you might have said or done in that scene or in that moment or imagine something different the other person could have said or done, even if that could never have happened. You can also imagine someone, who was not there at the time, coming in and doing something helpful (the Fairy Godmother from the Cinderella fairy tale, for instance). Or evoke Deus ex Machina ('God from the machine') from classical Greek theatre, who would help

to resolve the conflict and protect your best interests, or protect both parties' interests, if you choose so.

Greek Theatre Deus Ex Machina

The term has evolved to mean a plot device, where a seemingly unsolvable problem is suddenly and abruptly resolved by one of the Greek gods (a machine is used to bring actors playing gods onto the stage). The idea was used in Greek tragedy as a strategy to resolve the conflict, to bring the tale to an end, or find the resolution to the emotional tension and conclude the drama.

---

7.   Allow your imaginative and inventive mind to create a more pleasing outcome of the entire event. Observe how you feel with this new and happy ending, and where you sense these new emotions in your body. Notice the different and more positive thoughts you have about yourself. Give yourself permission to experience a sense of satisfaction with this new ending. Let your imagination resolve the situation in the best possible way for you.

8.   Then, gently go back to the original negative experience for a moment or two. Return to the new outcome and rest in the experience of the new ending. Then go back to the negative experience again (just briefly) and notice any shifts in your perception or the way you feel now. Then go back to the negative experience from the past, let it go, and rest in the feelings and thoughts of the new and happy ending.

Depression and panic attacks

Many people who have experienced abuse suffer from depression and anxiety, and sometimes even have symptoms of panic attacks. There are many reasons why we experience anxiety and panic attacks, and many rea-

306

sons and causes for depression, but there is an interesting relation between panic attacks *and* depression.

While fear refers to an unpleasant anticipation or reaction to external danger, free-floating anxiety, on the other hand, is a sense of a danger whose source we are not always aware of. Such vague anxiety can be a warning signal that a threat is present, but what is it? It can be a sign that something is threatening to arise in our consciousness, yet it has still to be discovered.

In many cases, what anxious people are afraid of is their own subconscious. The people who suffer from panic attacks may also be unaware of what causes or triggers them. The majority of them start experiencing panic attacks at a time when life is not joyful, positive expectations are turned down, when they face problems in life or dreams haven't come true. If they see a doctor and complain of unpleasant panic attacks that affect their everyday functioning, they may be prescribed antidepressant medication, too.

Is there a connection between panic attacks and a depressed mood? Aspectology could offer an explanation. Different aspects in the psyche have different voices, desires and agendas. We are not always fully aware of the emotional states in each of them as some may be suppressed or dissociated. For instance, when we are under pressure, or exposed to continuous stresses such as chronic health problems, interpersonal conflicts or abuse, we may feel emotionally drained, exhausted or depressed. We may feel disillusioned not only with our job or marriage but with life in general, so it becomes increasingly difficult to find motivation for everyday functioning. The 'disillusioned' aspect in our personality may react with an attitude like 'I am sick and tired of this crappy life'. However, it does not mean that we are actively suicidal or have a clear plan how to 'check-out' from the body and escape this 'awful, barren and hopeless human existence on the prison planet Earth'. And yet, the mind has detected vague fantasies about 'escaping' everyday existence or 'how it would be nice to fall asleep and never to wake up again', and identified them as some kind of unclear life threat. We may react with intense panic as though we were in mortal danger, but without a real understanding of what these attacks are all about because the fantasies about 'escaping' are very vague or suppressed.

If the blurry suicidal ideation or unclear messages that 'I do not want to live any longer' are reinforced with a gloomy emotional tone from the hopeless aspect disappointed with relationships or disillusioned with life, and have not been clearly recognised and understood, it is hard to put a finger on it and undoubtedly identify 'the danger'. The unclear fantasies about 'escaping' or messages from the subconscious ('I don't want to be here...') that trigger panic attacks, accompanied by physical sensations such as heart palpitations, chest pain, shortness of breath, are often misinterpreted as signs of a heart attack, stroke, mysterious but serious illness, madness, etc.

However, they can be understood if we engage in an imaginary dialogue with the aspect disillusioned with life. The insights into our emotional inner situation gained through dialoguing with the depressed aspect could help us realise that what frightens us the most is not that we may have a heart attack or that we are 'going crazy'— which means that we'll lose control over our behaviour and do something dangerous, for example, kill ourselves! Sometimes the fear that we are going crazy and that we may 'lose control over our behaviour and do something dangerous' actually means that we believe that we could lose control over the subconscious fantasies about dying.

What frightened us actually is that we might succumb to the depressed aspect's hidden self-destructive impulses and wishes to leave the body and this miserable life.

How to Deal with Unpleasant Emotional States

Jung's technique of active imagination is very helpful when we experience prolonged unpleasant emotional states such as depressed mood. The first step is to personify the affect. Use it as a starting point and try to find out what sort of fantasy-images express this mood. Let the emotional state come up in some form... perhaps as a personality aspect or even in the form of a human being. Then communicate with the imaginary person or the aspect—charged with intense or unpleasant emotions—as if it were a real being. You can ask questions such as: 'What is that you want to express?'; 'Is there something that you are afraid of showing or something that you are hiding, and why?'; 'Do you want me to know something about you?'; 'What do you want me to do?'; 'Do you feel suppressed by another aspect/person; or 'Are you suppressing; avoiding; pushing down something/someone else, or keeping someone under your control?'; 'Is there something I need to remember in order to release you?'; 'Do I need to forgive myself or someone else, so you'll let me off the hook?'

Hatred and Forgiveness

Children are loving beings. Their love is a gift to the world, and when the 'gift beyond price' is rejected, ridiculed, devalued or abused, the flow of love from the child's heart gets frozen. Then hatred says, 'I'll never love again!' Its function is to protect the heart from bleeding pain. Some women who have been abused by their intimate partner say the same: 'I'll never love again!' Some others want to forgive and stop hating but if we are to heal hatred, the pain must be drained first. Only after that is it possible to forgive.

There is nothing wrong with 'forgiveness therapy', but sometimes forgiveness is seen as some kind of a shortcut in the healing process. 'Forgive and forget, and go on with your life. Stay angry and you'll get stuck in the existing circumstance.' Directly dealing with loathing and hatred is avoided. Hate is suppressed into the shadow of the psyche while forgiveness is glorified. In this school of thought, forgiveness and anger are set up as opposite forces: forgiveness is 'good'; anger and, especially, hatred is 'bad'. But avoiding these feelings doesn't help.

The strongest argument of those who promote forgiveness as an important part of healing emotional wounds is that as long as we don't forgive, we are bound (or glued) to the other person with bonds of pain, rage or yearning for revenge. 'Holding onto hatred is like drinking poison and expecting the other person to die,' they say. And it makes sense. Chronic hatred indeed binds us into a negative psychic connection with the other person, but when we forgive, we break the bond and set ourselves free. Some healers even claim that after a long period of being trapped in a violent relationship, forgiveness can help us to cut the invisible energetic cords with the perpetrator.

The bottom line is that forgiveness—whether we ask others for forgiveness or we forgive others—is about letting go of the painful past. However, we have to deal with grief, anger, or even hatred, first.

At some stage of coping with the aftermath of domestic violence or crimes that affect the masses, such as terrorist attacks or mass shootings, someone will mention forgiveness. There is a belief that forgiveness would put an end to the distress or suffering, and someone will say, 'We have hated enough; now it's time to forgive!'

But forgiveness can be given prematurely. Some people who tend to forgive prematurely want to forgive out of their unconscious fear of intense hatred or emotions of spite and vindictiveness professed as 'not-okay'. Others rush to forgive before their traumatic experiences have been healed, but after some time notice that they still hate the person they seemingly forgave. They then may judge themselves for being 'small' and incapable of forgiveness.

Some people have a tendency to transform their hatred into a false acceptance and fabricated love, or even get engaged in social activities that aim to 'heal the world', 'end injustice' or 'right wrongs'. They mean well and want to create positive changes in society, yet they drag their unconscious shadow emotions right into the heart of the noble cause they fight for.

The problem here is that if we want to forgive in order to suppress hatred or to forget the painful experiences, we only move the distress into the shadow. The pain goes underground, and it might start festering there. It will find its way out, in one or another way, often through various physical symptoms or medical conditions.

On the other side of the coin are those who cannot stop hating. They will never forgive and, instead, decisively hold on to the need to see those who have hurt them keep paying for their transgressions. They claim that their perpetrator must experience the same pain and abuse that has been inflicted onto them, but even after 'justice has been done', they are still not ready to release the culprit from their lives. The problem with 'Never!' (being able to let go or forgive) is that whatever we hate ultimately binds us to itself. The desire to keep punishing the perpetrators is often equated with holding on to the injury, yet some people believe that revenge is the best method of healing the wound.

Another reason people may withhold forgiveness is fear. They may unconsciously believe that hatred keeps them alert and resentment shields them from potential aggressors. If they believe that their anger and a need for revenge have self-protective functions, forgiving the other person would mean that they are no longer protected from potential new attacks. And not just that. Some people will not give up easily on hatred because this feeling can help them to avoid pain and even feel better, at least briefly.

In the state of intense and long-term hatred, the focus is more on those who wounded you and less on the wound. Besides, when you hate your perpetrators or enemies, you see them as miserable or malicious creatures, not as glorified victors who defeated you. Thus, 'I'll never forgive you! I'll hate you forever!' can serve to protect the wound of defeat and degradation inflicted by the enemies or perpetrators, and it can keep you from sinking deep into despair and suffering, grief or depression.

Another benefit from 'Never forgive!' is that passionate hatred can give meaning and purpose to an empty life. We may also have difficulty letting go of the past simply because our pain and suffering hasn't fully been understood or recognised by others. Our hatred can then serve to indicate that the healing process hasn't been finished yet.

In practice, victims of domestic abuse can forgive only when they are well protected against further attacks from an abuser, and when they have already healed their emotional wounds, at least to some extent. (Imagine yourself in hospital, with a broken leg. It was an accident caused by your partner's negligence. As long as you are in pain, it's difficult to think about forgiving him).

In some cases, there are layers and layers of emotions—anger, rage, hatred or even murderous fury, sadness, despair, shame or degradation—that need to be addressed, metabolised and released before we are truly ready to forgive.

Forgiveness is not an emotion, nor is it a polite, saintly gesture made with a bowed head and modestly folded hands while we say the sentimental nonsense: 'I forgive you, because I see that you didn't know what you were doing'. When serious wounding has taken place, the perpetrator must be identified and brought to justice. Genuine forgiveness does not make excuses for abusive, improper or violent behaviour, and it is not about finding a way to say, 'Let them go'.

Forgiveness is a decision that can be made after the significant part of the healing work has been done. It does not make what happened okay, but, indeed, it can set you free and help you move on. Forgiveness can really add something significant to the recovery process. How does it do this? The victim has welcomed and consciously experienced the terror and dread she found herself in, but now she feels safe. She has gone through the pain and healed her broken heart, so she will be able to love again. She has managed to release bouts of rage and fury; therefore, she is ready to forgive. As though it raises her up from the pit of her suffering and testifies: 'It's over. You can't hurt me anymore. You have no power over my life any more. Now, I can forgive you'.

A topic for consideration: abuse and reconciliation

If any underlying rage and hatred have not been unveiled and worked through, the reconciliation between two parties in conflict—either in a war conflict between nations or in a private war between individuals—is an illusory one. Such attempts at reconciliation usually end up as a 'diplomatic cover' over the animosity that has been bottled up, or the hatred has been directed outside the conflict and against others.

It can help if the abuser feels genuine remorse and offers to repair the damage done to the victim. But the great majority of perpetrators are incapable of doing that, for one reason or another. Consider psychopaths who express zero empathy for their victims, or terrorists, war criminals and their supporters. The majority of them live in total denial of what they have done or what kind of ideology they have supported. If they face the fact that the organised mass hatred, dehumanising the enemy for specific political or personal interests, or their 'noble cause' ('We have only defended our people!') was nothing but collective programming, they would perceive themselves as victims of such propaganda. Nothing takes power away quicker than the self-perception of being a victim of something, so not many people would admit that they have been misused and manipulated to join the 'wrong side' in the war or political conflicts.

The same is true when it comes to perpetrators of domestic violence. Some of them will not change; if they could, they would keep inflicting pain onto their partners indefinitely. Does it mean that victims cannot heal their emotional wounds or even forgive their perpetrators? Of course not. He might not have changed, but his victim will be able to forgive because she will have changed. Ultimately, forgiveness is not about something between us and others; rather, it is about letting go of what we have been holding onto.

Post-traumatic growth

In some cases, letting go of the painful experience, and even the experience itself, can help us in our psychological growth and development. Bus is it really possible to find new meaning and purpose in life *because of* and *thanks to* the trauma? Or is the story about post-traumatic growth that raises us to a higher level of consciousness just another fairy tale?

Studies show that a great majority of people experience at least one traumatising event in their lifetime, but only a small percentage will develop full blown post-traumatic stress disorder (PTSD). What can help us to survive trauma without long-term consequences, and even support post-traumatic growth, the positive psychological change experienced as a result of adversity?

Here is a list of items that are considered the most useful in the recovery process:

Acceptance of the reality and significance of the traumatic events. The ability to accept the reality of tragic events, and their consequences, has been identified as a significant predictor of post-traumatic growth. The awareness of our reactions to what has happened—with compassionate acceptance of our reactions, no matter what they have been—has an important role in the recovery process. We also need to accept not only the events and our reactions to them, but the recovery process as our new reality. We know that the healing could go on for some time.

Communicating about the trauma. Creating a coherent narrative of your life—with the traumatic events integrated in the life timeline—while getting some emotional distance from the event(s) when communicating what happened, or journaling about events and personal experiences, can be very helpful in the healing process.

Taking in the good. Finding pleasant moments even during 'the dark night of the soul'. Taking in the good of a positive or bright moment is not about distracting yourself, 'so you don't think about what has happened to you'. A smile, a good meal, a stroll in the park, or a moment of laughter can provide a necessary respite from grief or distress. Such moments can even help the mind to shift gears and change the point of view or uplift you and open your perception to a larger perspective.

Positive re-framing. Finding the hidden gift in the experience. Developing the capacity to reframe the events and 'turning a regrettable moment into a teachable moment'—to understand it on a deeper level—is an important point in recovery from trauma. This includes forgiving yourself for any part of the event or painful experience.

Appreciating that new life came because of the catastrophe, not just in spite of it. The disappointments, difficulties, and even disasters can be the catalyst for growth or taking an entirely new direction in life, often with new purpose and meaning.

Helping others. Volunteering and helping others can bring us out of isolation into a larger community where we can find a place in the world again. Volunteering also helps metabolise what happened to us and pass along to others what has been learned. Helping others empowers us, and we regain a sense of competence that can help master our own recovery process.

Getting support. Get the support from family, friends, community or people who believe in your recovery. The support is not about a quick gloss-over of 'You're strong; you'll survive that', or 'Oh, don't worry, you'll be fine!' but genuine empathy for the pain and suffering of the victim. Support groups are significant places of healing, where people with the same problems gather to share experiences and help. The friendly community of the survivors of the same type of trauma—the people who 'have been there and who know'—helps with the perspective of the positive outcomes in the future: 'I may not be well now, but I will be fine someday'.

Women forming a network

In times of stress, we react with the fight-or-flight response. We fight against a threat if overcoming the threat is likely, or we flee if overcoming the threat is unlikely. However, when it comes to the fight-or-flight response, men are given a distinct physical advantage over women by having higher levels of testosterone. With testosterone comes the physical strength to both defend from danger and run away from a threat. Women do not have that level of physical strength. Besides, when they run to escape from danger, they often run carrying their children.

Yes, we all respond to threat with fight or flight, but research has shown that women have an additional coping response to stress. In 2000, Shelley Elizabeth Taylor, a professor of psychology, and her colleagues proposed the idea of a unique female tend-and-befriend behavioural pattern in response to stress: 'Although fight-or-flight may characterize the primary physiological responses to stress for both males and females, we propose that, behaviorally, females' responses are more marked by a pattern of "tend-and-befriend." Tending involves nurturant activities designed to protect the self and offspring that promote safety and reduce distress; befriending is the creation and maintenance of social networks that may aid in this process.'[8]

Thus the tend-and-befriend response is about the tendency to affiliate or to come together in groups in threatening times. It refers not to the biological, but the behavioural response of managing stress. It involves caring for offspring and seeking social support—tending to the young and befriending those around—to increase the likelihood of survival.

Tend-And-Befriend in The Bosnian War: Indira's Story

During the war in Bosnia and Herzegovina, I was living in an apartment building in Sarajevo. My neighbours were mostly women with small children. While their husbands were either at work or on the front line, the women would stay in their apartments taking care of their kids.

The city had been transformed into a living hell as sniper fire, bombardment and shelling from the nearby hills rained down on us daily. Without warning, shelling would start, and shells often exploded in someone's living room. When they would hear the familiar and frightening sound, the mothers' reactions were predictable. They would grab their small children and get together with the other women in the building to consult each other on what to do. 'Should we go to the shelter, or should we hide in my kitchen?' (The question made sense because the kitchens were sometimes better protected from the shells than improvised shelters in the basements).

The women in my building spontaneously but swiftly created a social network they could rely on and through which they could support each other. The unspoken yet clear agreement between them was forged, 'If something happens to you, I will take care of your children. If something happens to me, you will take care of mine!' A mother's worst fear in these situations is triggered by frightening

318

thoughts about what would happen to her small children if she were injured or killed. But the mothers in my building had each other. This tend-and-befriend type of response—tending to children and creating a supportive social network among women—helped the Bosnian women to reduce their level of helplessness and cope better with the horrors of the war.

Many believe that women are more likely than men to seek support from others in traumatic or stressful situations, especially during pregnancy and nursing. Women are more vulnerable to an outside threat during pregnancy, nursing or caring for children, so they naturally tend to get together and form female support networks, create friendships and self-help groups in order to protect themselves and their children. This female network also serves to protect the women from males, even within the home environment.

> It was the other abused women living in our street that assisted my mum. Part of the women's 'secret code' was: If anyone had not been seen for a few days, the children would be sent to check up on the woman to see if she was not badly injured and in need of medical attention. For us, this women's watch was a constant blessing.[7] **Elsie's story**

Women tend to call up their sisters when they are under stress or abused by their partners. Feeling powerless to deal with the atrocities of family violence, victims turn to women for help. Studies show that females who emigrate and are unable to form a female network, characteristic of female befriending, are more likely to become victims of abuse than women who are able to form these ties.[9]

Knowing that she is not alone and that there are people who can help her is often crucial in re-establishing a sense of safety, or in healing the trauma of abuse once the woman has managed to escape from the 'domestic war zone'. And if she hasn't? For women who still live in abusive relationships, counselling programs or self-help and support groups can be a tremendous help in breaking free from domestic violence. The woman may decide to remain in the violent relationship or return to the abuser after a temporary separation, and yet get support. Other women, who may have gone through similar experiences or quandaries, can help her make a safety plan and encourage her to think about steps she can take if her partner becomes abusive again. They can also help her to acknowledge that she may be in the most danger when she's trying to leave.

Some researchers believe that women's tendencies to actively seek emotional help from others, and men's tendencies not to seek help, might be one of the most distinct gender differences in adult human behaviour. But is it really true that women are more likely than men to seek out and use social support in stressful situations? True or not, the tend-and-befriend stress response could be just as adaptive for men as for women in certain contexts.

Chapter 15

THE FEMININE AND MASCULINE IN ALL OF US

The feminine and masculine are not bound to gender; they live in all of us: women and men. A woman carries the *animus*, the masculine component in a woman's personality as Jungian psychotherapists would describe it, with male principles and traits of assertiveness, athletic leanings, rationality, practical skills, etc. A man has the *anima*, the feminine component in a man's personality, with qualities and characteristics such as receptivity, intuition, creativity, etc. It is only the union of these two principles that constitutes a complete human being. When a person emphasises only one (masculine *or* feminine) of these inner 'packages' of principles and characteristics . . . and suppresses the other into the subconscious . . . the result is that only half a person is manifesting and developing.

The fear of looking 'womanish'

Some argue that establishing the male identity is more delicate and complex than establishing the female identity as masculinity is not what men are born with but something they must achieve. They suggest that the reason for this is because men are born from a body that is a different gender from themselves. A boy must define his identity *against* his mother's. If he doesn't, he just falls back into her non-masculine identity. No evidence has as yet been found to substantiate this assumption that the boy must dis-identify from his mother and identify with his father to develop a masculine identity. It is a well-known fact, however, that both girls and boys have equally developed an unambiguous sense of which sex they are from by about the age of two. Boys do not need to be 'initiated into manhood' and they do not need to 'develop' their masculinity. Something else plays the key role in the formation of their masculine identity: social influences and cultural norms.

The concept of masculine identity is what the patriarchy is based on, and it is something that has to be constantly lived up to. Societies, especially patriarchal societies, prescribe what men should be: how men should look, think, feel and behave to be seen and accepted as male. Many men claim that the fear of not being seen as male can be so intense that they tend to avoid not only the external feminine appearance but even internal emotional experiences that are not sanctioned to be 'masculine'. Within such masculine value-systems, feeling needy, vulnerable or frightened are regarded as 'feminine' feelings; therefore, they are a big no-no in the stereotype of a 'real man'. Men must prove they are not a sissy; otherwise, they'll be humiliated, shamed and ridiculed by 'real men'. Hence the male fear of the feminine.

When our client Senad was held at gunpoint while playing a homosexual to entertain his torturers in the concentration camp in Bosnia, he was humiliated not only because they had power over him, but because he had to play a 'womanish man'. It took him a while to realise that his deepest fear was the fear that others might see him as soft or feminine. Once he was ready to deal with that fear, he disclosed that he himself used to participate in derogatory stereotyping that allowed 'real men' to amuse themselves at the expense of men who look 'too soft'.

Under the influence of rigid social conditioning, we tend to label the feminine—in ourselves or in others—as 'womanish', thus inferior. And whatever we consider inferior, including half of a man's own being, we tend to attack, oppress, repress or dissociate from. So-called feminine men deviate from their prescribed gender roles; they are not adhering to societal norms and expectations, and deviation from the norm is seen negatively. Hence the never-ending story about the oppression of the 'inferiors': women, blacks, indigenous people, homosexuals, especially homosexuals. Not conforming to expectations makes people who embrace their prescribed gender roles uncomfortable because of associations with their own suppressed feminine, even when that feminine side in every man has nothing to do with homosexuality.

Patriarchy and Homophobia

Why are homosexuals hated and bullied? If we look up homophobia in the dictionary, it will tell us that the term is defined as 'hatred or irrational fear of homosexuals', so some claim that fear is behind bullying boys with long hair and men who look 'too feminine'. But fear of what? Yes, religious people may feel the fear of eternal damnation in that they will burn in heal if they or their children are homosexuals. The Abrahamic religions of Judaism, Christianity and Islam have traditionally forbidden homosexuality believing and teaching that such behaviour is a sin; but there is more to it, not just the fear of God.

There is a popular theory that those who bully homosexuals have been harbouring homosexual urges themselves. As such urges are unacceptable, 'latent' (closeted) homosexuals project them onto homosexuals and abuse or hate them instead of themselves. However, there is no evidence for the 'homophobia-as-repressed-homosexuality' hypothesis. Lots of people who are homophobic—and who bully and attack everything that is perceived as feminine in men—harbour no homosexual urges. So what are they afraid of, then? The suppressed feminine in themselves, even when that side of their being has nothing to do with 'homosexuality'?

There are many 'macho' men who live under the social pressure that they must repress and conquer their 'softer' feminine side. They tend to oppress and abuse women, too. In many cases, the oppression of women, especially in the age of the patriarchy, could be seen as a mirror reflection of the tendency to suppress anything that smacks of the feminine in men. Through repetitive patterns of mocking and abusing women and homosexuals, macho bullies inflate their egos and assure their superiority not only over external females and 'feminine' men, but internal femininity as well.

TOXIC MASCULINITY: Dean's story

In the year 2000, I was assigned to work with juveniles and young offenders after graduating from Her Majesty's prison officer training program. The prison population consisted of up to 1000 young men aged 15-21 years, incarcerated for criminal offenses that ranged from minor theft and non-payment of fines to that of the most horrific murders.

Unlike adult prisons, the young offender prisons do not catergorise their prisoners by the seriousness of their offence. This means that highly volatile prisoners incarcerated for extremely serious crimes will be mixed with prisoners who have committed petty crimes.

Initially, I experienced mixed emotions about working with juvenile and young offenders. The staff prison community is relatively small and word travels around fast. It was during my prison officer training that I'd heard rumours from other serving officers, mostly referring to their own experiences of working with 'juvees', which is the shortened version describing juveniles.

'Juvees' were well known amongst the staff for being the most challenging, reactive and unpleasant prisoners to work with. This reputation was due to their unpredictable behaviours that were full of volatility, poor self-control, emotional immaturity, and to top it all off, pubescent bodies filled with raging hormones.

So what makes juveniles (15–18 year old's) so volatile?

To gain a better understanding of a teenager's mind, I reflect on my teenage years growing up. I clearly remember the troubled years and brushes with the law I experienced that could have easily led me down similar paths as these boys.

I remember clearly that I was no angel growing up in West London. My most serious incident landed me before a Crown Court Judge. Only sheer luck and the unconditional love of my mother, who provided the most admirable character witness statement, helped me to avoid a considerable lengthy prison sentence . . . along with an understanding and experienced judge, who considered the change in my life circumstances as one of the main reasons for triggering the self-destructive behaviours that led to my arrest.

Interestingly, the lead-up to getting arrested took place over a 24–hour period, which saw me join up with several youths from my local area. I remember at the time I was extremely angry with the world; I was full of hate and wanted to lash out at whoever and whatever was in front of me.

A month prior, I was sitting in my lounge at home after being summoned there by my mother for a family meeting. It was unusual because in my family we never sat down as a family and talked. Alarm bells were going off in my head, and I was a little confused as to why my mother had called us all together. Thoughts were running through my head:

'Was I in trouble? What trouble have I gotten into that's made its way back to my parents?'

As my mother and father entered the lounge, I was aware of fear building up inside of me. I could feel the butterflies in my stomach and a queasy, sickly feeling. I did my best to avoid eye contact with my parents, looking down at the floor towards my own feet. I hunched over and waited to hear my mother's words.

My mother and father had chosen to sit at opposite ends of the lounge room, which I found highly unusual at the time. This only added to the uncomfortable feelings I was already experiencing. My mother did most of the speaking and started by saying, 'Your father and I are getting a divorce.' Immediately the fear and queasiness turned to anger. I lashed out with a torrent of abuse, 'You whore,' I blasted at my mother. 'You bitch.' I was relentless with my angry verbal attacks on her as I blamed her for breaking up our family. My safety and security within the family unit had become threatened, and ultimately my identity.

She didn't respond and instead became silent. She then began to speak again and expressed how hard this was for her, how she had been thinking about this for a long time, and how she felt that the time was right now for her to make changes to her life. I just watched her mouth move; however, I was unable to hear or interpret the words.

Fast-forward to my court appearance. As the judge reached his verdict, he considered my mother's character reference. She explained to the court that I was generally a good boy but the news of the divorce had impacted me greatly. It had led to me becoming emotionally distant and disconnected from my parents. She informed the judge of my running away from home weeks before the conviction, and how I had broken contact with my family.

She spoke of her despair after hearing that I had taken up with the local youths and had begun taking recreational drugs. She expressed her concerns about my lack of direction in life and the dubious relationships I was creating with males outside of the home, who seemed to be influencing the types of decisions and life choices I was making.

In summing up, the judge took the additional information from my mother and decided that the ordeal of watching my parents split up had caused enough emotional upheaval to initiate an uncharacteristic disruptive behaviour pattern that had moved me towards committing a range of serious criminal offenses over a 24-hour rampage.

Instead of the three years of incarceration that my barrister had predicted, the judge handed me and my family a lifeline and issued a two-year conditional discharge with strict conditions, stating if any criminal activity occurred in this time then a prison sentence would be issued.

Fast-forward again a few years, and it was that experience of narrowly avoiding prison that inspired my application to become a prison officer. Today, that same inspiration has led to the creation of the Young Men's Group primary prevention education program. This is a program focused on empowering and equipping boys with tools and strategies to live purposeful and fulfilling lives—lives not poisoned by toxic masculinity.

The term 'toxic masculinity' often appears in mainstream news, articles, popular feminist blogs, etc., and is generally used to denote how some aspects of masculinity—such as entitlement, homophobia and sexual aggressiveness—can harm women and cripple men's own wellbeing. Four major components that describe the concept of toxic masculinity are:

- Male domination over women and other men;
- Aggression or acts of violence like sexual assaults, gang rape, mass shootings;
- Suppression of anything stereotypically feminine;
- Suppression of emotions related to vulnerability like fear, sadness, or helplessness.

My attitude towards my mother would certainly have been associated with that type of 'toxic masculinity'. It was a toxic defence mechanism to springboard a transformation from the disempowerment of the fear of losing my parents into the empowering anger of attack. This manoeuvre—to quickly transform fear or shame into anger—often morphs into a pattern of abusive behaviour. The pattern is typical of boys who can't tolerate 'weaknesses' such as fear, guilt, shame... or anything that resembles the feminine in themselves.

Toxic masculinity is directly related to a man's devaluation or total unawareness of his feminine side. The man contaminated by toxic masculinity fails to recognise and respect feminine values in himself, in women and in life in general. How to deconstruct it? By regaining harmony and balance between the masculine and feminine within our being and in our world.

Yes, it is true that our present culture still tends to overvalue everything masculine, especially control and power over others... and undervalue the feminine principles that tend to unite. It is true that we are still living in a left-brain dominated society, driven by intellect, aggression and competition, but there are signs of increasing empathy, cooperation and compassion for all life on the planet. Hopefully we will see more right-brain feminine qualities develop in society. We need such qualities to neutralise the toxic masculinity. Only then can the human race evolve into beings of wholeness.

Satisfaction or a sense of pleasure when abusing, raping and oppressing whatever is 'womanish' can be highly addictive. The Bosnian women who survived torture and rape in Vilina Vlas, a hotel in the town Višegrad (turned into a rape camp for women during the Bosnian war), tell a story about the 'soft' and shy men who, in the beginning, were reluctant to rape. They had to be pushed by the machos to do that, but surprisingly quickly got hooked on raping and humiliating the women and girls.

Another consequence of amputating the feminine within is that we don't know how to deal with painful emotions. Macho men oppose the values considered to be feminine—compassion, empathy, intuition, emotionality, artistic, creativity or equality and sharing—and prefer competition, hierarchy and 'I dominant-You submissive' types of social games. Once they internalise this value system, it becomes difficult to cope with 'womanly' emotions such as grief or fear. They don't know how to deal with painful feelings and sensitivity, so act out instead.

Acting out is an unconsciously motivated behaviour that reduces tension, often created by conflicting feelings, or when one aspect in the personality feels something but another doesn't allow the expression of it. Inward tension builds up—it builds up on a physiological level—which these men discharge by 'acting out', usually not being able to realise what is behind such behaviour or what drives it. Senad also used to act out aggressively whenever he felt unpleasant inner tension. He 'learned' it from his father.

Men's power over women is only one characteristic of the patriarchy. Another characteristic is some superior men's power over other subordinated men. In patriarchal social systems, men gain power over other men by imposing strict patriarchal standards and rules, mostly through control, abuse, violence and fear.

Senad has personally experienced this. He was conditioned by his authoritarian and despotic father who imposed strict patriarchal standards and rules such as men are entitled to have power over women (so they protest when they don't have power over a woman), and men should be strong (aka boys don't cry). Senad noticed that he was conditioning his son in the same way he was conditioned by his father. But when he stopped believing that his 'feminine' Inner Boy aspect was 'all about weaknesses and vulnerabilities' and thus should be repressed, he stopped pressing his son to develop a powerful 'masculine' aspect centred around the values such as competitiveness, self-sufficiency, toughness and, above all, the 'I am dominant because I am a man' attitude.

Can we heal the wounds inflicted by the patriarchy? More and more men refuse to play that old macho game and want to integrate their more feminine characteristics and traits. They know that integrating the feminine and masculine principles is not about urging men to become effeminate or women to become mannish. For both men and women, recovery from the patriarchy comes when they learn to re-member, re-connect and embrace their other half, and cherish their own full humanity. It is perfectly possible for a man to retain sexual masculinity while at the same time allowing tenderness and nurturing to manifest in his personality. By the same token, a woman does not have to lose her femininity in return for allowing business, adventure, athletics or technical and intellectual achievements into her life.

Men and women: action and communication, thinking and feeling

Ask women to define a good partner, and we will hear about a person who has integrated both their masculine and feminine characteristics and personality traits. He is strong, reliable and firm yet warm, loving, tender, compassionate, empathic, nurturing and caring. Women say they need a man who is in touch with his feelings and responsive to his partner's feelings. He should be a strong guy who says what he thinks, stands up for what he believes in, who is a trustworthy and dependable protector and, on top of that, sensitive and able to empathically understand his female partners' emotional responses, especially in stressful life situations. Why do women insist on the qualities such as 'sensitive and empathic'? What is so appealing about these traits? It may be related to the ability to cope with the stressors in everyday life.

Women claim that they want a partner who can help them to feel more secure, stable and certain, especially in stressful life situations. Why certain? When women feel anxious and tense because they are unsure about the important issues they are dealing with—or when they doubt their internal psychological experiences and reactions—

they tend to talk about them with others who show empathy for their feelings and validate their point of view, or help them to change it.

Such conversations can help them to understand the problem better, or to feel more certain about problematic interpersonal issues or challenges and difficulties they face in their daily lives. This could be the reason why we claim women have a tendency to rely on communication with others more than men do, and react with a 'tend-and-befriend' stress response more often than men. When the woman finds herself in a stressful situation, her emotions can be overwhelming and create feeling of disorganisation or confusion. But if she has someone who is emphatic—someone who is genuinely emotionally present, responsive . . . who would create a safe environment for her to explore and understand what is going on . . . her overwhelming emotions would lose much of their toxicity.

That's why women may not be immediately concerned with finding practical solutions to stressful situations or annoying frictions in relationships. They rather seek relief by articulating the problem and expressing themselves first. When they are heard, they feel that their emotional responses to the situations are understood and validated.

Here lies the problem: men, of course, want to be understood and their emotional states recognised and acknowledged, but men's and women's perception of security or sense of certainty tend to come from different places. For a man, reaching a conclusion—whether it be through completing a job or making a decision—helps him with a sense of certainty, while finalising and getting a job done allows him to feel secure. In other words, men are inclined to rely on their own ability to take action and make things happen in order to feel okay. If they want to talk with others and open up about their problems and issues, it is because they want to solve them.

When a man finds a solution to his problem or reaches a conclusion, he feels better. When a woman shares with others her feelings and thoughts about stressful experience or challenging relationship problems, she feels better. And while the feminine likes to get on the phone and connect, feel the feelings and sometimes talk regardless of what is being talked about, the masculine prefers to get on the phone, discuss a topic, reach a conclusion and get off.

But are we talking about real differences between men and women, or about gender stereotypes? Everybody knows that gender is not a good predictor of academic skills, interests or any other characteristics. Gender stereotypes are defined as generalised beliefs about the characteristics and qualities attributed to men and women, and no individual fits the male or female stereotype perfectly. We say, for example, that girls talk about feelings more often than boys, but many of us know at least one boy who is very sensitive, immensely talkative about feelings, and doesn't do the 'boy way of doing things'. 'Differences between individual girls or between individual boys are much greater than those between the "average" girl and the "average" boy, yet we tend to generalize from the "average" girl or boy,' researchers claim.[1]

And yet, we cannot overlook the fact that, regardless of social influences and cultural norms, men are different from women, both physically and mentally. Scientists have already discovered significant differences between the male and female brain structure, as well as psychological differences between young boys and girls. Intelligence testers generally agree that women, on average, excel on tests requiring verbal fluency and attention to detail, while men excel on spatial abilities—men are better able to think of objects three dimensionally than women are. 'The right and left hemispheres of the male and female brains are not set up exactly the same way. For instance, females tend to have verbal centers on both sides of the brain, while males tend to have verbal centers on only the left hemisphere. This is a significant difference. Girls tend to use more words when discussing or describing incidence, story, person, object, feeling, or place,' Dr Gregory L. Jantz writes in the article 'Brain Differences Between Genders: Do you ever wonder why men and women think so differently?'[2]

Why do the researchers claim that men have better motor and spatial skills, and women are better at intuitive thinking? That's because 'male brains have more connections within hemispheres to optimize motor skills, whereas female brains are more connected between hemispheres to combine analytical and intuitive thinking. Roughly speaking, the back of the brain handles perception and the front of the brain handles action; the left hemisphere of the brain is the seat of logical thinking, while the right side of the brain begets intuitive thinking. The findings lend support to the view that males may excel at motor skills, while women may be better at integrating analysis and intuitive thinking.'[3]

We also believe that women, in general, are emotionally more intelligent and better at empathy. On top of that, when it comes to discussing emotional states, females, regardless of their cultural and social background, have more interest in talking about emotions, have more words and can better describe them. But Daniel Goleman, an author of a number of the books on the topic, cautions that things are not that simple. 'Emotional intelligence has four parts: self-awareness, managing our emotions, empathy, and social skill,' he writes in the article 'Are Women More Emotionally Intelligent Than Men?'[4]

There are also three kinds of empathy: cognitive empathy (being able to know how the other person sees things); emotional empathy (feeling what the other person feels); and empathic concern, or sympathy (being ready to help someone in need). Women on average may be better than men at some forms of empathy, but men may do better than women when it comes to managing distressing situations and emotions: 'Here's where women differ from men,' Goleman writes. 'If the other person is upset, or the emotions are disturbing, women's brains tend to stay with those feelings. But men's brains do something else: they sense the feelings for a moment, then tune out of the emotions and switch to other brain areas that try to solve the problem that's creating the disturbance'.[5] So, instead of ruminating or revisiting emotional memories, males, after reflecting briefly on an unpleasant emotive memory, tend to mentally analyse it and try to solve the problem that is creating the disturbance. They may also choose to do something practical about the problem, or move onto the next task unrelated to the distress, rather than reflect on their emotions.

We often tend to 'choose a side' and say the feminine way is better than the masculine, but is it? The feminine characteristics and skills such as multitasking, intuition, empathy, recognising feeling, etc. may be particularly valuable in dealing with babies and small children; however, logical, rational thinking and the strategic operations in stressful situations can be contaminated by intense emotions. If we have an instant action to be performed—when we face the dangerous situation and must act now—male brains, on average, are more attuned to it.

When we need to fight for our life, the 'masculine tendency' to shut off feelings might be more useful in such critical circumstances, the researchers claim. And these are only a few examples of how the typical masculine response is different, but equally valuable, to that of the feminine.

However, if we study not the differences between men and women, but between so-called feminine and masculine energy—characteristics and qualities in everyone regardless of their gender—we clearly realise that they are designed to complement each other in the same way the left and the right brain hemispheres in every human brain cooperate and complement each other. But what are masculine and feminine energies, anyway? How do we define these terms beyond simply our gender?

In traditional Chinese Medicine, these differences are described as differences between yin and yang. Yin energy is considered feminine; it is receptive because it moves inward from the outside. Yang energy is masculine; it is active and moves outwardly from within. The feminine is associated with receiving and attracting; the masculine is about doing and giving. It values analytical, rational thinking and practical models of productivity (the 'get it done' attitude) that acts as the foundation for many workplaces in today's society. The masculine is also protective, supportive and reliable.

Both men and women carry feminine and masculine principles symbolically represented in the yin/yang symbol. The symbol exemplifies the holistic union of the feminine and masculine (yin/yang)—the swirling interaction of equal forces—and such unions should be present in every man and woman. However, sometimes one or both of these energies is out of balance, oppressed, silenced, wounded, misunderstood, disrespected. They are often 'in war' instead of 'in love'. Without balanced, harmonious relationships between the feminine and masculine, yin and yang, emotional and mental, we may find ourselves in trouble. For example, without emotions and intuition, a rational decision may not always be the best possible choice.

Rational decision making is what separates humans from other creatures, and decision making is traditionally viewed as a process where reason calculates the best way to achieve results. But being overtly analytical and pragmatic or devoid of emotions that support mental ability and add depth to the logical approach can easily limit a deeper understanding of the complexity of a problem. Intellect cannot work at its best without emotional intelligence. Daniel Goleman writes, 'In the dance of feeling and thought the emotional faculty guides our moment-to-moment decisions, working hand-in hand with the rational mind.'[6]

Why men don't express their feelings as women do

We often hear comments that men tend to suppress their painful emotions or that they are conditioned not to ask for help. While their female partners may release tension by talking to their girlfriends about an unpleasant event or relationship problem, men may protect themselves from feeling overwhelmed by emotionally shutting down. They prefer to withdraw themselves for a while, or find refuge in isolation, in an attempt to metabolise a stressful life event or painful circumstance.

However, this male response may perplex their partners, or it can easily be misunderstood and judged by their female family members. Why don't they want to talk about their feelings and problems?

We claim that men in most cultures are socialised in ways that reinforce norms of stoicism, invulnerability and avoid emotions such as fear or sadness. 'Men have to live up to the tyranny of masculinity and prove that they are not insecure and weak,' we say. We believe that if men were not conditioned to bottle up their feelings, they would be more open to communicating about their painful emotional states (dabbed as 'vulnerability') in a similar way that women deal with internal stresses. 'If only our men could open up and just talk about what they are going through,' their wives believe, 'they would experience the same sense of relief that we women experience when we work through a problem by communicating with each other.'

But what works for women does not necessarily work for men. It may be true that men have to help themselves by breaking out of the patriarchy and stop suppressing the 'feminine within', including tender feelings. However, men claim that they do not find as much emotional relief by sharing and expressing their emotions as women do. A man whose focus is more on thinking and analysing rather than verbally communicating says he wishes to be understood rather than to 'share feelings' with others.

While his wife may want him to acknowledge and validate her emotions, he feels good when she understands not his emotions but the meaning behind what he is trying to explain. Some men say that if we want to help them, we should honour their male 'solution-based approach' in dealing with issues, rather than using the 'don't-be-afraid-of-your-vulnerability' and 'share-your-feelings' approach. Conclusion: men, at times, need different strategies for stress release than women.

For a man, especially an introvert, to share how he feels and what is going on in his private world can be uncomfortable and even awkward. When an introverted man is under stress, he may prefer to go inside to find the solution for the issues he is dealing with. While extroverts may want to talk with someone—so that they can process their thoughts and emotions out loud—an introvert would rather go inside his head to figure out the problem. For many men, talking about problems without finding solutions can be more of a distraction than a help. Besides, the man's sense of self as competent and capable to deal with issues is often defined through his ability to create results and achieve goals. So, if he wants to talk about his problem with a professional, it is because he needs expert advice. To share feelings and talk without coming to a conclusion is just a waste of time!

However, this does not mean that men should not be encouraged to open up about their inner emotional experiences. Counselling is not about 'sharing emotions' or babbling about feelings; it's about gaining deeper insights that can promote a shift in consciousness, thus change the attitude, mood, behaviour and consequently the person's life. Cognitive insight is not enough. Feeling is not the poor cousin to reason. There is no self-knowledge or wisdom without deep emotional experiences. Many men know that, but the problem is that a man's need for independence and self-sufficiency often does not allow him to seek out help even when he does need help, so his 'internal orientation'—to 'go inside' when under stress—can work against him, especially when he is depressed or suicidal.

Males and females in conflict

If you ask men what they don't like about their female partners, they will often say, 'complaining'. Men define complaining as talking about problems without the intention to do anything to remedy the situation. While women may feel that they are just processing something unpleasant or stressful, or simply expressing their frustrations or irritations, their men find it nothing but critical and negative.

Criticism: A Destructive Attempt to Get One's Needs Met

Verbal attacks or personal criticism is the common reaction to frustration in a relationship. Criticism is often fuelled by the unfounded belief that if we criticise and punish our partners with nasty comments, they will care for our needs. Or we believe that they will be sorry for the hurt they caused, so they will be kind and give us the attention we want. However, criticism is the most destructive attempt to get one's needs met or to rectify an unpleasant situation. What's the solution? The solution is to identify what you want and express it directly, instead of criticising what you don't want. Many men claim that it is a big relief for them to hear what their wives want them to do about the distress they are experiencing. Instead of long debates and deliberations about problems and issues, many men feel relieved when they realise that there is something they can do to change the situation or correct their behaviour and improve themselves. One more thing: When a man does not feel that a woman is blaming him for her unpleasant emotional state, he is much more motivated to take a corrective action in her favour.

What do women complain about? Many women complain that their husbands offer only rational or practical solutions to their problems rather than emotional support, as though they do not care how the woman feels. 'I don't want him to fix it. I want him to listen and understand what I am going through,' they say. So, why is it that men want to fix their partners' problems, and if they can't, tend to withdraw or shut down? Men say it is not easy to be immersed in their partner's painful feelings without trying to cure them. 'Especially difficult are the situations when you can't do anything to protect or help the woman you care about,' they claim. So when men feel overwhelmed by their wife's distress and powerless to take her pain away, they cope by withdrawing and disengaging from the problem, or distracting themselves by doing something else.

The Man's Hero Instinct

Is it true that men are afraid of a strong, independent and competent woman? Do they have a problem being in a close, committed relationship with her because they feel insecure and intimidated by her? There might be another reason men find it difficult to be in an intimate relationship with a woman who is strong, tough and totally independent: they fear that they have nothing valuable to offer her because she already has everything she needs. They say if a man feels he is not needed and that there is nothing he can bring to the woman's life that she could not have without him, he feels incapable of being 'a man' with her; nor can he be her hero.

Evolutionary biologists claim that the man's protector instinct is a biological drive. Most men have a built-in need to take care of their women, just as women have a built-in need to take care of their children. It often means that a man prefers a woman he feels he can make happy. Naturally, when in relationship with the woman he cares about, he wants to be needed, useful and appreciated for what he has been doing for her and their family.

If he is jealous, the most painful thought he struggles with is that there is someone else out there who can make his wife or girlfriend happier than he can. This becomes mental torture and strikes at the heart of a man's fear that he is not good enough or he is not man enough. He cannot make the woman he loves happy! But when he makes his woman satisfied, he is pleased. Yes, he is pleased because

she is happy, but he is also pleased to know that he can satisfy her. Yet men claim that to be able to fully express their
hero's instinct they need to feel safe in the relationship with
the woman. Safety is defined as 'not being constantly criticised'.

Some men try to support their female partner in the
same way they support their male friends. How do men
support each other? Men believe that the best way to
support another man—and the best compliment you can
give him—is to tell him that he is strong or capable
enough to overcome the difficulties he is dealing with.
'Try to support a woman in the same way, and you can
easily come across as being insensitive or indifferent,' relationship counsellors warn. The woman who expects
compassion and empathy from her partner hopes that he
will provide emotional comfort. If he reacts with 'Oh,
you'll be fine, I'm sure you can deal with it,' she believes
that he doesn't care or doesn't understand her.

Of course, there are many men who are compassionate
or capable of understanding and empathising with their
female partners. Empathy is defined as the ability to put
yourself in the other person's place, being able to listen
and respond to another human being without getting
caught up in your own point of view, and many men are
very good at that. However, even the compassionate and
empathetic man can feel overwhelmed and inundated by
the barrage of words and emotional expressions that
come from their female partner when she is stressed. No
doubt, men can listen and be emotionally supportive, but
it does not always come as easy for them as it does for
women. Why not? If they are goal-oriented and practical
problem-solvers, they may still ask 'What's the point in
discussing something and expressing emotions if you
can't do anything about it!'

Resentment and unfulfilled needs

Some men and women tend to offer help that they need and give the kind of love they would like to receive, and not necessarily what their partner needs or would like to receive. For example, when a woman shares that she is upset, or talks about her problems, a man may assume she is looking for assistance or advice. He will offer solutions because this is his way of trying to help. In his world, talking about problems is an invitation for advice—that's what he would expect from his male friend. So he wants to help his partner feel better by solving her problems, but she protests. She says she does not need his unsolicited advice!

Reflective Listening and Consultancy Work

Consultants are trained to listen to their clients even though they know what the client is going to say. Consultancy work is not only about giving advice, but letting the client know that they have been heard and understood. A good consultant mirrors what the client says, validates their point of view and shows empathy for how they feel.

Definition of **MIRRORING**: *Reflecting back to the client an understanding of their inner states so the client feels acknowledged and understood.*

Professional consultants know that the same advice can be viewed differently. The advice is perceived as pure gold when the client feels listened to before the advice is given, but as insignificant when the consultant jumps ahead without listening and letting the client know that they have been heard. When not allowed to talk and elaborate on their problems and issues, clients may feel that the consultant has not fully understood their situation, so the consultant's advice is often (unconsciously) devalued. This is the whole idea behind reflective listening—mirroring back to someone what you have heard them say in order to convey that you understand what has been communicated.

Many husbands complain that their wives do the same thing. Women too, tend to give unsolicited advice to their male partners. They claim their female partners often point out what men need to do differently, which may not be welcomed by the man. Indeed, why do women give unsolicited advice about what their men should do and how their men should be?

There is a general belief that the feminine tends to nurture, support growth and create beauty. When a woman bonds with her man, she has a desire to make their relationship beautiful, to please the man she loves, help him feel good about himself and improve himself. However, when she offers unsolicited advice, and helps without being asked, her man may believe that she does not trust his ability to do it himself. If she does not realise that her need to care for him and improve him may instead humiliate him, she may keep giving him what she thinks he needs and doing the things for him she believes needs to be done. And when she anticipates his needs, or gives instructions and directions believing she is helping him, he may feel offended. He may also change his perception of his partner—for the worse.

A man may perceive a woman who is too pleasing or too helpful, especially when he does not ask for help, as either being a doormat or being controlling. Both types of women—'doormats' and 'control freaks'—may trigger his sense of resentment. When she points out that what he did was wrong, she becomes his mother, or even worse: the enemy. He feels offended, resentful, degraded or controlled. When he feels resentful or controlled, he may react defensively or offensively.

On the other hand, the woman gets offended too. She feels taken for granted that the man is not grateful for what she has done for him. When she feels taken for granted and unappreciated for her efforts, her deep sense of bitterness starts festering. The bitterness builds up, and she gradually collects a ton of toxic waste, buried as resentment.

Definition of **RESENTMENT**: *Resentment is a by-product of expecting something and not getting it.*

Chronic resentment is the most common reason why relationships become difficult. How do we heal resentment? Most complaints about partners are actually statements about our unmet needs and a counterproductive attempt to get the partner to meet them. The revealing question about this emotional relationship breaker is: 'What is the need that is not getting met that causes the resentment in the first place?' The answer to that question can help us to understand the problem better and find resolution for our interpersonal conflicts, arguing, frictions and hurtful criticism.

In some cases, if we openly ask our partner for what we need, without blaming them, and show that we are ready to meet their needs, they are more open to changing their behaviour. If we do not judge, blame or criticise, they will not feel the urge to explain, defend, shield, and protect themselves from what we are saying. They are able to listen to us, instead of investing energy in self-defence strategies and focusing on their own counterattacks. When we are the enemy, our partners will react defensively or offensively. But if they do not have to counterattack or compete with our words—because we relate to them by telling them what we genuinely feel or experience—our partner is able to hear us when we are opening up to them.

The relationship shifts from romance into a battlefield when important needs or expectations such as 'My partner will love me like my parents never did' are not met. It feels as if our partner is deliberately withholding gratification, and some people may have a strong impulse to retaliate. They may try to get their partner to understand their suffering by inflicting a similar pain on them, or try to get what they want by using behaviours like withholding affection, blaming, shaming, being sarcastic and cold, or threatening, abusing and physically attacking their partner into 'loving them right'.

A partner's resentment can also be the result of an accumulation of suppressed anger and disappointment from feeling they are giving more than they are receiving, or that their partner wants to dominate them. As a result, the power struggle starts. In such relationships the power struggle between two people is about how the bond between them will be defined—who dominates and who is submissive. If the imbalance of power is chronic—one party is continuously getting more than the other—it is just a matter of time until the simmering resentment will work its way closer to the surface and starts poisoning the relationship. What to do?

Identifying and naming a power struggle between partners can help them to deal with it better. When we clearly see what is going on in the relationship, we can make choices, alternatives, and corrections. Identifying and addressing the problem can also defuse a sense of powerlessness and frustration and allow resentment to dissipate. When resentment dissolves, so too does the underlying need for revenge. But when nothing is discussed—perhaps out of fear that the discussion could cause dangerous eruptions—the problem goes underground and becomes more difficult to recognise and heal. An example is when a wife feels that her complaints about her husband's inappropriate behaviour have gone unheard or ignored.

Men's defensive withdrawal and women's reactive criticism

Many men who attend couples therapy sessions say they would like to have some magic words that would stop their wives from complaining and being upset. They worry that if they talk with their female partners about emotions, it'll be just like the arguments they have at home. They will hear their wives complaining about them, saying she is disappointed with the relationship, while the man doesn't even understand what's really wrong with their relationship. Talking about this is almost like a danger zone, a client said, so he gets frustrated and just wants 'all this fixed'. And when he can't fix it, he leaves. 'I just leave the house and go for a walk. What's the point of arguing? I can start fighting or I shut the door on her and go for a walk. There's nothing else to do', he says.

Not being able to understand what her husband is going through, and that he might be fearful of his intense emotions and inner tension that could 'explode uncontrollably', the client's wife experiences his withdrawal as a sign of abandonment, and then protests his withdrawal by further complaining and criticising. Not understanding his reaction—his defensive withdrawal is unconsciously designed to protect him from overwhelming emotions or inner tension and frustration—she may even run after him yelling, 'You just walk away like I don't matter! I'll not let you just walk away!'

Her hurt feelings are a combination of reactive anger, on the surface, and her hidden fear of abandonment and rejection. Underneath her fear is the deep sadness her Inner Child aspect had never fully experienced at the time she lost her parents, as it was too much for the six-year-old girl.

The more her husband turns away, to avoid the conflict between them, the more she feels disrespected, lonely and abandoned. The loop has taken over and it's painful for both of them.

As a real-life example, only when a couple learned to use the formula 'XYZ': *When you did X, it made me feel Y, and I'd rather you did Z instead*, could they stop the pattern of her reactive criticism and his defensive withdrawal. As she opened up to her deeper emotions of sadness and fear of being abandoned, she moved past her rigid, angry stance and started telling her husband about her loneliness. Her experiences and insights into her suppressed emotional states evoked new responses in the communication with her husband. He saw her sadness and felt compassion for her. His hidden, suppressed fear, 'I don't know what to do... We are falling apart... So I run away, what else is there to do...' disappeared. The therapist helped him to recognise and name the 'scary' emotion (fear of being lost; not knowing how to fix the problem), and expand a felt sense of his experience. Recognising and naming what he experienced (fear) helped him to stay engaged with, but not be overwhelmed by, his emotions. He could pay attention to his wife's messages about the impact his defensive distancing had on her, and both partners could see how they generated the pattern of her reactive critics and his defensive withdrawal—the pattern that would trigger their distress over and over again.

Once difficult feelings or suppressed and never-fully metabolised emotional states become addressed and worked through, partners can hear and empathise with each other. They move past surface responses (reactive anger, acting out, etc.) and take a different perspective on what is going on in their relationship, correcting their interpersonal responses and behaviour.

Some people believe that they should 'get rid of negative emotions'. However, when the core emotion is experienced (instead of being suppressed or expressed), owned and integrated, we change our sense of self and the way we engage with others.

A character assassination

A warning sign that a relationship is in danger, relationship counsellors claim, is a character assassination—a critique of the person, not the person's actions. There is a big difference between criticising a partner and pointing to a partner's behaviour in a particular situation, stating how it made you feel. Harshly criticising a partner's personality has a far more corrosive impact then saying, 'When you forget to do what you promised me, it makes me feel like I am not important to you.' People usually respond to an attack on their character either by fighting back—lashing out in anger, so the conflict ends in a fruitless shouting match—or retreating into stony silence, often with the facial expression that conveys contempt. (If it is not safe to get angry at her partner, the woman may project all of her anger and frustration at a safer target—children, for example, or someone who will not fight back).

'Resentment issues'—the ones that stem from situations where a man invalidates a woman's feelings and a woman tries to change a man's behaviour by offering unsolicited advice—and showing contempt for a partner can seriously poison the relationship. What to do? Instead of arguing (arguing defined as trying to prove your point), fighting, endlessly discussing the same themes and going around in circles, try some communication techniques.

The Exchange of Monologues Technique

The most common problem in communicating with an intimate partner is that neither side feels the other person has really heard them. They get resentful because they feel their partner does not understand them. If they don't feel understood, they are neither capable nor willing to listen to another.

Women often complain that men do not listen because they do not care. While it is true in some cases, the major reason a man is unable to display empathy towards his partner is because he feels she is not listening to him or she refuses to understand him and his point of view. Her critical tone of voice makes him feel defensive.

When people fight, they want to win. If they are lectured, shamed or yelled at, they fight back not only because they want to defend themselves but because these things are an invitation for them to compete. So, when a man shuts off his feelings of empathy or compassion and goes into fighting mode with his female partner, he is setting the stage for competition with her. But if a man who is not abusive sees his woman in pain, he feels the need to take her pain away. Most men, who are not violent or abusive, instantly relate to their partner who is genuinely expressing her feelings without blaming him for them. That's why the *exchange of monologues technique* can help couples to improve their communication.

Instructions:

The exchange of monologues is a process of speaking and listening when the disclosure of one partner is met with empathy from the other. There are different levels of empathy. Harville Hendrix, the author of the popular book *Keeping the Love You Find*, makes a distinction between first-level empathy—the communication to another person that you hear and understand his or her feelings—and second-level empathy—when you not only hear and understand but you are *experiencing* his emotion inside yourself. This second level is difficult for most of us, so Hendrix recommends couples to strive for the first level to begin with.'[6]

- The focus is on your own feelings or needs in relation to the discussed topic, or in connection with a specific incident. Instead of blaming or criticising: 'Whenever we (go shopping...) you (do something inappropriate...!)' you choose 'Yesterday when we (went shopping...) and you (did that...; said that...), I felt (angry, hurt, frustrated...) because (I needed you to be reliable; I wanted you to do...; I expected you to be...).' Psychologist Haim Ginott, the grandfather of effective-communication programs, recommended that the best formula for a complaint is "XYZ": "When you did X, it made me feel Y, and I'd rather you did Z instead." For example: "When you didn't call to tell me you were going to be late for our dinner appointment, I felt unappreciated and angry. I wish you'd call to let me know you'll be late" instead of "You're a thoughtless, self-centered bastard," Daniel Goleman writes in the book *Emotional Intelligence*.[7]

- After you have spoken, your partner reflects back to you the essence of what they heard you say. If they did not understand, you repeat the segment until you are clear that they have understood what you want to communicate. Then it is your partner's turn to speak. When they have finished, you similarly repeat back what you heard. Your partner clarifies what they said until they are satisfied that you heard them accurately.

- One person talks for a certain period of time (let's say ten minutes) while the other partner only listens. When they finish, they say thank you for listening, and the partner takes over.

- The focus in the monologue is on 'me; how I think or feel about something; what are my preoccupations, concerns, fears or frustrations, and what are my needs, desires and expectations in the relationship with my partner.' The focus in the monologue is not on 'you are...; you did that...; you made me feel like...!.' If *you* is mentioned in the monologue, it is only to point to the circumstances and situations in which the speaker felt triggered or experienced something that they want to elaborate on. The intention is not to blame or criticise your partner. Even when the speaker expresses anger, there is a big difference between blaming their partner for the emotion of anger and just telling him/her how they feel about their partner's behaviour.

Why does this technique work? The exchange of monologues technique can help to de-escalate the tension and settle the coupler's disagreement effectively.

When you are able to listen and convey empathy, the other person will feel more empathic and ready to hear you in return. Both partners benefit from it. A wife feels that her husband hears her complaint or distress (instead of offering a practical solution too early on) and empathises with her feelings about the problem or the matter even when he doesn't agree with her. Often a wife interprets her husband's advice or practical solutions as a way of his dismissing her feelings as unimportant or trivial. But when she feels heard and her feelings are validated even when her husband disagrees, she feels respected, so she can calm down.

The same is true for men. A major problem for men is that they feel overwhelmed when their wives are too intense in voicing their criticism and complaints, and/or when their wives attack them as a person. Her angry personal attack will either lead to a husband's getting defensive or he'll 'stonewall'. However, when he is heard and understood, there is no need to be offensive or defensive.

Just marital conflict or domestic abuse?

Many long-term couples have 'intense moments' from time to time when they fight. Where is the point when the intimate partners' conflicts morph into domestic abuse—either psychological or physical?

The serious problem in a relationship begins when one partner feels overwhelmed by the behaviour of the other partner. He or she is almost constantly on guard for emotional abuse or violence and hypervigilant for signs of on-coming verbal or physical attacks. This means that the other partner's abusive behaviour has become a pattern. As these patterns of behaviour tend to escalate, similar to the patterns of addictive behaviour, the marital problems get worse.

The creation of the pattern is a dangerous turning point: the point when the relationship becomes toxic. Small issues now trigger serious and even dangerous bat-tles; the abusive partner can't calm down unless they inflict pain or cause distress in other. Their 'righteous in-dignation' or feeling like an innocent victim continually fuel their anger and an urge to hurt their partner. They frequently scan what their partner does, looking for something that might confirm the view that they are vic-timised (discounting or ignoring everything the partner does that would question that view) and using it to justify the attack. Have they become addicted to abusing their partner?

What our mothers, sisters and daughters need to know

In their almost decade-long research in which they fol-lowed 63 couples with a history of battering, psychology professors Neil Jacobson and John Gottman described two distinct types of men who repeatedly abuse their partners. As discussed previously, they named the batter-ers 'Cobras' and 'Pit Bulls'.

Just to reiterate, Pit Bulls are domestic violence perpe-trators whose emotions tend to explode quickly. Jacobson and Gottman's research confirmed that once battering starts, there is nothing the victim can say or do that can effectively stop the physical battering. Pit Bulls may be insecure or oversensitive to even the slightest criticism, and they often have an excessive and unhealthy dependence on their partners. They may fear being abandoned or being betrayed, so they are often extremely jealous, possessive, and paranoid. They can be relentless and dangerous stalkers, too.

Pitt-Bull abusers are capable of feeling remorse, but they defend themselves by blaming the woman and arguing that they are victims, and their partner is the perpetrator. The pattern tends to increase in frequency and/or severity. Typically, even if physical battering does decrease over time, or even completely stop, it is replaced with emotional battering. The abuser behaves as though he has become addicted to abusing his partner; he feels compelled to inflict pain.

Unlike Cobras, Pit Bulls have been known to respond to therapy or men's behaviour change programs, but they first have to take responsibility for their actions and actively seek to change.

Cobras are different. They are about 20% of the men who commit domestic violence. They are often diagnosed with anti-social personality disorders. They can be dangerously violent or abusive towards their partners. They do so in a cold, calculating state rather than being carried away in the heat of fury. Gottman and Jacobson found that as their anger mounts, their heart rate drops: Cobras grow physiologically calmer, even as they get more belligerent and abusive. Their violence appears to be a 'calculated act of terrorism'; that's why the Cobra style of abusing a partner is often called 'intimate partner terrorism'. They tend to dominate and control their partners, and may use physical violence as a method for instilling fear and coercing the woman into fulfilling their desires or complying with their wishes, rules and regulations.

They play the 'I dominant-You submissive' nasty game, and their 'relationship' with their partner is often nothing but a power struggle.

Is the power struggle in a marriage with Cobra only about his sense of entitlement and 'getting a partner' to meet the Cobra's needs, especially the need for power and control? Can a Cobra become addicted to the 'I dominant-You submissive' game of abusing the woman? We believe he can. The sense of satisfaction can be seductive, so domestic violence perpetrators continue with controlling and dominating strategies even when power and control strategies are not directly about 'getting their partner to meet their needs', but to get high on the sense of satisfaction when she is compliant and submissive.

There are many explanations why a domestic violence perpetrator re-offends, but we maintain that the man who repeatedly abuses a woman often does it because he craves it. Of course, he may not be aware of this. Instead, he'll tell her 'You made me do it!' Or he'll tell her she is too sensitive, or her hurt feelings are her own fault. Or he'll simply tell her she is crazy, stupid and deranged if she thinks that he feels compelled to act abusively in a similar way a gambler feels compelled to gamble.

A serious re-offender is akin to an 'energy vampire'. The ongoing nature of the repetitive pattern of his abuse and violence is designed to elicit particular responses in his victim. Like vampires who feed on the victim's blood, he feeds on the energy-in-motion (emotion). The woman's hurt feelings, her sense of degradation or humiliation and/or her fear of him is what he is after. Why? The woman's emotional reaction helps him to feel better. It helps him to reduce unpleasant inner tension and can even give him a sense of pleasure. Some feel rise in self-esteem when they 'punish' (abuse) the woman.

The idea that your intimate partner craves to hurt you is hard to believe. So, many abused women may accept his excuses ('He has problems with alcohol; drugs; stresses at work or in his family; poor communication skills; childhood trauma...') or she may refuse to believe that what he does to her is intentional, so she'll try to bring him to reason. Like a wife of a gambler who is hoping that her husband would stop gambling if he realised the negative consequences of his habit, the victim of domestic violence may believe that if her partner just understood the impact of his deeds or words on her, he would not abuse her again.

This is why some victims feel the need to explain to their abusers how they feel and in what way his abuse is hurting them. But the problem is not his lack of insight or information about the consequences of his behaviour. On the contrary, he is very aware of the effects of what he is doing to her! The woman's shame, pain, humiliation or her fear of him is precisely what he intends to 'extract' from her. However, he might not be ready to see and acknowledge that fact.

The re-offender often becomes progressively more abusive. This is a truth universally acknowledged by those who have professional or long-term personal experience with intimate partner abuse or domestic violence. But the victim may not clearly see it because she has never heard a plausible explanation as to why this repetitive pattern of abuse tends to escalate in frequency and severity. The woman may try to explain it away by the increased stresses in the man's daily life, at work or in the family, and even comes up with ideas, solutions or suggestions how to change things. But her solutions and suggestions do not address the root causes and hidden reasons for his abuse, so nothing much changes in the way he treats her.

When she realises that the usual strategies—complaining, blaming, threatening him, explaining the problem to him or attending counselling programs with him—do not yield positive results, she may feel powerless, trapped, start sinking into depression or alcoholism. Or she may attempt to justify his abuse by blaming herself for it.

However, if she could pause and not go into her head to explain away the patterns and cycles of his abuse, she would realise that her mere need to explain his repetitive attacks on her is a sign that something is deeply wrong with the man's behaviour towards her. And if she stopped justifying, rationalising or going through endless cycles of blaming and criticising him . . . she would be able to turn inwards and hear the voice of the Wise Woman within. The Wise Woman's advice is clear and straightforward:

> 'With an abusive partner, rather than having a long speech with him or explaining how you feel when he abuses you, you say one sentence, "If you do (or say) that again, you will lose me forever." Then you get up and leave the space, or if you can't leave, you stop arguing.
>
> You say the sentence without harsh words, without raising your voice, without preaching or teaching him, or pointing out his flaws. With that clear message, you convey to him that you don't come across as demanding something from him, but as someone who is okay with whatever he decides. Now it's up to him to do or to say that again, or not.
>
> He may initially dismiss, ridicule or ignore what you said. But you are fully aware of what you need to do if he repeats hurting you. You're not going to give in simply because you feel lonely or anxious about living without him, nor you deceive yourself with false hopes that he'll change. You are sure that the man you want to stay with is the man who says, "You know what, you're right. I apologise. I don't want to lose you"—and who never does that again.'

Chapter 16

SOME CLOSING THOUGHTS

Sydney, February 2021

Shocking statistics have revealed that since the start of the coronavirus lockdown in early 2020, domestic violence has dramatically surged in big cities all over the world. Official figures suggest that violent crime, including murder, rape and assault, has plummeted, but as lockdowns began, domestic violence—a crime committed in private homes—has increased. The UK's largest domestic abuse charity, Refuge, reported a 700% increase in calls to its helpline in a single day, while a separate helpline for the perpetrators of domestic abuse seeking help to change their behaviour received 25% more calls after the start of the COVID-19 lockdown.[1]

Specialists have worked around the clock to ensure that frontline domestic abuse services remain open and accessible to victims. The campaign, promoted under the Twitter hashtag #YouAreNotAlone# has encouraged the public to show their solidarity for those trapped in the horrific cycle of abuse. Many people and organisations have responded with empathy and compassion. Hotel chains and numerous charities have offered alternative accommodation to help women and children escape domestic violence.

Abusive men have been seeking help, too. We may say that the 25% increase in calls to the Refuge helpline from the perpetrators who need help to stop abusing their partners is nothing in comparison with the increase in the number of calls from the victims; however, we cannot neglect the fact that there are men who are genuinely motivated to stop. They too feel trapped in the cycle of abuse, no matter how hard it is for them to realise that. The moment they accept and acknowledge that their own behaviour is the real issue, they find the reason to change it. If only they knew how. Some don't even understand why they repeatedly abuse their partners in the first place, or why they can't control themselves.

Our intention in writing *Toxic Love* is to inspire these men to look for answers to their *why* and *how* questions. We want to help the victims of abuse free themselves from the domestic violence trap, as well. Ultimately, we would like to empower both men and women to create healthier relationships and ways of relating. This book is also aimed at researchers and practitioners working in the field of domestic violence and intimate partner violence. It challenges the current understanding of the nature of intimate partner abuse.

We believe that the sustained pattern of male-on-female abuse—the pattern that tends to increase in frequency and/or severity and/or diversity—is not just about power and control. It is also about feeding an addiction. Thus by posing the question, 'Why does the pattern of abuse tend to escalate in frequency and/or severity?' we invite the readers to search deeper and view the abuser's behaviour within a behavioural addiction paradigm.

We also invite abusive men to view the pattern from this new angle. As long as they believe that domestic abuse is all about power and control and nothing else, it is hard to change the underlying addictive behaviour. The reason for that is very simple: When we don't understand what motivates us to do the same thing over and over again, it's hard to quit. Therefore, changes in the basic assumptions are necessary. For example, the shift in perspective from power and control to behaviour addiction can help abusers to understand that they may have unintentionally created a dangerous aspect in their personality—an aspect that has become addicted to abusing their partners. However, understanding the *why* is not enough if they are to break the repetitive cycle of abuse in their relationships. They also need to know *how*.

So far, the existing treatment programs for abusive men haven't been very successful in treating perpetrators or protecting victims. We need to expand our knowledge and address the deeper layers of the challenging problem we are dealing with.

We, the authors, are big believers in a psychoeducational approach to changing these addictive behaviour patterns. The psychoeducational slant in the book reflects our background in psychotherapy with the victims of torture, trauma and abuse, and in counselling work with boys and men who use violence. In our experience, helping the victims of trauma to understand the nature of their disturbing symptoms (especially the symptoms of intrusion—intrusive thoughts and images; traumatic nightmares; flashbacks; and traumatic re-enactments), and *how* to stop them, is extremely important if we are to help victims improve their psychological condition. The same premise applies when we work with the men who want to change their abusive behaviour.

The insights into the nature of repetitive patterns of abuse—the information about how we create various aspects in our personality and how to dismantle them—have enormous implications for the treatment and prevention of domestic abuse. Just as the knowledge about the coronavirus is crucial in making a COVID-19 vaccine, so is the knowledge about the addictive nature of repetitive patterns of abuse in dealing with the domestic violence pandemic. The better we understand the pattern, the inter-generational transmission of abuse and the factors that contribute to the conversion from terrorised into terrorising . . . the better we will be inoculated against this type of malice.

And yet, the perennial question, 'Why do we abuse each other?' still remains. Being harmless (committing no harm) is an essential characteristic of higher levels of consciousness. The evolution of human consciousness may be a slow process but there is a belief that even a small number of people who resonate higher on the 'scale of harmlessness' can significantly contribute to the mission of eradicating the violence on the planet. This includes domestic violence and intimate partner abuse. Imagine what might happen if more people cease deriving pleasure from another person's suffering and commit to not hurting others? It is our hope that this book can contribute to reducing the current epidemic of harm, for the sake of the victims, perpetrators, their children and their children's children.

Indira and Dean

ENDNOTES

INTRODUCTION

1. GLOBAL STUDY ON HOMICIDE Gender-related killing of women and girls UNODC Research 2018. https://www.unodc.org/documents/data-and-analysis/GSH2018/GSH18_Gender-related_killing_of_women_and_girls.pdf

CHAPTER 1

1. Initially, Johnson argued that there were two distinct forms of intimate partner violence (IPV): 'common couple violence' (now known as situational or conflict-initiated violence), and 'patriarchal terrorism' – the pattern of violence primarily perpetrated by a man against his female partner.
(Johnson MP. 'Patriarchal terrorism and common couple violence: Two forms of violence against women'. *Journal of Marriage & the Family*. 1995;57:283–294).
Later, he renamed 'patriarchal terrorism' as 'intimate terrorism'; this has been amended in recognition that not all domestic abuse is rooted in patriarchal structures and attitudes. (Johnson MP. 'Domestic violence: It's not about gender – or is it?' *Journal of Marriage and Family*. 2005;67:1126–1130)
2. *Domestic violence – is there a risk of death* Western Centre for Research & Education on Violence Against Women &Children. Canadian Domestic Homicide Prevention Initiative. http://makeitourbusiness.ca/warning-signs/domestic-violence-is-there-a-risk-of-death
3. Ibid.
"The Domestic Violence Death Review Committee (DVDRC) found that in 81% of the reviewed cases of domestic homicide, the couple was either separated or in the process of separating. This shows that victims are most vulnerable and at risk for death when they have left or plan to leave the abuser. But why does leaving an abusive relationship put a victim at greater risk for being killed? The motive for post-separation violence, including death, has been grouped into three categories: 1) retaliation, 2) restoration, and 3) reconciliation".

4 Mindy B. Mechanic, Terri L. Weaver, and Patricia A. Resick, 'Intimate Partner Violence and Stalking Behavior: Exploration of patterns and correlates in a sample of acutely battered women', PMC, US National Library of Medicine National Institutes of Health, Violence Vict. 2000 Spring;15(1):55-72. . https://www.ncbi.nlm.nih.gov/pmc/articles/PMC2977930/
"The length of time a woman was out of the violent relationship was the strongest predictor of postseparation stalking, with increased stalking found with greater time out of the relationship".
5. Ibid.

CHAPTER 2

1. Eric Berne, *Games People Play: The Psychology of Human Relationships* (London: Penguin Books, 1964), 15.
2. Ibid (p.13, 14)

CHAPTER 3

1. Lenore E. Walker, *The Battered Woman* (New York: Harper & Row, Publishers, Inc., 1979), Introduction xi.
2. Ibid. p. Introduction xv.
3. Prevalence of Domestic Violence in the United States – "On average more than three women a day are murdered by their husbands or boyfriends in the United States" (Family Violence: Legal, Medical, and Social Perspectives, by Paul Harvey Wallace, Cliff Roberson, Chapter 1, p5)
https://edition.cnn.com/2013/12/06/us/domestic-intimate-partner-violence-fast-facts/index.html   CNN Domestic (Intimate Partner) Violence Fast Facts
Prevalence of Domestic Violence in Australia – "On average, one woman a week is murdered by her current or former partner".
https://www.ourwatch.org.au/understanding-violence/facts-and-figures
4. Linda G. Mills, *Violent Partners: A Breaking Plan for Ending the Cycle of Abuse* (New York: Basic Books, 2009), p. Introduction xii.
5. Joan McClennen, PhD, *Social Work and Family Violence: Theories, Assessment, and Intervention* (New York: Springer Publishing Company LLC, 2010), 230.
6. Thomas J. Dishion, James J. Snyder, *The Oxford Handbook of Coercive Relationship Dynamics* (Oxford: Oxford University Press, 2016), [Critique of the Duluth Model p.218.]
7. Jess Hill, *See What You Made Me Do: Power, Control and Domestic Abuse* (Black Inc, 2019), 107.
8. Richard C. Howard, 'The quest for excitement: A missing link between personality disorder and violence?' October 2011 *Journal of Forensic Psychiatry and Psychology*, 22(5):692-705, p2.

362

https://www.researchgate.net/publication/233258548_The_quest_for_excite
ment_A_missing_link_between_personality_disorder_and_violence

9. Heng Choon (Oliver) Chan, *A Global Casebook of Sexual Homicide* (Springer
Nature Singapore Pte Ltd., 2019), 68.

10. Liam Ennis, Carissa Toop, Sandy Jung, Sean Bois, 'Instrumental and
Reactive Intimate Partner Violence: Offender Characteristics, Reoffense
Rates, and Risk Management', *Journal of Threat Assessment and Management*,
Vol 4(2), June 2017, (p.5)
https://www.researchgate.net/publication/315933849_Instrumental_and_Re
ac-
tive_Intimate_Partner_Violence_Offender_Characteristics_Reoffense_Rates
_and_Risk_Management

11. Ibid. (p.13)

12. Ibid (p.13)

13. Neil Jacobson and John Gottman, *When Men Batter Women: New Insights
into Ending Abusive Relationships* (New York: Simon & Schuster, 1998), 121.

14. Ibid (p.29)

15. Ibid (p.84)

16. Ibid (p.92).

17. Ibid (p.29)

18. Ibid (p.38)

19. Evan Stark, *Coercive Control: How Men Entrap Women in Personal Life*
(New York: Oxford University Press, 2007), 5.

20. Evan Stark , Ph.D, MSW, 'Re-presenting Battered Women: Coercive
Control and the Defense of Liberty' (Prepared for Violence Against Wom-
en: Complex Realities and New Issues in a Changing World, Les Presses de
l'Université du Québec (2012), (p.11)
https://www.stopvaw.org/uploads/evan_stark_article_final_100812.pdf

21. Ibid (p.12)

22. Ibid (p.9)

23. Ibid (p.11)

24. Ibid (p.13)

25. Ibid (p.10)

26. Jess Hill, *See What You Made Me Do: Power, Control and Domestic Violence*
(Black Inc. 2019), 19.

27. Evan Stark, Ph.D, MSW, 'Re-presenting Battered Women: Coercive
Control and the Defense of Liberty' (Prepared for Violence Against Wom-
en: Complex Realities and New Issues in a Changing World, Les
Presses de l'Université du Québec (2012), (p.13)

28. Ibid (p.9)
https://www.researchgate.net/publication/14715739

29. Janet R. Johnston, Ph.D., and Linda E.G. Campbell, Ph.D, 'A Clinical Typology of Interparental Violence In Disputed-Custody Divorces', *American Journal of Orthopsychiatry* 63(2):190-9, May 1993, (p.191)
30. Ibid (p.193)
31. Ibid (p.193)
32. Ibid (p.194)
33. Richard C. Howard, 'The quest for excitement: a missing link between personality disorder and violence?'
The Journal of Forensic Psychiatry & Psychology, 2011, 1–14 (p.1)
https://www.researchgate.net/publication/233258548_The_quest_for_excitement_A_missing_link_between_personality_disorder_and_violence
34. Ibid (p.7)
35. Ibid (p.4)
36. Ibid (p.11)
37. Neil Jacobson and John Gottman, *When Men Batter Women: New Insights into Ending Abusive Relationships* (New York: Simon & Schuster, 1998), 62.
38. Richard C. Howard, 'The quest for excitement: a missing link between personality disorder and violence?'
The Journal of Forensic Psychiatry & Psychology, 2011, 1–14 (p.8)
39. Ibid (p.11)

CHAPTER 4

1. Jennifer Schnider M.D. website: 'Addiction, Tolerance, and Dependence: An Interview with Dr. Jennifer Schneider'
http://www.jenniferschneider.com/index.php/81-articles/23-addiction-tolerance-and-dependence-an-interview-with-dr-jennifer-schneider
2. Loretta Graziano Breuning, PhD, *Habits of a Happy Brain: Retrain Your Brain to Boost Your Serotonin, Dopamin, Oxitocin, & Endorphin Levels* (New York: Adams Media An Imprint of Simon & Schuster, 2016.), 9.
3. Ibid, (p.13)
4. Ibid, (p.36)
5. Ibid, (p.50)
6. Ibid, (p.51)
7. Ibid, (p.51)
8. David R. Hawkins, M.D., Ph.D., *Power vs Force: The Hidden Determinants of Human Behaviour* (Australia: Hay House Australia Pty Ltd, 2000), 84.
9. Ibid (p.85)
10. Ibid (p.84)
11. Ibid (p.85)
12. Ibid (p.84)
13. Nancy M Petry, *Behavioural Addictions: DSM-5 and Beyond* (New York: Oxford University Press, 2016), 228.

http://www.insightonfoods.com/wp-content/uploads/2013/05/Moreishness-and-Drinkability-Insight-on-foods.pdf

14. Aleks Milosevic, David M. Ledgerwood, 'The subtyping of pathological gambling: A comprehensive review', *Clinical Psychology Review*, 2010. https://www.uni-hohen-heim.de/fileadmin/einrichtungen/gluecksspiel/intern/SubtypingPG.pdf

15. Ibid, (p.9)

16. Robert Weiss, 'Sexual Addiction, Hypersexual Disorder and the DSM-5: Myth or Legitimate Diagnosis?' *Counselor, The Magazine for Addiction Professionals*, Feature Articles, 2012/Sep-Oct. http://www.robertweissmsw.com/wp-content/uploads/2012/09/Counselor2012.pdf

17. Richard Irons, M.D. and Jennifer P. Schneider, M.D, 'When is Domestic Violence a Hidden Face of Addiction?' (1997) *Journal of Psychoactive Drugs* 29 (4):337-344. http://www.jenniferschneider.com/articles/domestic.html

18. Sam Vaknin, 'Narcissists, Narcissistic Supply And Sources of Supply', *HealthyPlace.com* https://www.healthyplace.com/personality-disorders/malignant-self-love/narcissists-narcissistic-supply-and-sources-of-supply

19. Jeanna Bryner, 'Humans Crave Violence Just Like Sex', *LiveScience Staff Writer, LiveScience.com*, Jan 17, 2008. https://www.livescience.com/2231-humans-crave-violence-sex.html

20. Bill Buford, *Among the Thugs:The Experience, and the Seduction, of Crowd Violence* (New York: W. W. Norton & Co Inc. 1992), 217.

21. John H. Kerr, *Understanding Soccer Hooliganism* (Open University Press, Buckingham, 1994), 88.

22. Richard Irons, M.D. and Jennifer P. Schneider, M.D, 'When is Domestic Violence a Hidden Face of Addiction?' (1997) *Journal of Psychoactive Drugs* 29 (4):337-344. http://www.jenniferschneider.com/articles/domestic.html

23. Ibid

24. Ibid

25. Ibid

CHAPTER 5

1. Eric Berne, *Transactional Analysis in Psychotherapy: The Classic Handbook to its Principles* (A Condor Book Souvenir Press, Educational and Academic, Ltd, 1961), 47.

CHAPTER 6

1. Freda Briggs, Russel M.F. Hawkins, Mary Williams, *A comparison of the early childhood and family experiences of incarcerated, convicted male child molesters and men who were sexually abused in childhood and have no convictions for sexual offences against children* (University of South Australia, Magill Campus, South Australia, 1994), p.3,4. https://crg.aic.gov.au/reports/30-92-3.pdf
2.Ibid, p.3
3.Ibid, p.39
4.Ibid, p.45.
5.The cycles of violence: The relationship between childhood maltreatment and the risk of later becoming a victim or perpetrator of violence Key facts Violence and Injury Prevention Programme WHO Regional Office for Europe, (© World Health Organization, 2007).
http://www.euro.who.int/__data/assets/pdf_file/0008/98783/E90619.pdf

CHAPTER 7

1. Susan Chenery, 'Call me changed', *The Sydney Morning Herald*, November 21-22, 2015 (p.32 News Review)
2. Ibid.

CHAPTER 8

1. Quoted in: Thomas A. Harris, M.D, *I'm OK - You're OK* (New York: Harper & Row, 1969), 1.
2. *The term "Aspectology®" was coined by Geoffrey Hoppe and Tobias of the Crimson Council to explain the different roles and identities that we have used to help answer the fundamental question: Who Am I? We create helpful aspects of ourselves to meet situations in life, such the parent, the business owner, the healer, etc., and sometimes less helpful aspects appear in response to traumatic situations. Ultimately, all these parts of self can be welcomed home and integrated back within the true Self. More information on Aspectology® can be found at www.crimsoncircle.com.
3. Janina Fisher, *Healing the Fragmented Selves of Trauma Survivors* (New York: Routledge, 2017), 10.
4. Ibid, p.8
5. Richard C. Schwartz, Robert R. Falconer *Many Minds, One Self:Evidence for a Radical Shift in Paradigm* (Illinois: Trailheads Publications, 2017), 10.
6. C.G.Jung, *Memories, dreams, Reflects* (London: HarperCollins*Publishers* 1995), 354.
7. Allen Carr, *Allen Carr's Easy Way To Stop Smoking* (Penguin Books Third Edition 1999), 34.
8. Ibid, p.

CHAPTER 9

1. Robert M. Sapolsky, *Behave: The Biology of Humans at Our Best and Worst* (New York: Penguin Press 2017), 74.
2. Smilja Teodorović, Bogdan Uzelac, *Genetic basis of aggression: Overview and implications for legal proceedings* (Romanian Journal of Legal Medicine Vol. XXIII, No 3(2015), p.195-196. http://www.rjlm.ro/system/revista/35/193-202.pdf

3. Sandra Maitri, *The Spiritual Dimensions of the Enneagram: Nine Faces of the Soul* (NewYork: Jeremy P.Tarcher/Penguin, 2000), 13.
4. Ibid, p.131.
5. Robert D. Hare, *Without Conscience* (New York: The Guilford Press, 1999), 145.
6. Michael R. Gottfredson and Travis Hirschi, *A General Theory of Crime* (Stanford University Press, Stanford, California, 1999), 5
7. Ibid, p. (Preface xv)
8. Ibid, p. 177

CHAPTER 10

1. Roberto Assagioli, M.D., *Psychosynthesis* (London: Thorsons, An Imprint of HarperCollins Publishers, 1993), 22.
2. Allen Carr, *Allen Carr's Easy Way To Stop Smoking* (Penguin Books Third Edition 1999), 34.
3. Ibid, p76
4. Internet Encyclopedia of Philosophy, George Santayana (1863 – 1952) https://www.iep.utm.edu/santayan/

CHAPTER 11

1. Bessel A. van der Kolk, MD., 'The Compulsion to Repeat the Trauma Re-enactment, Revictimization, and Masochism' *(Psychiatric Clinics of North America*, Volume 12, Number 2, Pages 389-411, June 1989).
http://www.cirp.org/library/psych/vanderkolk/
2. Fanita English, M.S.W, 'Episcript and the "Hot Potato" Game' (*TA Bulletin*, October 1969)
http://www.fanitaenglish.com/fileadmin/fanita_content/downloads/Episcript%20and%20the%20hot%20potato%20game.pdf

3. Richard Irons, M.D., FASAM, and Jennifer P. Schneider, M.D., Ph.D. 'When is Domestic Violence a Hidden Face of Addiction?' in *Journal of Psychoactive Drugs*, Vol 29, pages 337-344, 1997, authors
http://www.jenniferschneider.com/articles/domestic.html

4. Jess Hill, *See What You Made Me Do: Power, Control and Domestic Violence* (Black Inc. 2019), 17

5. Robert D. Hare, PhD, *Without conscience: The disturbing world of the psychopaths among us*, (New York: The Guilford Press, 1999), 53.

6. Ibid (p.49)

7. Ibid (p.38)

8. Ibid (p.145)

9. Ibid (p.172)

10. Ibid (p.173)

11. Ibid (p.6,7)

12. *Domestic violence laws passed in Queensland to make non-fatal strangulation a separate offence* By Gail Burke Posted 20 April 2016,
http://www.abc.net.au/news/2016-04-20/domestic-violence-laws-strangulation-new-offence-queensland/7340340

13. Stacy Sechrist, Ph.D., John Weil, & Terri Shelton, Ph.D. Evaluation of the Offender Focused Domestic Violence Initiative (OFDVI) in High Point, NC & Replication in Lexington, NC February, 2016 (p.7) (Suggested Citation: Sechrist, S. M., Weil, J. D. L., & Shelton, T. L. (2016). Evaluation of the Offender Focused Domestic Violence Initiative (OFDVI) in High Point, NC and Replication in Lexington, NC. Final report for Community Oriented Policing Services, cooperative agreement number 2013-CK-WX-K028. Washington, DC: U.S. Department of Justice.) https://ncnsc.uncg.edu/wp-content/uploads/2013/11/COPS-OFDVI-Lexington-High-Point-Evaluation-FINAL.pdf

14. Ibid (p.119-120)

15. Ibid (p.96)

16. Hayley Gleeson, 'Jess Hill's mission to understand abusive men' Posted SunSunday 23 JunJune 2019 at 6:05am, updated SunSunday 23 JunJune 2019 at 9:10am

https://www.abc.net.au/news/2019-06-23/jess-hill-domestic-violence-cruel-twist-abusive-men/11188842

CHAPTER 12

1. Darlene Lancer, *Codependency for Dummies* (John Wiley & Sons Inc. 2nd Edition, 2015), 52.
2. edited by Bonnie S. Fisher, Steven P. Lab, *Encyclopedia of Victimology and Crime Prevention*, Volum 1, (SAGE Publications, Inc. 2010), 257.
3. Ibid, p. 257.
4. Ibid, p. 258.
5. Lenore E. A. Walker, EdD, *The Battered Woman* (2nd Edition, Springer Publishing Company, 2000), 7.
6. Judith L. Herman, *Trauma and Recovery*, (Basic books, 1992), 92.
7. Mark Banschick M.D. 'Field of Intimacy, The physics of love and anguish'
https://www.psychologytoday.com/us/blog/the-intelligent-divorce/201205/field-intimacy
8. PositivePsychology.com Learned Helplessness: Seligman's Theory of Depression (+ Cure)
https://positivepsychologyprogram.com/learned-helplessness-seligman-theory-depression-cure/

CHAPTER 14

1. Bessel A. van der Kolk, MD 'The Compulsion to Repeat the Trauma Reenactment, Revictimization, and Masochism, (*Psychiatric Clinics of North America,* Volume 12, Number 2, Pages 389-411, June 1989)
http://www.cirp.org/library/psych/vanderkolk/
2. *Cultivating the Witness* Posted September 4, 2013 Excerpt from Ram Dass' newly released book Polishing the Mirror: How to Live From Your Spiritual Heart https://www.ramdass.org/cultivating-witness/
3. http://www.goddess.ws/kuan-yin.html
4.Jessica Griggs, 'Tetris blocks traumatic flashbacks even after the memory is fixed', *NewScientist*, 6 July 2015.
https://www.newscientist.com/article/dn27846-tetris-blocks-traumatic-flashbacks-even-after-the-memory-is-fixed/
5. Ibid

6. Emily A Holmes, Ella L James, Thomas Coode-Bate, Catherine Deeprose, 'Can Playing the Computer Game "Tetris" Reduce the Build-Up of Flashbacks for Trauma?' A Proposal From *Cognitive Science National Library of Medicine*, 2009 Jan 7. https://pubmed.ncbi.nlm.nih.gov/19127289/
https://www.sciencedaily.com/releases/2015/08/150813101535.htm
Playing Tetris for as little as three minutes at a time can weaken cravings for drugs, food and activities such as sex and sleeping by approximately one fifth, according to new research. ScienceDaily
7. http://www.abc.net.au/news/2014-11-25/elsie-you-believe-it-is-your-fault/5915514
8. Taylor, S.E., Klein, L.C., Lewis, B.P., Gruenewald, T.L., Gurung, R. and Updegraff, J. 'Biobehavioral responses to stress in females: Tend-and-befriend, not fight-or-flight.' *Psychological Review*, 107, 411-429. (2000)
http://dx.doi.org/10.1037/0033-295X.107.3.411
9. Cecilia Menjivar and Olivia Salcido 'Immigrant Women and Domestic Violence: Common Experiences in Different Countries' Source: *Gender and Society*, Vol. 16, No. 6 (Dec., 2002), pp. 898-920 Published by: Sage Publications, Inc.
https://www.peacepalacelibrary.nl/ebooks/files/Immigrant-Women-and-Domestic-Violence-Experiences-Menjivar.pdf

CHAPTER 15

1 Patricia B. Campbell, Ph.D., Jennifer N. Storo, *Girls Are... Boys Are...:Myths, Stereotypes & Gender Differences*, Office of Educational Research and Improvement U.S. Department of Education http://www.campbell-kibler.com/Stereo.pdf
2. Gregory L. Jantz Ph.D 'Brain Differences Between Genders: Do you ever wonder why men and women think so differently?' *Psychology Today*, Posted Feb 27, 2014 https://www.psychologytoday.com/intl/blog/hope-relationships/201402/brain-differences-between-genders
3. Tanya Lewis, 'How Men's Brains Are Wired Differently than Women's', *LiveScience* on December 2, 2013
https://www.scientificamerican.com/article/how-mens-brains-are-wired-differently-than-women/
4. Dan Goleman, Ph.D., 'Are Women More Emotionally Intelligent Than Men?' *Psychology Today*, Apr 29, 2011.
https://www.psychologytoday.com/us/blog/the-brain-and-emotional-intelligence/201104/are-women-more-emotionally-intelligent-men
5. Daniel Goleman, *Emotional Intelligence, Why It Can Matter More Than IQ* (London: Bloomsbury, 1995), 28.
6. Harville Hendrix, Keeping the Love You Find, A Personal Guide, (New York: Atria Books, 1992), 284.

7. Daniel Goleman, Emotional Intelligence, Why It Can Matter More Than IQ (London: Bloomsbury, 1995), 146

ACKNOWLEDGEMENTS

Dean Quirke

I want to thank Indira Novic for her invitation to join her in co-authoring this book. *Toxic Love* was inspired through a conversation we had about a book I was writing through my life lens, which focused on changing the patterns of self-destructive behaviours in boys and men

To my wife and most generous supporter, Fransiska Ingrati, your love, encouragement, wisdom and guidance has ultimately helped bring much of this material to life. I know Indira and I am so grateful for your editing of the manuscript's initial drafts. Thank you for your incredible attention to detail and endless conversations on restructuring the material into a readable format.

To my spiritual teachers, they inspire a willingness to seek answers to many of life's philosophical questions. Their generous sharing of the ancient knowledge and wisdom of the yogic tradition has guided me to go deeper into the origins of destructive behaviour patterns.

I have worked with the many young men who have restored my faith in human beings' abilities to change their behaviour and redirect their focus from self to others. With a joyful heart, I express my delight in observing the power of youth working in collaboration on projects that inspire a sense of connection through community.

To my family. My sister's strong spirit of keeping going while battling inner conflict and facing the demons of her own addiction, abuse and mental illness, with the attitude of using those learnings to help others overcome their suffering. I am also thankful for my dad's words of encouragement to share information and help find the answers to healing abuse. Thank you also to my extended families' continuous support.

To Dr Juliette Lachemeier, our editor, publisher and guide at The Erudite Pen, Indira and I express so much gratitude for your ability to take such complex information and simplify what we hope will bring understanding to a larger audience.

To the thousands of men sitting in group circles, they dare to be vulnerable in sharing and providing space for others to do the same, which will help men redefine masculinity and shape a new paradigm to help define what it means to be a good man.

And finally, I would like to acknowledge the power of community. This collaboration brings out the strengths, skills and heart of the collective working towards change for the benefit of the highest good.

Indira Haracic-Novic

The idea to write this book came to me during a farewell lunch for one of our dear STARTTS colleagues.

374

A group of us counsellors enjoyed food in our favourite restaurant, Jasmine, in the Western Sydney suburb of Auburn, and as usual, we discussed the future of our colleague who was about to leave us, as well as some work-related topics that concerned us all. At the time, we had just commenced the compulsory routine of screening female clients about their experience of domestic violence. We shared our first experiences and impressions, and agreed that screening may indeed encourage women who would not otherwise disclose abuse or recognise their experience as abuse.

I was eating a delicious Kafta kebab and babbling about the nature of the repetitive patterns of perpetrators' violent behaviours, and how the pattern of abusive behaviour is very similar to the pattern of addictive behaviour – my favourite conversation topic.

Since the beginning of the Bosnian war in 1992, I have heard so many stories about perpetrators who got hooked on humiliating, torturing and raping, similar to the way people got hooked on drugs or gambling...and I was developing my psychology narrative. I said that we can become addicted to seeking retribution against our enemies, or revenge addiction. That's why we can't seem to control our urges to lash out at perceived enemies and may even derive a great deal of pleasure from it. But my colleagues didn't take me seriously. "He just wants to control her. Domestic violence or intimate partner abuse is all about power and control," they said.

Perhaps I'm not able to explain it properly, I thought, a bit disappointed by their lack of interest in my favourite topic. Would I be able to inspire them to view the repetitive pattern of abusive behaviour within an addiction paradigm if I wrote about it?

I went home and started searching the internet. I wanted to see what had already been written about it. I was searching high and low, but the only article I found was 'When is domestic violence a hidden face of addiction', written by two American doctors, Richard Irons and Jennifer Schneider, in 1997. The article perfectly explained what I was trying to explain.

That's why I would like to express my deep gratitude first of all to Jennifer P. Schneider, M.D., Ph.D. She is a nationally recognised American expert in addiction-related fields: addictive sexual disorders and the management of chronic pain with opioids, but also a compassionate doctor committed to educating others in her fields of specialty. I have certainly learned a lot from her. She helped me with the manuscript, too. I was over the moon when I read her e-mail message: 'I was indeed very interested in your manuscript, a subject that Richard Irons and I wrote about in 1997.' My personal debt to her for her time and advice given to me during the course of writing the book is beyond measure.

I also want to express deep gratitude to my brother, Asim Haracic, MD, a psychiatrist in Washington, DC. His support, enthusiasm and long hours spent with me discussing a hundred and one clinical issues has given me so much energy. His insights and perceptions based on his own work with the victims of trauma and abuse are inextricably woven into the fabric of this book. Love you, bro.

To my colleagues at STARTTS, whose sincerity and dedication to the work with the trauma survivors make it an honour to work with them, I also want to express my thankfulness.

I would like to thank Jennifer Y. Levy-Peck, PhD. As a clinical psychologist and an expert in the field, Jennifer has worked with trauma survivors, co-founded a domestic violence program in Virginia, USA, and helped lead the development of services for sexual assault and abuse survivors. She is also an excellent editor, as well. Her preliminary review and suggestions about the book's content and structure helped me immensely. I am also deeply grateful to Professor Patricia Easteal, School of Law, University of Canberra, Australia, for referring me to Jennifer.

Much respect and gratitude to Amela Zukic, who provided feedback on several chapters.

ABOUT THE AUTHORS

Indira H-Novic, a clinical psychologist, has been working as a clinician, clinical consultant and writer in the area of war and refugee-related trauma, since the beginning of the war in Bosnia and Herzegovina in 1992.

She has worked at STARTTS (NSW Service for the Treatment and Rehabilitation of Torture and Trauma Survivors) since 1996. She provides counselling treatment for the victims of torture, rape and abuse.

As a clinical consultant, Indira provides clinical supervision, training, consultations and support for clinicians, counsellors and case workers in their work with refugees and victims of trauma and abuse.

Her particular interest and expertise is in the use of a psycho-educational approach in psychotherapy to aid in the recovery of trauma survivors.

Indira is trained in Transactional Analysis (TA), EMDR and Trauma Therapy.

Dean Quirke is a wellness educator and facilitator who specialises in men's health and wellbeing, primary prevention education and community development. His area of expertise is in the use of behavioural science and primary prevention strategies to help empower boys and men.

In 2018, Dean consulted with the Department of Veteran Affairs (DVA) as an experienced Community Support Advisor, delivering key health initiatives to promote health and wellbeing amongst the veteran community. In his role with DVA, he provided advice in planning, developing, implementing and evaluating programs such as the Men's Health Peer Support program, which assists the DVA in its commitment to the DVA Social Health Strategy 2015–2023.

In 2015, Dean founded the Young Men's Group and Empowering Youth, Changing Lives Program. These initiatives have since made an impact in the lives of over 500 young men from all walks of life across Sydney, including Fairfield, Bankstown, Canterbury, Mosman, Maroubra and Botany.

Dean has twenty years' experience as a speaker and facilitator, delivering a variety of early intervention and health promotion programs to individuals, groups and corporate clients in schools, charities and prisons.

He has worked and partnered with key stakeholders within the community to tackle a variety of social issues that impact the lives of young men, including domestic violence, community, youth violence, suicide, social isolation, addictions, unemployment and lack of purpose and direction.

His skills in facilitating workshops are highly sought after in the areas of youth and men's wellness and community development.

For more information about the book or breaking the addictive cycles of or domestic violence, you can reach out to the authors at:

www: toxiclove.com.au

Email: **deamymg@gmail.com;**
      indira_novic@yahoo.com

Facebook: facebook.com/toxiclovecommunity

WHO CAN I CONTACT?

If you or someone you know is the victim of domestic or intimate partner abuse, here are some helpful contact details:

1800RESPECT on 1800 737 732 or visit 1800RESPECT.org.au.

This is a 24-hour national sexual assault, family and domestic violence counselling line for any Australian who has experienced, or is at risk of, family and domestic violence and/or sexual assault.

Mensline Australia on 1300 789 978 or visit www.mensline.org.au

Mensline supports men and boys who are dealing with family and relationship difficulties. It provides 24/7 telephone and online support, and is an information service for Australian men.

Men's Referral Service on 1300 766 491 or visit www.ntv.org.au/get-help/

This service from 'No to Violence' offers assistance, information and counselling to help men who use family violence.

Lifeline on 13 11 14 or visit www.lifeline.org.au

Anyone across Australia experiencing a personal crisis or thinking about suicide can call 13 11 14. Someone will help put you in contact with a crisis service in your state or territory.

Kids Help Line on 1800 551 800 or visit www.kidshelpline.com.au

Free, private and confidential, telephone and online counselling service specifically for young people aged between 5 and 25 in Australia.

Beyond Blue on 1300 22 4636 or visit www.beyondblue.org.au

Information and support to help everyone in Australia achieve their best possible mental health, whatever their age and wherever they live.

Heavy M.e.t.a.l Group: Mens Education Towards Anger and Life on 0401 766 877 or visit www.heavymetalgroup.com.au

Support for men who need help with anger management to lead a non-violent lifestyle. Programs that help men to identify, understand and take responsibility for their behaviour, attitudes and emotional reactions. This helps contribute towards safer situations for family members and encourages men to treat women and children with respect and equality.

www.ingramcontent.com/pod-product-compliance
Lightning Source LLC
Chambersburg PA
CBHW011432050426
42334CB00070B/2981